PENGUIN BOOKS

SEE JANE HIT

James Garbarino, Ph.D., holds the Maude C. Clarke Chair in Humanistic Psychology at Loyala University Chicago, and from 1985 to 1994 he was president of the Erikson Institute for Advanced Study in Child Development. He is a Fellow of the American Psychological Association. Dr. Garbarino has served as consultant or adviser to a wide range of organizations, including the National Committee to Prevent Child Abuse, the National Institute for Mental Health, the American Medical Association, the National Black Child Development Institute, the National Science Foundation, the U.S. Advisory Board on Child Abuse and Neglect, and the FBI. He lives in Chicago, Illinois.

see jane hit

WHY GIRLS ARE GROWING MORE

VIOLENT AND WHAT

WE CAN DO ABOUT IT

James Garbarino, Ph.D.

PENGUIN BOOKS

PENGUIN BOOKS
Published by the Penguin Group
Penguin Group (USA) Inc., 375 Hudson Street, New York, New York 10014, U.S.A.
Penguin Group (Canada), 90 Eglinton Avenue East, Suite 700, Toronto,
Ontario, Canada M4P 2Y3 (a division of Pearson Penguin Canada Inc.)
Penguin Books Ltd, 80 Strand, London WC2R 0RL, England
Penguin Ireland, 25 St Stephen's Green, Dublin 2, Ireland (a division of Penguin Books Ltd)
Penguin Group (Australia), 250 Camberwell Road, Camberwell,
Victoria 3124, Australia (a division of Pearson Australia Group Pty Ltd)
Penguin Books India Pvt Ltd, 11 Community Centre,
Panchsheel Park, New Delhi – 110 017, India
Penguin Group (NZ), cnr Airborne and Rosedale Roads, Albany,
Auckland 1310, New Zealand (a division of Pearson New Zealand Ltd)
Penguin Books (South Africa) (Pty) Ltd, 24 Sturdee Avenue,
Rosebank, Johannesburg 2196, South Africa

Penguin Books Ltd, Registered Offices: 80 Strand, London WC2R 0RL, England

First published in the United States of America by The Penguin Press,
a member of Penguin Group (USA) Inc. 2006
Published in Penguin Books 2007

5   7   9   10   8   6   4

Grateful acknowledgment is made for permission to reprint
excerpts from the following copyrighted works:
*Creating True Peace: Ending Violence in Yourself, Your Family,
Your Community and the World* by Thich Nhat Hanh.
Copyright © 2003 by The Venerable Thich Nhat Hanh. All rights reserved.
Reprinted with permission of The Free Press,
a division of Simon & Schuster Adult Publishing Group.
"Girl, 12 accused in death of 4 year old," Associated Press, October 31, 2004.
Used with permission of The Associated Press Copyright © 2004. All rights reserved.

THE LIBRARY OF CONGRESS HAS CATALOGED THE HARDCOVER EDITION AS FOLLOWS:
Garbarino, James.
See Jane hit : why girls are growing more violent and what we can do about it / James Garbarino.
p.   cm.
ISBN 1-59420-075-0 (hc.)
ISBN 978-0-14-303868-9 (pbk.)
1. Girls—United States—Psychology.   2. Girls—United States—Social conditions.   3. Violence
in Children—United States.   4. Violence in adolescence—United States.   I. Title.
HQ777.G37 2006
303.6'0835'20973—dc22   2005049341

Printed in the United States of America
Designed by Claire Vaccaro

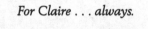

For Claire . . . always.

Contents

Part Three: When Things Go from Bad to Worse for Girls, Then and Now

Part Four: What Now?

Part One

What's Going on with Girls?

1

The New American Girl
Gets Physical

Youth violence is in the news. After two decades of public outcry about juvenile violence the newspaper headlines may seem unremarkable at first glance: TEEN HAZING TURNS VICIOUS, GANG BEATS MAN SENSELESS, TEENAGERS INDICTED FOR MURDER, SCHOOL SHOOTER SOUGHT REVENGE FOR PUT DOWNS, YOUTH ARRESTED IN MURDER PLOT AIMED AT PARENTS. Many people will be surprised to hear that the perpetrators in all these cases were girls. The violence perpetrated by boys has been on our minds as a serious issue for many years. But violent girls? What's that all about?

According to the U.S. Department of Justice, while criminal violence among teenage boys today still far exceeds criminal violence among teenage girls, the gap is narrowing. Twenty-five years ago for every *ten* boys arrested for assault, there was only one girl. Now there are only *four* boys arrested for each girl arrested. Put simply, the official arrest data indicate that girls today assault people and get arrested more often than did the girls of generations past.

But the news from the front lines about American girls today is not just about criminal violence. Here are some other headlines worth noting: GIRLS' RUGBY IS THE FASTEST-GROWING PHENOMENON IN THE COUNTRY, KIDNAPPER FOILED AS GIRL RECALLS DAD'S LESSON: FIGHT, GIRL SAVES PARENTS FROM MUGGERS, TRAINING PROGRAM TEACHES GIRLS SELF-CONFIDENCE, GIRL ATHLETES COMMAND NEW RESPECT FROM PEERS. This too is the American girl.

Girls in general are evidencing a new assertiveness and physicality that go far beyond criminal assault. They are apparent in the girls' participation in sports, in their open sensuality, in their enjoyment of "normal" aggression that boys have long enjoyed in rough-and-tumble play, and in the feeling of confidence that comes with physical prowess and power.

We should welcome the New American Girl's unfettered assertiveness and physicality. We should appreciate her athletic accomplishments, like the way she stands up for herself, and applaud her straightforward appreciation of herself as a physical being. But I believe that the increasing violence among troubled girls and the generally elevated levels of aggression in girls are unintended consequences of the general increase in normal girls' getting physical and becoming more assertive. *All* this, the good news of liberation and the bad news of increased aggression, is the New American Girl.

While it's true that female adolescents make most of the headlines, the real story starts in childhood. Many people believe that adolescence typically brings about dramatic and unpredictable changes in kids. In her classic book *Children Without*

Childhood, Marie Winn speaks of the Myth of the Teenage Were-wolf to express this belief: "A pervasive myth has taken hold of parents' imagination. . . . Its message is that no matter how pleasant and sweet and innocent their child might be at the moment, how amiable and docile and friendly, come the first hormonal surge of puberty and the child will turn into an uncontrollable monster."

But systematic research belies this expectation. The overwhelming majority of children (about 80 percent) avoid dramatic tumultuous change as they enter adolescence. Instead they become teenage versions of the children they were. Childhood is the time when basic patterns of behavior emerge. These patterns provide the foundation for what happens in adolescence. For most girls—and boys, for that matter—adolescence is the coming to fruition or intensification of childhood patterns of behavior and development, not some dramatic change of course or profound transformation of character. For example, most high school dropouts were struggling academically in elementary school. Most depressed teenagers were sad children. Most teenagers who have trouble with relationships were socially unskilled as children or had problems with attachment. Most violent youth were aggressive children. Research reveals that many personality traits show a great deal of continuity despite the fact that when you ask individuals directly, they "think" they have changed. This is one reason why the myths about adolescence endure.

There are exceptions, of course, but mostly adolescents are what they were in childhood, only more so. This is not to say that there are no special features of adolescents that distinguish them from children. Their brains do mature. Thus, for example, while many young teenagers have great difficulty assessing the emotions of others correctly, most older adolescents have achieved adultlike competence in this area. Similarly, most adolescents become capable of more abstract thinking than they were capable of in childhood, and this has implications for everything from their schoolwork to their moral judgments, from their concepts of themselves to their ability to argue with their parents and peers.

Teenagers do struggle with the rapid and dramatic physical changes brought on by puberty. Many have heightened concerns about body image that translate into issues of self-esteem. Teenagers have to work out emotionally loaded issues revolving around their orientation to peers. The impulse to peer conformity peaks as kids leave childhood and enter adolescence, and the judgment and behavior of teenagers are vulnerable to distortion in response to peer influences.

What's more, adolescence does bring on shifts of allegiance, with attachments that were once principally focused on parents shifting more to peers. This does highlight the importance of the cultural content of peer relations. Research reveals that antisocial and self-destructive elements of peer culture are particularly likely to get transmitted to kids in adolescence.

This perspective on adolescence has important implications for our understanding of how physical aggression fits into the life of the New American Girl. Specifically, the increasing problem of violent female teenagers is mostly *not* a matter of nonaggressive girls learning to be more aggressive when they reach adolescence. Although the ramifications and severity of aggression may shift as girls enter adolescence, the basics of aggression do not lie in the developmental changes brought on by adolescence. No, they start in childhood.

The fact is, children—boys and girls—start out aggressive, and for the first three years of life girls and boys are almost equally aggressive. But traditionally most little girls have been more ready and able than most little boys to exchange physical aggression for more subtle, effective, and socially acceptable tactics for getting what they want and for expressing themselves. Why? This difference emerged for two reasons. First, little girls developed more social competence than little boys and as a result did not need the clumsy tool of physical aggression to get their needs met. Second, powerful pressures were applied to girls to persuade them to "give up" physical aggression because it was not "feminine" to hit. What is more, they were told to give up assertive physicality more generally in favor of verbal interaction and, eventually, passive sexuality.

Following this traditional pattern, girls then reached adolescence having learned the social competencies necessary to get what they wanted *and* to forgo physical aggression when they didn't as well as to forgo rough-and-tumble physicality generally (and sexually). When they didn't get what they wanted, girls learned to redirect their aggressive impulses to nonphysical modes of assault, using words and manipulating feelings in what has come to be known as relational aggression. These same forces encouraged passivity in relation to boys and put young women at risk for being victimized by predatory males in general. But none of this is written in stone.

As the conditions that cause girls to learn to be socially competent change and the pressures to give up physical aggression decline, girls can and will become more and more likely to hold on to physical aggression in their early years and make use of it later on. They will also become more likely to behave violently when they are troubled and socially ineffective. In this they re-semble the boys I have known who have trouble with childhood aggression that blossoms into violence when they enter adoles-cence, particularly when they face social and emotional depriva-tion and trauma.

For more than thirty years my professional life has revolved around my efforts to understand, prevent, and resolve violence in the lives of children and youth—in families, in schools, in neigh-borhoods, and in war zones around the world. Mostly I have been concerned with the violent and aggressive behavior of boys, with girls appearing in my writing mainly as victims. Twenty books, hundreds of lectures and articles, and a million air miles later, I find myself starting over, focusing on aggressive girls rather than boys because the new social and psychological realities demand such a shift of focus.

In my 1999 book *Lost Boys*, I wrote as a psychologist about the pathways from childhood aggression to youth violence in boys. Why boys? Because violence has long been a predominantly male issue. Historically males have accounted for 90 percent of mur-ders in America and for most of the serious violence that reaches the court system and finds its way into our prisons. When in 1986 I addressed a social work conference in Michigan on the topic "Toward a Violence-Free Michigan" I began my presentation with the tongue-in-cheek suggestion that if "a violence-free Michigan" were the goal, an effective strategy would be "to round up every man and boy and move them to Indiana." Today I could not make that joke with quite the same scientific confidence.

According to the U.S. Department of Justice, the last decade of the twentieth century witnessed a dramatic shift in criminal violence rates for girls and boys. I believe this shift transcends the problems with changing definitions and policing policies noted by some criminologists. Criminal violence perpetrated by adolescent females increased at a time when the rate for adolescent males was decreasing. From 1990 to 1999 the rate of aggravated assault among girls under eighteen went up 57 percent, while for boys it went *down* 5 percent. During that same period weapons violence increased 44 percent for girls and *decreased* 7 percent for boys. If we move beyond these potentially lethal forms of violence to look more generally at criminal aggression, we see that during the 1990s the growth of offenses against people (as opposed to property crimes) for U.S. girls was 157 percent while for boys it was 71 percent. In Canada the comparable figures are 68 percent for girls and 22 percent for boys. Criminal violence among girls has been increasing across North America.

But so has more "normal" aggression. Girls are learning martial arts, participating in contact sports like hockey and rugby, and generally roughhousing more than ever before. Girls are getting physical in dramatically new ways, throwing and catching balls, lifting weights, and running track, as never before. They are also hitting people more and more on the playing fields of our communities, in our movies and television programs, in the classrooms, hallways, and cafeterias of our schools, and in the living rooms and kitchens of our homes.

The targets of this aggression are still all too often themselves. Troubled girls have long engaged in self-destructive behavior, mainly by internalizing negative views of themselves, by getting depressed, by accepting victimization by predatory males, and by manifesting their pain and sadness through physical symptoms like headaches, stomachaches, and eating disorders (what is called somaticizing). Now girls are becoming more physical when they are assaulting themselves, cutting and starving, poisoning and shooting themselves in record numbers. Why?

I believe it is because at the same time that girls are being liberated from many of the constraints of rigid and oppressive sexual stereotypes (the pervasive message that "It's not ladylike to do X, Y, or Z"), they have been confronting an ever more toxic social environment. The elements of this social toxicity include spirit-deadening superficial materialism, reduced benevolent adult authority and supervision, civic cynicism, and fragmentation of community, all promulgated through the vehicle of pop culture that often undermines legitimate adult authority and promotes a vivid linking of assertive sexuality with explicit aggression. All these social toxins stimulate aggressive behavior. This is decisive, when coupled with the fact that girls have the innate capacity to be aggressive and that the cultural pressures for girls to give up physical aggression early and seek alternatives have been declining.

Thus the issue we face is not simply the thousands of criminally violent girls who make the headlines and go to prison or the hundreds of girls who kill themselves each year, but the larger question of how and why the role of physical aggression in girls is changing across the board. It's about the changing lives of our daughters, our nieces, our sisters, and our granddaughters, for better *and* for worse. It's time to take a good hard look at changing patterns of physicality and aggression in girls. More and more parents, teachers, and counselors are beginning to confront this issue. It is starting to come into focus as parents observe behavior in their daughters that takes them off guard.

Barbara is a friend of mine, a teacher. She is in her mid-forties, and I've known her for ten years. I've been to her home and met her family, including her husband and her daughter, Melissa. Over the years Barbara has talked often and with pride about her daughter's achievements and activities. She's obviously pleased with the way her daughter takes on the world in an assertive way, riding horses, playing sports, having relationships with boys that are friendly, without the constraints that Barbara remembers from her own childhood. Melissa is now fourteen, and Barbara recounted this story about Melissa's recent high school tennis match:

> Melissa is a high school athlete. She plays tennis and soccer. Last week she played against another team from a neighboring community. I was there to cheer her on, and it was clear that the other team's girls brought a real "attitude" with them to the match. They were insulting my daughter and her teammates, making nasty remarks, that sort of thing. After the match my daughter said to me, "Mom, that girl was such a bitch, and there was nothing I could do about it. That's the trouble with tennis: It's such a polite sport. If this were soccer, I could have just knocked her over and that would be that."

Barbara doesn't know quite what to make of Melissa's statement. On the one hand, she is proud that her daughter is not cowed into submission by her opponents' verbal aggression. On the other hand, she's not sure that she likes the fact that her daughter seems to be part of a trend in which more and more girls are adopting a traditionally male approach to conflict: Hit them and be done with it. What's a mother to do?

Here's another example. A young father sought me out after a public lecture based upon my book *Lost Boys*. He's a thirty-five-year-old up-and-coming executive working for a high-tech company and is very serious about being a husband and father. With a worried look on his face he said: "Yesterday I took our three-year-old daughter to the park. At one point I told her she had to get off the slide because it was time to go home for dinner. As I went to pick her up, she slapped me! I was so stunned I didn't know what to do. If our son had done that, I would have known how to respond, but what do I do when it's my daughter? Boys hit, of course, but girls? *My little girl?*" What's a father to do?

I think most effective parents have a whole toolbox of techniques for dealing with aggression in boys, tools that generally work pretty well and have stood the test of time, based upon evidence showing that by the time boys leave adolescence only about 5 percent have problems controlling their aggression. But many parents seem perplexed by physical aggression in girls. Why? For the most part they never thought they needed to deal with this issue before because the culture around them uniformly and homogeneously taught girls it was not ladylike to hit. That has changed, and now parents need new child-rearing techniques. Part of raising girls today is figuring out how to find a balance between encouraging assertive physicality and avoiding problematic aggression. But how to find that balance?

To understand better what is going on, I have been asking teenage girls and young women to reflect upon their experiences with physical aggression—against others and against themselves. I have been posing these questions to the "normal" girls and young women I know in the university classroom and to the troubled girls and women I meet in my professional capacity, dealing with criminally violent youth. I have been asking them to reflect upon their experiences and those of their peers, reaching back into childhood and early adolescence, and then to report back to me in the form of brief memoirs. I have drawn from the two hundred reports I collected to put a human face on the body of research on aggression that provides the foundation for my analysis of the New American Girl and the role of social toxicity

in her life. To protect the privacy of my informants, I have
changed details in their accounts and altered identifying information, keeping the essence of the reports.

What can we see of the role of aggression in the lives of our
girls? The German poet Goethe once wrote: "What is most difficult? That which you think is easiest, to see what is before your
eyes." I feel this way about the topic of girls' physical aggression.
Having committed myself to putting aside preconceptions and
comfortable traditional assumptions about girls and aggression, I
see it before me now much more clearly.

Consider some of the statistics:

- A study of physical aggression in young children reports
  that at age four girls are nearly as likely to use physical aggression as boys (24 percent versus 27 percent).

- Thirty years ago research showed that the effects of TV
  violence in stimulating aggression were mostly confined
  to boys. Now the effects are equally apparent for girls and
  boys.

- A study of aggression in eleven thousand children ages six
  to twelve reported that "girls initially declined but then
  caught up with (and exceeded in the case of hostile attribu-
  tion biases) boys in each of the variables. . . ."

- U.S. Department of Health and Human Services data reveal
  that each year 7 percent of female students have been involved in a physical fight on school property (versus 18 percent of male students).

- According to the most widely cited study of spousal violence in the United States, the rate of physical assault by
  women against men in couples is 12.4 percent versus 12.2
  percent for men against women; for severe assault, it is 4.6

percent for women against men versus 5 percent for men against women.

- According to the American Humane Association, the majority (59 percent) of cases of physical child abuse involve women (mothers) as perpetrators; for 32 percent of the fatal cases, it is the mother acting alone.

The wisdom of Goethe's insight is brought home to me regularly. These data have been hiding in plain sight.

I think something important is happening in the lives of our girls as we begin the twenty-first century, but we haven't yet seen it for what it really is. The first challenge we face is seeing what is in front of us. That's not as easy as it sounds. Often, important social trends are hidden in plain sight. Few commentators detected the growing mental health crisis in middle-class American high school boys, precipitated by homophobic bullying, harassment, and emotional violence and coupled with the onslaught of violent images present in popular culture (TV, video games, movies, and music), until they exploded in the school shootings of the 1990s, exemplified by the Columbine High School massacre in April 1999. Only then was there a significant national response, heralded by the White House Summit on Youth Violence held in May of that year. Sometimes it's hard to see things happening right in front of us.

Some big events emerge through rapid crystallization of trends long in the making but mostly hidden from view. This is one reason for our frequent historical blindness toward social change. In these cases, a dramatic change occurs once a social trend has crossed a previously undefined line, a threshold. Students of disease transmission (epidemiologists) call this a tipping point, as when a flu virus already present in the population rapidly spreads to become an epidemic. We see it most clearly when an apparently slow and orderly process of change suddenly escalates rapidly, and there is a wholesale transformation that is often stunning in its dramatic appearance. We may be witnessing a tipping point in the changing nature of physical aggression in American girls.

Another cause of our blindness to emergent social change is suggested by findings from the branch of science that has come to be best known as chaos theory. Chaos theory tells us that social and physical systems are often interconnected in ways that are complex, hard to detect, and sometimes the result of influences that are impossible to measure with complete precision. As a result, it is difficult to predict the ultimate effects of even small changes in one or more of these systems because the pattern of changes does not take a simple form that we may describe easily or arises suddenly in a manner that defies conventional predictions.

Sometimes very tiny influences, even those too small to measure precisely, can set in motion events that produce major shifts that escalate and magnify as they move from their origins in one particular system to connected systems. This process of escalation then results in giant effects. In meteorology this is called the butterfly effect, referring to the fact that it is possible for a butterfly flapping its wings in the Amazon River basin to set in motion events that could culminate eventually in a hurricane in the South Atlantic Ocean. The butterfly effect is real. It is also not confined to the science of meteorology. It may explain initially puzzling phenomena in the lives of children and youth, like the recent dramatic increase in violence by troubled girls.

As awareness of all the above sets the stage for looking at the role of physicality and aggression in the New American Girl, I offer four main ideas:

First, we are seeing the beginning of a dramatic shift in the forms and extent of physical aggression in American girls. Also there may be butterfly effects at work in our society and culture that are moving us toward a tipping point when it comes to female aggression. When I write this, I think of Amanda, a nineteen-year-old A student and cello player. Her parents are divorced, and she and her younger teenage sister live with their mother in a small city in upstate New York. She told me this:

> My mom was out with her friends, and I was home alone and had all the doors in my house locked. It was about ten p.m., and I was upstairs doing homework. My sister came home while I was upstairs and because she didn't have a key was banging on the door for me to let her in. I was in the middle of a paragraph and wanted to finish it before I let her in. It took about two minutes until I went downstairs to unlock the door and let her in. When I opened the door, she was furious because I had made her wait. She started yelling at me and getting in my face. When I tried to push her away, she started hitting me, and when I held her hand so she couldn't hit me anymore, she started kicking me. I was not looking for a fight, so I just let her go and started backing up slowly. But she continued to come at me, kicking. When she got too close, I put up my hands to block her, and she went after my hands. I couldn't move in time, so she kicked me in the hand with her foot. She broke my right-hand middle finger, and I had to go to the hospital the next morning and was in a splint for almost a month.

Girls are hitting people more than in the past, and this represents a challenge to adults charged with the responsibility for rearing and teaching those girls.

Second, girls are getting physical and learning the very positive message that their bodies can be physically powerful in ways that are not sexual. These very positive changes in girls result from unleashing them from the traditional bonds of femininity and are evident in assertiveness, participation in sports, and active rather than passive psychological coping strategies.

Consider the case of Sarah. Tall and athletic-looking, she is eighteen now, the youngest of three children in her family. Her father is an accountant, and her mother a nurse. They live in a Philadelphia suburb. This is Sarah's report:

> At around the age of twelve, I became interested in playing basketball. I practiced all the time and soon was ready to play in games. I always felt I had to prove myself and break free of the stereotype that girls can't play hard. I would push, set picks, and run harder than the guys on the court. I played aggressively because I thought I had to. By the end of most games the boys would admit that they were surprised at how well I played and how aggressive I was. During every game I played, whether it was varsity or pickup, I tried to be as physically aggressive as possible. In fact, during my sophomore year of high school I was given the Most Aggressive Player Award.

Participation in sports can lead to opportunities for enhanced character development or to heightened aggression. Which way it goes depends upon how adults use athletic experiences as teachable moments.

Third, the issue of social toxicity compounds the risk that physical aggression will become destructive violence because the problem of violence is fundamentally tied to spiritual well-being. Keeping physical aggression in check depends in large part on kids having positive social and cultural anchors, so that they may internalize a sense that they live in a meaningful universe with moral limits and an ethic of caring. This is what spirituality is about and why preventing violence is tied to spiritual well-being (which is not synonymous with the practice of religion, although the two are related for most of us).

Spirituality suffers in a materialistic culture like ours, where kids, girls and boys, are exposed to the delusion that they really are what they own, what they buy, what they wear, and how sexy their bodies are. Violence taps into our deepest issues of meaningfulness. Without positive meaning in their lives, girls (like boys) will be drawn to the spiritually empty dark path of nihilism and aggressive sexuality where violence flourishes. Spiritual emptiness lets loose primitive aggressive impulses; spiritual fullness leads to higher standards of behavior and to character. I think this is evident in Caitlin's experience.

At nineteen, Caitlin is a quiet and shy young woman. She grew up in Los Angeles living with her mother because her father died when she was five. She is an only child and expresses a strong interest in working with young children when she graduates from college. She recalls:

> It was the first day of high school. I was fourteen, and I remember feeling a bit out of it on the bus because it seemed all the other girls were wearing hot clothes and cool jewelry, and I wasn't. My mother wouldn't allow me to go to school like that. There were two girls in particular who looked the way I wanted

to look. Then, when I stepped off the bus, the first thing I saw was a fight. One of the two cool girls started screaming at another girl. It was all "fuck you, bitch" and that sort of thing. I tried to walk by calmly, but before I knew it, one girl had grabbed the other girl's long blond hair and used it to throw her onto the sidewalk. She proceeded to jump on top of her and began scratching viciously. At this point the driver got off the bus and broke up the fight. It was like being in a reality show on TV! Later that day in the cafeteria I learned that the girl who had gotten grabbed by the hair and thrown down had been having sex with the other girl's boyfriend. That afternoon the boyfriend broke up with her during lunch period. He took her out into the hallway and said that he wanted to end it. She slapped him across the face and then walked away. The next period she had gym class, and she walked into the locker room and punched the lockers. She hurt her hand pretty badly. She was very upset with him because he had taken her virginity. I guess that made her violent. The thought of being beaten up by another girl scared me to death. I had no idea of how vicious girls could be to each other until that day.

Remember that these girls were only fourteen. They were awash in social toxicity.

Fourth, we must adapt to the changing nature of physicality and aggression in girls as parents—with a new emphasis in our rearing of girls—and as professionals and citizens—through our support of programs to address the changing nature of physicality and aggression in girls, particularly among troubled girls who are acting out in more dangerous ways than ever before.

Robin is an eighteen-year-old honor student. She is a sensitive, compassionate young woman whose parents are elementary school teachers. With great sadness she recalls coming face-to-face with cutting in a female peer:

> Carrie came to high school sophomore year. From the beginning everyone could tell she was driven and committed to doing well. However, she did not seem to relish her success. One day after English class I heard her crying. She was having a cell phone conversation with her mother. I approached her afterward, and she told me that she had gotten only a B+ on her midterm exam and her parents were furious. That was the last time she mentioned her grades. As the weeks passed by, she began to get extremely thin. Her face became gaunt and sallow. She almost became one of those invisible people. As spring came, she continued to wear long, loose-fitting clothing that completely draped her body. One day in history class she fainted. The teacher and I carried her to the nurse's office. I sat with her while the nurse pulled up her shirtsleeves to take her pulse. When Carrie's sleeves were pulled up, I gasped at the wounds on her arm that appeared to be fresh. Her arms were covered with gashes, some of them quite deep. Her arms were pitted with old scab wounds and fresh slash marks. When Carrie woke up, she was terrified to realize we had seen her arms. She was more frightened by the fact that her secret was out than by the fact that she was a "cutter" in the first place. She told me later that when the tensions in her life built and her chest tightened with fear, she cut herself to get relief. She enjoyed watching the blood flow because she said it almost made her feel as if she were cleaning her self and her self-abuse was the key to her freedom. Since then I have known other girls who cut themselves, but I'll never forget Carrie.

Rachael is also eighteen. She lives in Chicago with her parents and her two brothers. She is studying psychology and wants to become a therapist when she graduates from college. Perhaps that career interest is related to her memory of Naomi's crisis:

> One afternoon when I was in sixth grade, I received a phone call from my friend Naomi. She began speaking to me in a panicky voice. Through her tears she told me that she had a bottle of pills and was going to kill herself. She told me how she hated her life and how she wanted to end it once and for all. I was so shocked. I tried to calm her down and told her that she was a great person and that everyone loved her. After being on the phone for thirty minutes, she said she would dump the pills in the toilet. Soon after that she said good night and hung up. I thought she was OK. The next morning she wasn't at school, and one of my friends told me she heard that Naomi was in the hospital because she had tried to kill herself by taking pills. I lost track of Naomi in high school after my family and I moved to another part of the city. But last year I was visiting a friend from my old neighborhood, and she told me that Naomi had shot and killed herself.

It's not of course that physical aggression has been totally foreign or is totally new to girls and women. In *The Don Flows Home to the Sea*, Mikhail Sholokhov's 1943 historical novel about the civil war that engulfed the Soviet Union in the 1920s, the author describes the fate of a group of male prisoners of war: "Twenty miles they were driven through village after village, greeted at each by crowds of tormentors. The old men, women, and elder children beat them, spat in their bloodstained swollen faces, threw stones and clods of hard earth, cast dust and ashes into their eyes. The women were especially brutal, resorting to the most cruel and ingenious tortures."

Jennifer Hargreaves's account of the history of female boxing includes descriptions of fights that are gruesome to read even today. An account of two women fighting in 1794 is exemplary:

Great intensity between them was maintained for about two hours, whereupon the elder fell into great difficulty through the closure of her left eye from the extent of swelling above and below it which rendered her blind through having the sight of the other considerably obscured by a flux of blood which had then continued greatly for over forty minutes—not more than a place even as large as a penny-piece remained upon their bodies which was free of the most evident signs of the harshness of the struggle. Their bosoms were much enlarged but yet they each continued to rain blows upon this most feeling of tissue without regard to the pitiful cries issuing forth at each success which was evidently to the delight of the spectators since many a shout was raised causing each female to mightily increase her effort.

Such accounts stand out because the physical aggression described is so atypical for traditional females by not being confined to domestic violence and child abuse. These are highly unusual situations and individuals. But girls and women *can* be physically aggressive when their situations encourage and validate it, as contemporary social science research well documents. One reason for this is that even physically nonaggressive girls may harbor aggressive impulses and desires. For example, psychologist Larry Aber and his colleagues reported in their study of eleven thousand school-age kids that at age twelve, girls actually had *higher* levels of aggressive fantasies than did boys of the same age.

Traditionally, these fantasies mostly do not translate into much physical aggression directed by girls at their peers (mostly being confined to assaults against romantic partners and younger children in their care). When it comes to peers, most of the girls' aggressive fantasies have either remained hidden behind the feminine facade or been displayed in the form of verbal attack and indirect emotional assault through social manipulation of relationships (relational aggression).

Here's a girl who represents the traditional female experience with this form of aggression. Brady is a savvy nineteen-year-old from a middle-class family in Denver. Asked to comment on her experience of aggression in girls, she said:

> Girls by nature are different. They are usually not the ones to throw a punch when they are mad. Girls for the most part have a different form of violence. Because girls are said to be more emotional and more likely to express their feelings through words, they usually lash out with words when they are mad. However, this is not to be underestimated. Lashing out among girls can get just as ugly, and I daresay uglier than, the physical fights among boys. Girls can be manipulating, crude, and downright cruel with their words, resulting in worse injuries.

That is the traditional view of girls, but today, more and more of the aggression displayed by girls is physical. This aggression is often portrayed in a positive light, both in its own right and as a positive alternative to relational aggression, *which I believe it often is.* Here's one example. Soon after the third Harry Potter movie (*Harry Potter and the Prisoner of Azkaban*) was released, my daughter and I went to see it. Amid all the wizardry there are the heroic actions of Hermione, "the smartest witch of her age." In a pivotal scene toward the end of the movie, thirteen-year-old Hermione punches the easy-to-despise bully Malfoy in the nose and sends him packing. "That felt good," she says with a smile, to the approving looks of her compatriots and the cheers of the laughing audience.

It's the kind of act that has been cheered and celebrated in American movies for decades. The obnoxious bully is put in his place though an act of decisive physical aggression. But it is a role that has long been reserved for boys. The fact that it is the otherwise very feminine Hermione who takes on this important mission is a reminder that things have changed. In fact Hermione is, if anything, more physically aggressive than Harry Potter himself.

I thought of Hermione when I read Tasha's account of her friendship with a real-life example of the heroically aggressive girl. Tasha, now nineteen, comes from New York City and attended what many would regard as a tough city school. A temperamentally timid girl in a very aggressive world, she tells a story that rings familiar to many a timid boy. She writes:

> When I made the change from my small elementary school to the much bigger middle school, I found myself being threatened. I was appointed captain in a game of field hockey/baseball during gym. As captain I was supposed to regulate the game and make calls as to who was out. In one instance I called out a girl named Jeannie, who immediately threw down her stick and came toward me. She pushed me and yelled that I would be sorry that I had ever messed with her because she was the biggest bully in her old school. Unfortunately, she had two sidekicks with her, and they also approached me. At that moment the gym instruc-

tor (who had been dealing with another group) saw us and asked if there was a problem. I told her no. But as we lined up, Jeannie said that she would beat me up after school. I was worried about what she might do to me, so I confided in my best friend, Natalie. When I went to my locker that afternoon, I was still fearful, and my fear did not subside when Jeannie approached my locker. Rather than hit me, however, she surprised me by apologizing for having pushed me. When I saw Natalie later that day, I told her about what had happened with Jeannie at my locker. Natalie wasn't surprised at what had occurred. She herself was bigger than Jeannie, and after hearing my story earlier in the day, she had gone to Jeannie to tell her stop messing with me—"or else." Apparently this worked because Jeannie never bothered me again for the rest of middle school.

I have heard many stories from girls and young women about physical aggression against self and others, some of it prosocial like Natalie's intervention with Jeannie, some of it predatory, like Jeannie's threats to Tasha. When I was a boy, I lived in the world these girls inhabit, the world of threats and counterthreats. I can relate to these stories and recognize the positive qualities inherent in them, just as I resonate with the negative images they contain.

Of course, as a man approaching sixty years of age whose last physical altercation with a bully occurred nearly five decades ago, I should prefer kids to have a wide range of nonaggressive skills to resolve conflicts and prevent bullying. Still, I regard strong girls like Natalie's standing up to bullies like Jeannie as more positive than passive acceptance of victimization of her or her friend.

I hear many stories from girls that deal with physical aggression. Some negative; some positive. Many speak to a broader experience with physicality, comfort with using the power of their bodies for something other than sex. These are often the sports stories, the girl athletes who are physically powerful and proud of it, and having been a high school athlete myself, I can relate to these stories too.

Elizabeth is a twenty-year-old college student who exudes health and comfort with her body. In class she often sits with a group of male students, and the feeling among them is clearly that of camaraderie. The youngest of five children, Elizabeth works at a sports camp during the summer break and aspires to be a pediatrician. Here's her account of what being an athlete means to her: "When I play soccer, I feel free. My body feels strong, and I feel like I can do anything I want to do. Running up and down the field, I feel powerful. Sometimes when I leg tackle another player and she goes down on the ground, I feel really good. I suppose I shouldn't, but I do. Even if I don't score a goal, it still feels good to know I have this power."

The New American Girl's experiences of physical power through sports stand in stark contrast with the stories of yesterday's girls deprived of these opportunities. These are stories of regret at being forced away from positive physicality because of the prison of being "a lady." There is great sadness in forty-year-old Sheila's account of her childhood. Although she is now a successful executive in an insurance company, Sheila's memory of childhood sports is dominated by her sense of loss, of having missed out on something positive because she was a girl. She tells it this way: "My father wouldn't allow me to play Little League baseball. My brothers could play because they were boys. All I could do was keep score while my brothers played ball. Why? Because playing baseball wasn't 'ladylike.'" Three decades later her anger and her sadness are still palpable.

That's not the end of it. When I told Sheila of research into aggression by Canadian psychologist Richard Tremblay documenting the importance of fathers' teaching their kids about normal physical aggression by playing physically with them—wrestling and play fighting—she replied, "My father never wrestled with me. It would have been inconceivable." It's a sad moment, one replicated by many women of her age as they watch their daughters and nieces happily playing on fields around the country.

It reminds me of my own sadness when nearly two decades ago my own daughter and I sat watching the Chicago Bulls on television in Chicago. Joanna, who was an avid Bulls fan at age five, turned to me at one point and asked, "Are there girls in the NBA?"

"No," I replied, "but lots of girls do play basketball."

"Dad," she asked after a moment's reflection, "is there a girls' NBA?"

"No," I replied, "but girls play on teams in college."

"Oh," she said.

We continued watching the game, but I think her interest was never as keen again.

I console myself with the fact that Joanna and I did wrestle together—and dance. Also, Joanna became a horseback rider, and her physical encounters with horses made her physically strong and able—with biceps that today are the envy of many boys her age. Now she is a young woman very comfortable with her physical self. But how glad I shall be if someday I have a granddaughter who asks the question Joanna did because I could then proudly tune in the Women's National Basketball Association.

The point is that sports have long been the normal social institutional setting for boys getting physical and that in the last twenty years they have opened to girls dramatically and decisively. Where once there were thirty-two boys playing high school sports for every one girl, the current figure is approaching one to one. That is an *enormous* shift! The change extends to all forms of athletic activity. Consider, for example, that most physical of team sports, rugby. A report from Oregon entitled "Girls Can Hit Too," includes remarks from several young women about the sport. One teenage girl says, "It's kind of like soccer, but a lot more intense. It's both mentally and physically demanding. It's so physical that it's hard to get up sometimes after a hit. But we have some very strong girls on this team." Adds another girl: "I just expect the bruises; it's part of the game. This is my first year playing and I'm having a great time." A third puts it this way: "There's no pads, no helmet. There are a lot of tough girls out there . . . and we shouldn't be underestimated because girls can hit too."

I see it myself. Several times each week when I am home in Ithaca, New York, I troop off to the gym for an exercise class. I have been doing this on and off for more than twenty years. When I began (at a gym in Chicago), the classes were all more or less one form of aerobic dancing or another. You know the drill: step, step, step, hop. But now I attend two classes developed and marketed by the Les Mills training program that go well beyond old-fashioned aerobics, Body Pump and Body Combat.

Body Pump is weight lifting to music. Most of the participants are women—young, middle-aged, and old—and it's great to see them getting pumped up. For some it is the first time they have done anything athletic in their lives, and they have learned to sweat right alongside the men (who are a very small minority in the classes).

Body Combat is still aerobics, but with a twist: The moves are all boxing or martial arts—jabs, crosses, uppercuts, rips, chops, kicks, elbow slashes. It's a great workout. Like those in most aerobic classes I have attended over the years, the participants are mostly female (about 90 percent or more most days). The instructors (also mainly women) narrate the moves as we do them: "Aim for the nose with those jabs," "pummel your opponent with those rips," "go for the chin with that cross punch," "the back kick's target is your opponent's knee," etc. etc. etc. A review on iCircle.com (a women's lifestyle Web site that bills itself as "for women who love life") says of Body Combat: "Who'll like it? Tomboys rather than girlie girls who like dancing and prancing in aero-boogie classes. Psychologically, it's an empowering workout, with regular participants claiming improvements in their self-confidence and a reduction in their stress levels. . . . And though we can't guarantee it will turn you into Lara Croft overnight, Body Combat could be the first step in your quest to a *Tomb Raider* style body."

Frankly, as a psychologist concerned about aggression I'm sometimes a bit embarrassed to participate. I find the aggressive narration a little bloodcurdling at times, even though it's been more than thirty years since I was actually in a physical fight of any sort (playing ice hockey, truth be told). But I have often wondered what the young women in the class think and feel about all the aggressive talk and practice. So I asked a few of them. Here's what twenty-year-old Katie had to say, as she retied her ponytail and donned her black gloves in preparation for class: "It makes me feel powerful. I hear all these stories about girls who get pushed around by their boyfriends or who get assaulted on the street. I don't want to be one of them. But there's more to it than that, really. I like the moves. I like to feel strong. It feels terrific. I leave feeling I can take care of myself."

That doesn't stop at the gym. A fifteen-year-old Florida girl recently foiled a kidnap attempt by fighting back. She reported that when the man grabbed her she remembered her father's message: "Fight. Go down fighting. Don't give up at all." That's good, right? We all want girls to feel strong and powerful, not always on the defensive, not trapped in some depressing prison of conforming to some concept of what is "ladylike" and what isn't. But there is no such thing as a free lunch when it comes to aggression. Letting the genie out of the bottle can result in all kinds of consequences that are not apparent at the start of the process.

The first law of human ecology is: "You can never do just one thing." Why? Because human systems are so interconnected every action has multiple consequences, some of them unintended and often negative. Is it possible to do just the one thing of freeing girls from the prison of being "ladylike," without (as the iCircle Web site suggests) forcing them to choose between being a "tomboy" and a "girlie girl"? Is it possible for girls to take on the world of physical aggression on terms more traditionally masculine without also having to take on all the negative aspects of male psychology and behavior? We are facing these issues at a time when the socially toxic mass media saturate kids with images that link violence, sex, and materialism for girls. These socially toxic influences conspire to increase the likelihood of adverse consequences and the magnitude of those consequences when they do occur. That's the way social toxicity works.

Kids in general will test the limits wherever those limits are set. Thus troubled kids will be bad at the outer limits of their social environment. I have watched that in kids for my entire professional life. I have seen boys who would have fought with fists and knives thirty years ago just as readily take up guns today. I have known sixteen-year-olds who would have agonized over whether or not to kiss on the first date thirty years ago today nonchalantly report on their multiple sex partners. I have seen the rate at which American kids are "troubled enough to need professional mental health services" double from 10 to 20 percent during that same time period. I worry how the changing relationship of girls to aggression will play out in this socially toxic environment in which they live, with declining support from benevolent and authoritative adults, being infused with an ever more nasty and vicious pop culture, and being faced with soul-starving shallow materialism at every turn.

Are there safeguards built into girls that prevent them from walking down the same path from acceptance of physical aggression to acting out violently? If we need them, do we have in place for girls the socialization experiences that have proved necessary and largely successful in channeling aggression for boys? Remember that while most little boys are physically aggressive at some point, only about 5 percent of men end up having trouble controlling aggression and behaving prosocially in adulthood.

Are the forces that put women into professional basketball the same forces that put U.S. Army Private Lynndie England in the position of torturing Iraqi prisoners at the Abu Ghraib prison? Is there a link between the cultural messages that enable my female Body Combat classmates to feel physically strong and powerful and the forces that lead troubled girls with traumatic hard lives to follow the path from physical empowerment into criminal violence and prison? Questions abound. Let's look for some answers.

2

To Hit or Not to Hit: Are Girls and Boys Wired Differently for Aggression?

There is a long-standing debate in our culture about what used to be called the nature of man, today more appropriately referred to as human nature. The underlying issue is whether humans are born with moral predispositions or with a neutral orientation that makes them completely open to being shaped by experience. Writing in the fourth century A.D., theologian St. Augustine saw the human infant as arriving on the scene tainted by badness and needing the benevolent interventions of society to become good. Seventeenth-century English philosopher John Locke saw the infant as a blank slate upon which experience would write the child's values and personality, for better or for worse. Eighteenth-century French philosopher Jean-Jacques Rousseau spoke of the child as a pure "noble savage" who is tainted by the evils of the world. Twentieth-century psychoanalyst Sigmund Freud spoke of the id—an aggressive life force that sought only gratification—and of the efforts of rationality (ego) and civilization (super ego) to tame the savage beast (even while they serve id by seeking socially appropriate and safe ways to gratify its impulses).

Each of these famous approaches to human nature implies something about whether aggression is learned or innate in human children. The view from contemporary evolutionary biology focuses on the adaptive survival value of human traits. Its message is always the same: If a trait increases the odds of survival, it is passed to the next generation; if it doesn't, it won't be. Thus evolutionary biology sees aggression as innate and serving a purpose in human evolution. As the human race evolved, the strong and powerful could protect themselves and their kin, and this ensured the survival of their genes in the next generation, while the weak died out. From this perspective, aggression is hardwired into human beings and thus is a matter of nature.

In contrast, many contemporary psychologists see human nature as open and the persons we become mostly the product of our learning and experiences. B. F. Skinner's behaviorism, which focused on human development as simply the product of reinforcement, is an extreme version of this view. It exemplifies the judgment that aggression and peacefulness are mostly matters of nurture. This nature-nurture debate is centuries old, and we continue to struggle with the question of whether we as human beings are naturally peaceful or instinctively aggressive.

How we answer this question says a lot about how we approach aggressive behavior in girls. When does it start and where does it come from? If the natural state of the infant is to be peaceful, harmonious, and nonaggressive, then we must inquire into the corrupting influences of experience. But if aggression is the norm, we must discover why and how girls give it up and avoid the developmental pathway to violence. The question becomes, Why do girls stop hitting? At its root, then, the core question is whether aggression in young girls is an aberration or the norm.

Although my own background is Christian, in wrestling with these questions, I have found myself drawn to the spiritual psychologist and Buddhist teacher Thich Nhat Hanh. There are few observers of human development whom I respect more. Understanding violence has been a matter of lifelong dedication for him, and his experiences with war and peace have offered him many opportunities to observe and reflect upon the origins of human aggression. In Nhat Hanh's view, there is no simple, one-dimensional human nature. Rather, human reality includes elements of both aggression and peacefulness. He writes: "We begin by recognizing that, in the depths of our consciousness, we have both the seeds of compassion and the seeds of violence. We become aware that our mind is like a garden that contains all kinds of seeds. We realize that, at any given moment, we can behave with either violence or compassion, depending upon the strength of these seeds within us. When the seeds of anger, violence, and fear are watered in us several times a day they will grow stronger. . . . Yet when we know how to cultivate the seeds of love, compassion, and understanding in us every day, those seeds will become stronger, and the seeds of violence and hatred will become weaker and weaker."

This is an insightful observation from the perspective of a spiritually grounded applied psychologist. It provides a useful language with which to discuss aggression in children, and I respect it greatly. Nhat Hanh's observations lack the statistical rigor that we expect of empirical psychological science, but fortunately we can find that necessary statistical rigor in the work of the more conventionally scientific psychologist Richard Tremblay.

Public opinion polls reveal that most people think teenagers are the most aggressive human beings, but the empirical evidence collected by Tremblay and his colleagues belies this belief. In fact, infancy and early childhood, not adolescence, are the most aggressive stages of life.

Are infants aggressive? Tremblay's research (based upon reports by mothers) reveals that 80 to 90 percent of seventeen-month-olds, girls and boys, evidence some physically aggressive behavior. This aggression often emerges first in response to simple frustration, but as the infant becomes more mobile and engages in social interactions, it results increasingly from conflicts over toys and territory. Just watch babies and toddlers for a time, and you will eliminate any doubts on the validity of Tremblay's view. Infants and toddlers bite. They pinch. They hit. Tremblay puts it this way: "If you put your four-month-old to bed one night, and went in in the morning and he was suddenly six feet tall and 200-plus pounds, you should just run away. Because he will really beat you up."

Most toddlers of both genders, according to Tremblay's research and the studies of others, engage in physical aggression—hitting, slapping, pulling hair, and biting, for example. In fact, toddlers average one act of physical aggression for every four social interactions, and most commit aggressive acts on numerous occasions in any twenty-four-hour period. Aggression actually peaks at about thirty months of age and declines thereafter.

Tremblay's research provides a definitive set of data to address the issue of whether aggression is innate or learned. Whereas conventional social learning theory has defined the task for psychological research as one of explaining how aggressive behavior arises in young children, Tremblay's empirical research stands this issue on its head. His data demonstrate that physical aggression is the natural response of infants to the frustrations of human existence, that the frequency of physically aggressive behavior starts to decline in the second year of life, and that this decline continues across the life span for most human beings (with only about 5 percent of adults struggling with aggression issues). What is more, in these data it is not until fifteen months that a gender difference in aggression emerges. Up to that point little girls and little boys are equally aggressive; it is only then that the girls become less physically aggressive than boys.

It's only the relative powerlessness of the infant and toddler that makes it safe for parents to live with and socialize them. That makes evolutionary sense; the odds of human survival increase when biology gives socialization time to work things out. Two-hundred-pound infants and toddlers would kill off their parents and then starve to death themselves when they couldn't successfully navigate the world.

Think of Lennie in John Steinbeck's classic novel *Of Mice and Men*. Lennie is a giant toddler (mentally and emotionally retarded but physically imposing and strong), and he commits acts of extreme physical violence: crushing a man's hand out of anger, smothering a puppy out of love, snapping the neck of a young woman out of fear. Each incident exemplifies the impulsive aggression you might see when your four-month-old bites your fingers, your one-year-old hits you in the face with a toy car, or your two-year-old pinches you. The difference is that Lennie's aggressive behavior is backed up by adult strength. In my work as an expert witness in murder trials I have met men like Lennie in prison, emotional and intellectual toddlers in the bodies of adults. Few combinations are so dangerous.

When you approach very young children with open eyes, when you are fully present and aware, their aggression registers. Consider these notes from a college student completing her class assignment to spend a day observing young children.

Three-year-old Laura is getting ready to eat dinner. Her father makes something she is not interested in, so she pushes the food away. He tells her that it is time to eat and puts the food back in front of her. She pushes his hand away and then starts screaming. When Laura's father picks her up, she punches him and throws her arms all around while screaming that she wants to be put down.

Jesse, age three, starts building blocks in the corner of the room. He is having fun by himself and enjoying his creation. A few minutes later two-and-a-half-year-old Zack comes over to play. They are making creations together when all of a sudden Zack puts a block in the wrong place and Jesse throws a fit. He throws a block at Zack and then steps on Zack's hand.

Ashley, age three and a half, is playing with her younger brother, Peter (he's two). They are in the sandbox, each at an end. When their mother walks inside to answer the phone, Ashley requests the shovel from Peter. He's not done playing with it, and he holds on tightly. She starts yelling at him, yanks it out of his hand, then pushes him over on her way back to her end of the sandbox.

Twenty-one-month-old Stephen is playing on the ground near the play structure when his mother tells him it is time to leave. She picks him up, and he bites her and then pushes her to get free.

We often gloss over the aggression manifest in infants and toddlers. Why? Because they do little damage, and as time passes and they become more civilized, our memories of their early aggression fade. Tremblay's research deals with this phenomenon as well, revealing that the frequency of aggression reported by mothers in the behavior of their children is lower when recalled years later than when reported at the time it occurred. The process of retrospection drops the proportion of seventeen-month-old children committing acts of aggression from 90 percent when reported on by parents at the time of its occurrence to 5 percent when reported on ten years later.

Tremblay's data make it clear that the task before us is to understand why and how most children learn to contain, control, subordinate, and channel their aggressive impulses and behaviors, how they water the seeds of nonviolence, to use Thich Nhat Hanh's terminology, while others—a minority—do not and thus water the seeds of violence.

Early childhood behaviors may set developmental trends in motion, but it is later experiences that either redirect and weaken or reinforce and strengthen these early patterns. Conflicts provide "teachable moments" with respect to aggression and where adults stand on the issue of hitting. Tremblay writes: "During these conflicts children learn that they can hurt and be hurt. Most children quickly learn that a physical attack on a peer will be responded to by a physical attack and that adults will not tolerate these behaviors." I might add that traditionally girls received these messages more uniformly than boys. Tremblay's research demonstrates that almost every child he studies is more aggressive at age six than at sixteen. To a large extent, the socialization of aggression works.

Think of puppies. It's a race against time; you have to train them early so that you have control before they get big, or you will be dragged around at the end of a leash. Of course, with some dogs there are more than control issues involved. Some breeds have a greater disposition to aggression than others, raising the stakes immensely. I used to walk our mild-mannered Labrador retriever in the park most mornings. We routinely encountered a man walking two pit bulls, neither of which was on a leash. Both my dog and I knew that what stood between us and assault by those dogs was the goodwill and the controlling influence of the pit bulls' owner.

Is it too much to say that some children are pit bulls and some are Labs? Perhaps, but there are some variations in aggression that emerge early in life. All kids are aggressive, but some children have stronger aggressive impulses than others. It is what parents, peers, and others do about these impulses that matters. Of course one of our big concerns about girls is precisely the actions of these "others," specifically the mass media. This is a topic to which we shall return later. Here I shall just say that one of the most dramatic changes in the experience of girls vis-à-vis physical aggression is the changing nature of the mass media's treatment of female aggression, from a consistently negative message ("girls don't hit") to an ever more positive message ("girls kick ass").

Here's Tremblay again, speaking about the core process of teaching children the norms about aggression: "If children are surrounded by adults and other children who are physically aggressive they will probably learn that physical aggression is part of everyday social interaction. On the other hand, if a child lives in an environment that does not tolerate physical aggression and rewards pro-social behavior, it is likely that the child will acquire the habit of using means other than physical aggression to obtain what he or she wants, or for expressing frustration."

Do parents differentiate the messages they give to boys and girls regarding aggression? That's a crucial point. Research from the 1950s to the 1990s demonstrated that parents and others traditionally have differed in their tolerance for physical aggression by boys versus girls. This differentiation has been evident in everything from parental attitudes toward aggressive behavior ("boys will be boys" versus "it's not ladylike to hit") to their selection of toys (guns for boys; dolls for girls). Girls were taught by word and deed that for a girl to engage in physical aggression was "weird," "unnatural," and "unfeminine."

At the same time that this training regarding the ins and outs of aggression is going on in the lives of young children, differences are emerging between boys and girls in the kinds of social skills that provide effective alternatives to physical aggression as a tactic for meeting needs and getting what is wanted. As child development researcher Beverly Fagot and her colleagues report, by two years of age children are becoming aware of the key gender stereotypes: that males and females are expected to behave differently. With that recognition, overt aggression drops off more sharply for girls than for boys.

The greater attachment of boys to aggression has a biological basis as well, although the links are not simple and direct. Prenatal exposure to the male sex hormone androgen predisposes children to a high level of physical activity. This impulse to be physically active can be channeled into rough-and-tumble play, the roughhousing that many young children delight in. Different from aggressive fighting, it is a good-natured, sociable activity.

As child development expert Laura Berk puts it, "Children's rough-and-tumble play is similar to the social behavior of young mammals of many species. It seems to originate in parents' physical play with babies, especially father's play with sons. . . . Boys' rough and tumble consists largely of playful wrestling, restraining, and hitting whereas girls tend to engage in running, chasing, and only brief physical contact." While not really aggression per se, rough-and-tumble play is one of the raw materials for physically aggressive behavior. The more you like to crash into people, the more you are inclined to listen to messages validating physical aggression. The more you find crashing into people distasteful, the more easily you will be persuaded to give up aggression.

What is the cumulative effect of the sex-typed responses to the issue of aggression by parents and other agents of socialization, the generally greater social competence of girls, and the biological basis for greater physical activity in boys? It is the traditional pattern of behavior with respect to physical aggression: increasing differentiation between boys and girls in childhood as boys tend to hold on to aggression while girls tend to give it up.

Although most little girls may well be less disposed to rough-and-tumble play than most little boys for a mix of biological and social reasons, this does not mean all girls are immune to the dynamics that release and reinforce aggression in boys. The biological differences are relatively small, and there is significant overlap; some girls are more inclined to high-activity rough-and-tumble play than some boys. Tremblay's research and Thich Nhat Hanh's observations speak to the fact that most children of both genders have many of the raw materials out of which they can build lives of physical aggression. What matters is whether or not socialization and culture intervene to send messages and teach skills to suppress and redirect aggressive impulse and, in so doing, water the seeds of nonviolence.

This all takes place of course in the context of another major traditional influence on the behavior of children—namely, the distribution of power. In 1982 Carol Gilligan published her landmark book *In a Different Voice*. In it, she argues that females travel a different path in the development of moral thinking and as a result speak with a "different voice" in processing social issues. Gilligan sees girls speaking with a voice that reflects an ethic of caring, a cooperative spirit, and a commitment to emotional connection. Boys, on the other hand, speak with a voice that emphasizes objective principles of justice, hierarchy, and a commitment to independence. *In a Different Voice* quickly became a classic and spawned numerous intellectual and programmatic spin-offs focusing on the "voice" of girls, on how it arises and when and why it is heard rather than silenced.

Gilligan's influence has been enormous, despite the many challenges to her work. Some of these have come from feminists who are suspicious of anything that posits differences between females and males (because of the justified concern that traditionally anything that shows women to be different from men quickly becomes defined as a deficit). Some have come on scientific grounds. These challengers question Gilligan's claim that females and males actually do speak in different voices when they consider moral issues. The data addressing this issue are mixed but seem to demonstrate more similarities than differences.

Another challenge to Gilligan's work concerns the origin of whatever differences in "voice" are observed. From this perspective, the different voice of girls is not intrinsically related to their gender. Rather, as the critics put it, this different voice is actually the one that comes from being in a subordinate position in the social hierarchy. Put this way, the differences are primarily a matter of power, not gender, and it is only because of the traditionally subordinate position of girls that their voice is different from boys'. That there has traditionally been a power imbalance between males and females in our society and that it favors males hardly need fresh documentation.

The evidence on this score is voluminous. Here's one small indication. Traditionally when a girl adopted a masculine persona, she was labeled a "tomboy," and traditionalists accused her of not knowing her place, of aspiring to a higher status she could never achieve. In contrast, when a boy was drawn to things feminine, he was called a sissy, his crime being that he was "lowering" himself to the feminine level. But evidence of how things are changing is to be found in the fact that today there is much less stigma attached to a girl's being called a tomboy—indeed, the word is much less common—and the word *sissy* has been replaced by words like *fag* and *gay*. The traditional power imbalance between the masculine and the feminine is being displaced and transformed.

The distinction between speaking with a different voice because of gender or because of gender-linked powerlessness is important. Why? Because it implies that if the power relations between the genders equalize, changes in voice will follow. Indeed, some people have been disappointed in the political and business conduct of powerful women, with Martha Stewart and Margaret Thatcher being two prominent examples. Women in power have not been the paragons of virtue that one might expect if indeed the feminine voice described by Gilligan reflects inherent female moral superiority (as some have argued). Women in power don't seem to be all that much better than men in power, and women voters have not shown themselves to be decisively more enlightened than male voters. What differences have emerged are relatively small, even when they do favor females. Lord Acton's famous adage seems to fit the facts of gender and development: "Power corrupts, and absolute power corrupts absolutely." All this is highly relevant to the matter of aggression in the lives of children. It is logical to assume that if girls are empowered, they will become more likely to engage in physical aggression. Of course that is exactly what I think is happening.

Perceived and real inequities in power have consequences for how and when children act aggressively and why they sometimes don't. Individuals with undisputed physical power can "afford" to be physically aggressive. They can act without fear of retaliation. Individuals with less power cannot. These individuals must cultivate alternatives to the assertion of naked power. This is one way to understand the commonly reported differences between boys who reach puberty early (early maturers) and those whose pubertal development is delayed (late maturers). The former tend to be dominant in the social hierarchy because of their physical power manifest in athletics, in appearance, and in the attributions that peers and adults make to them. Adults and peers attribute more adultlike characteristics to these early-maturing boys and treat them as more grown up with corresponding increases in social prestige and thus power.

What can late-maturing boys do to compensate? In the manner of all subordinate groups they can cultivate social power. They can ally themselves with the powerful boys. They can develop verbal skills (like being funny) that gain them influence. They can align themselves with adults and thus garner their protection. Sound familiar? Late-maturing boys exhibit many of the traits commonly thought of as feminine. This is no coincidence.

As for girls? Traditionally the advantage has gone to girls who are neither early- nor late-maturing but rather are right in the middle. Why? The explanation offered by researchers is that the early-maturing girl elicited rejection from both her peers (because she was different from everyone else in a peer culture that valued conformity above almost anything else) and from adults (who were suspicious of her precocious sexual maturation). In addition, early-maturing girls had to deal with the sexual interest of older boys, which placed these girls at risk for a variety of experiences that taxed their psychological resources. However, in the long run early-maturing girls ended up with an advantage because being "different" put them outside the traditional system of femininity and ultimately worked to their advantage by promoting more androgyny.

Late-maturing girls were spared the premature sexual interest of older boys and the suspicions of adults but did have to deal with the traditional feminine demand for conformity, in which any difference (better or worse) is cause for disapproval and pressure to conform. They did accrue advantage in the long run, however, like the early-maturing girls, by the sheer fact of having been different and thereby detached a bit from the traditional system of femininity.

But it is not this simple. In some settings, it seems, early-maturing girls are more popular because in a toxic sexualized culture "younger is better" when it comes to being sexy. However, this may not be good for their mental health. And even adults seem to be buying into the idea that sexy is good, no matter what age a girl is. Now in research it appears that early-maturing girls have an initial advantage but in the long run a disadvantage, and the situation is reversed for later-maturing girls. What is particularly fascinating is that it seems that more and more the impact of when a child matures is coming to be more similar between boys and girls than it has been in the past.

One of the driving forces that lead children to check their aggressive impulses and fantasies is the messages they receive about their power relative to others in their social environment. What are these messages? One is that there can be costs associated with hurting people and benefits associated with nonviolence. Some of these costs are in the form of physical retaliation. A child learns that when you hit, you may get hit back, and that hurts. (For example, Jane hits Robert after he refuses to give her a toy she wants. Robert pushes Jane down and hits her in the head with the toy. She cries and lets Robert keep the toy.) Some of these costs are in the form of the realization that in many situations you can achieve your goals more efficiently through means other than physical aggression; cooperation, altruism, deception, and manipulation are often more effective than frontal assault. (Let's say Sally wants the toy that Robert is now playing with. He refuses to give it up, so Sally goes and finds another toy that she knows he likes and she offers to trade it to him for the toy she wants. After a moment's reflection Robert accepts the deal.)

Another message is that positive physical interaction—stroking, hugging, kissing—feels good and soothes and meets some of the very needs that when frustrated stimulate aggression in the first place. (Alice wants to join in playing with Sally and Natalie. At first they refuse to let her join in. Holding her doll, she sits near them for a few minutes. Then, when she sees that Sally and Natalie are looking for some teacups, she goes across the room and gets them. When she offers the teacups to Sally and Natalie, they let her join in the play tea party.) There is a kind of power in being nurtured and cared for, although it is a kind of power that traditionally has been appreciated more by girls than boys. I should say, parenthetically, that by defining this kind of power as "feminine," we deprive boys of one of the most powerful ways to water the seeds of nonviolence. That is a topic well developed by many new books dealing with boys, such as Dan Kindlon and Michael Thompson's *Raising Cain*, William Pollack's *Real Boys*, Michael Gurian's *The Wonder of Boys*, and Joseph Pleck's *The Myth of Masculinity*. The more we water the seeds of nonviolence in children, the less aggressive they become, and the more socially adept and nonaggressive.

The kinds of power children believe are open to them have implications for the kinds of aggression they will "choose" to make use of. Traditionally this has meant that boys typically employ physical aggression and girls typically employ relational aggression. As child development expert Laura Berk puts it, "Boys more often attack physically to block the dominance goals typical of boys. Girls resort to relational aggression because it interferes with the close, intimate bonds especially important to girls." Psychologist Nicki Crick is one of the leading researchers studying relational aggression. She makes the same point this way: "Boys generally harm others with physical or verbal aggression because this behavior is consistent with the physical dominance peer group goals of boys. Girls, on the other hand, are apt to focus their aggression on relational issues with their peers. This behavior is consistent with the social peer group and intimacy goals of girls." So it goes traditionally.

Developmental psychologist Eleanor Maccoby, who is generally recognized as a pioneer in studying gender differences in child development, has also studied the differences between the relational styles of boys and girls. Speaking of kids from childhood to adolescence, Maccoby writes: "Boys are more concerned with competition and dominance, with establishing and protecting turf, and with proving their toughness, and to these ends they are more given to confronting other boys directly, taking risks, issuing or accepting dares, making ego displays, and concealing weakness. . . . Girls, though of course concerned with achieving their own individual objectives, are more concerned than boys with maintaining group cohesion and cooperative, mutually supportive friendships. Their relationships are more intimate than those of boys."

But these traditional formulations are breaking down as the cultural realities of power between boys and girls change along with the cultural images of physical aggression. Girls' interactions are not uniformly cooperative. Far from it. There is actually a great deal of competition among girls, mostly for boys (traditionally) but increasingly for worldly success. In a very astute analysis of girl culture, lawyer Cheryl Hanna lays out how the theme of competition among girls infuses their aggressive acts, whether relational or physical. She points out that three out of four victims of female violent offenses are themselves females and that in half the cases the victim is an acquaintance. She writes: "There is growing evidence to suggest that violent girls are not fighting back against boys. . . . In far too many cases, girls are trying to attract boys at the expense of other girls."

Allysia is a thoughtful sociology major who plays on her college women's basketball team. She grew up in Mobile, Alabama, with her mother, her stepfather, and three stepsisters. Hers is an insightful report of how aggression worked in her world as she was growing up:

> From my own experiences and those of my girlfriends, I believe that most aggression in girls stems from a territorial standpoint. I am very familiar with the aggression that girls show when jealous about a guy or simply trying to put a stamp on their property. I have seen firsthand that when females feel they are being threatened, they will do anything or act any way to make another girl stay away. One of my most disturbing experiences involved one of my best friends in high school, Jane. Breaking up with her boyfriend sophomore year was a whirlwind of craziness and hate spun out of control. After she started up with a new boy, she got phone calls from his former girlfriend

ranging from threats that if she were seen out in the streets, she would be sure to get beaten up to hang ups in the middle of the night. Jane did her best to avoid the other girl, but one day she caught Jane alone and kicked her ass in front of the Starbucks where all the kids hung out after school. When Jane called me afterward, I went straight over there, and I couldn't believe what I saw. My best friend's face was all scratched up, she had bruises all over, and for weeks she was scared to be left alone, especially to be alone anywhere near Starbucks.

This also brings up an interesting question: Are girls more or less likely to stop fights between two other girls? It seems to depend upon why the girls are fighting.

One way for girls to demonstrate their friendship may be to act aggressively against intruders, even when it is a friend's boyfriend, not their own, who is being claimed by a competing girl. Roberta witnessed this in her high school. Now a college student majoring in art history she speaks to the power unleashed by competition among teenage girls:

Throughout high school it was normal to hear stories of deceit and cheating within boy/girl relationships, mostly on the part of the boys. However smooth a person might think he was, it was only a matter of time before the entire school found out that he had been cheating. This was high school, and there was no such thing as secrets. A bunch of us went on a spring break trip together. My friend David was hooking up with the beautiful Jenna at the time. We all were seniors, and Jenna was a junior, so she couldn't come along on the trip. To make a long story short, David hooked up with another girl during the trip and got caught. Jenna's friend Allison walked in on David and the new girlfriend, Jo. That's when the screaming and fighting began. Allison rushed the couple and punched Jo in the face. The two started fighting and screaming loud enough that not only did all our friends run into the room but hotel security came charging in as well. The following week, on the first day back in school, Jenna slapped David in front of the entire school.

And this, from Tiffany, an eighteen-year-old girl from New York City whose adolescence was spent as a social heavyweight:

In tenth grade, nightclubs were a hot spot for people in our age-group who wanted to dance the night away and drink and drug without the intervention of parents. One night Karen, Marni, and I were hanging out with some other friends and Karen's boyfriend. As the night wore on, a girl from a rival high school appeared. Everybody knew that she had slept with Karen's boyfriend (which caused Karen to break up with him, but they got back together two weeks later). Karen knew who the girl was but had never seen her to confront her. When Karen caught sight of this girl at the club, she immediately stormed over with Marni in tow to bitch the girl out. The girl was with a couple of her girlfriends who backed up their friend in what was becoming a full-out argument. Words were exchanged, some so dirty all the toilet paper in the world wouldn't clean them up. At the height of this spectacle a nasty comment was directed at Marni, at which time Marni threw a fist at the opposing party. Then it was an all-out catfight. Hair was being pulled, and Marni's tube top was pulled down. Two bouncers watched the fight for a while and then intervened, pulling the girls away from each other and throwing us all out of the club.

Of course, it's worth asking whether the bouncers would have waited so long to intervene if it had been two teenage boys fighting. The answer is, probably not. The rules are clearer with respect to boys (and the assumption is that girls don't really hurt each other).

In our increasingly toxic social environment the onset of sexual interest is coming earlier and earlier in the lives of children. What Freud termed the latency period, when sexuality and sensuality were put on hold until adolescence, has eroded to the point of vanishing for many children. For example, the television program preferences of many eight-year-olds are the same as they are for most fourteen-year-olds. Clothing styles used to offer a sharp differentiation between childhood and adolescence but now mostly don't. I have heard eight-year-olds speak of childhood in the past tense; they see themselves not as children but as "preteens."

As a result, adolescent culture is more and more infusing the lives of preadolescent children. For example, girls' competition for boys starts ever earlier. Here's one girl's account of how the impulse to get the attention of boys expressed itself among a group of eight-year-old girls. It comes from nineteen-year-old Beverly, a sophisticated young woman who grew up in an upper-middle-class suburb in Michigan. She remembers:

> We were on the school bus one day in third grade, and we were making fun of this quiet, chubby girl who always sat in front of us with her seat belt on (this was an extremely "uncool" thing to do). She also wore her extremely long hair in one unappealing braid that dangled above her seat and to the front of the seat behind her. We were at the age when the male sex was start-

ing to appeal to us, and we always wanted to seem outgoing and tomboyish so boys would notice us. Every day we sat in the back of the bus, near the boys, joking about how "weird" this girl was. The boys always thought her long braid was "dirty" in some way. Challenged by a "triple dog dare," one of my female friends decided that she would take action and cut the girl's braid off. Holding arts-and-crafts class scissors, she marched to the front of the bus, grabbed the long braid, and made one long snip. The girl shrieked, and the bus came to an abrupt halt. All my friends were rolling around on the bus floor, laughing hysterically, while the "criminal" turned red and started to cry after realizing what she had done.

The traditional messages about power have generally been clear and convincing for girls in the peer-dominated world of school and playground, where the androgen-fed inclination of most boys to be more rough-and-tumble than most girls coupled with strict messages of what was feminine and what was not pushed girls away from physicality in general and physical aggression in particular. Only the tomboys among the girls contested the playing fields with the boys. The traditional messages about male physical domination became more salient in mid-adolescence, when the physical size of most boys comes to far exceed the physical size of most girls, and girls were mostly banished from the playing fields and relegated to the role of cheerleaders. Eventually even most of the childhood tomboys packed it in and surrendered to the imperatives of femininity in adolescence.

But when it comes to physical aggression, it is clear that traditionally girls have had little choice in the matter of shifting toward nonphysical expressions of their aggressive impulses. Parents and other adults have colluded with culture to make the option of physical aggression off limits for girls. By the same token, bigger kids (and particularly bigger males) are on average slower to learn this lesson because they are more likely to conclude from their experience that physical aggression *is* successful. Even some girls have been slow to learn this lesson.

Elementary school is still a time when many girls are relatively big and strong enough to believe that physical aggression and dominance are a winning proposition for them. Here's an account from a teenage girl, Anne, who grew up in a small midwestern town with her parents and three sisters. As she looks back on her elementary school experience, she recalls with a mixture of awe and sadness another girl from her town, a girl who came from "the wrong side of the tracks," a girl who opened Anne's eyes to the world of physical aggression that was alien to her:

> Her name was Elizabeth, but everyone called her Liz. I was lucky to count her among my friends. She grew up in a bad part of town, with two older brothers who both had the reputation of getting into a lot of trouble and getting into fights. I knew she grew up quickly, learning to defend herself. But her aggression in school became more than defense. She showed me where a pressure point was on the back of the neck and that by pinching it in a certain way, you could cause a person a lot of pain. She enjoyed chasing some of the boys she didn't like in the class and pinching the backs of their necks during gym class. As we got older, I grew apart from her, and by high school she had the reputation of being a troublemaker, tough, someone you didn't want to get on the bad side of. She had the image of being someone who wouldn't back down from a fight.

The key to Liz is not that she was physically aggressive in elementary school but that she didn't make the shift to nonphysical aggression in adolescence when even most boys get the message. When physically aggressive little girls don't make the shift away from physical aggression, they often head down a path that spells increasing troubles of all sorts, including delinquency, sexual acting out, and escalating violence. We shall meet some of these girls in Chapter 5.

Physically dominant girls who *do* make this shift to nonphysical aggression can become powerful social forces to be reckoned with in high school, central figures in the competition for power and prestige. They may do this by shifting their aggressive energies to relational aggression or even to positive leadership roles, and they are often recognized as student leaders.

In my childhood in the 1950s it was my classmate Ann Ruffalo who epitomized this pattern. In elementary school she was at the top of the heap when it came to physical dominance. Each winter when the snow fell, we would choose teams for snowball fights, and no one was picked ahead of Ann Ruffalo. No one messed with her in elementary school because she was able and willing to use her superior physical power. But by the time we all reached high school Ann had gotten the message that there were better ways to be powerful than sheer brute physical force, and she became the dominant social force in our class. Each year when it came time to organize the school-wide competition involving dramatics, sports, construction, and art projects that was judged by a panel of community representatives and teachers, Ann was the unanimous choice to direct our efforts. And direct it she did. Her power was undeniable. I might add that at our thirtieth high school reunion I saw that Ann was still a force to be reckoned with, now a grandmother who organized community-based literacy programs.

But the traditional messages about physical power have sometimes been less clear for girls inside families, and this trend is increasing. The family has traditionally been the place where physical aggression by females was to be found if it was to be found at all. Recall from Chapter 1 that women constitute the majority of child abusers and that the rates of assault by wives against husbands is about the same as it is for husbands against wives (with the important caveat that in most cases the harm inflicted by men against women is much greater than that by women against men).

And so it is that in the family girls have been slower to learn the rules of feminine aggression. This is either because of the special circumstances they faced (such as being the oldest child and therefore the strongest) or because of parental ideology that preached gender equality in the matter of aggression. Here's one teenage girl's report on this phenomenon. Natalie is an eighteen-year-old student majoring in psychology. She's also a college athlete and was president of the student council in high school. She grew up in a suburb of Toledo with her parents and two siblings. She describes her neighborhood as "solidly lower-middle-class and very traditional."

> In my family I am the oldest. I have a little brother who is two years younger than I am and a little sister who is three and half years younger than I am. As we were growing up, my younger brother and I would always wrestle. My younger sister always wanted to join in, but whenever we allowed her to, she would inevitably get hurt and start crying and run to my mom. My mom

would yell at us for hurting her, and we would get in trouble. As time wore on, we did our best to exclude her, either that or when she got hurt, we would convince her to hit us as hard so she could "pay back" for our hurting her. She finally realized that she was so much younger and weaker than we were that she couldn't really hurt us, but by that time she had also learned that if she wanted to join in, she had to be tougher. What was also really interesting was that since I was two years older than my brother and naturally a pretty strong person, I was always stronger than he was.

But could this last? She continues:

People always taunted me that as he got older, he would get stronger and be able to beat me up, but I couldn't believe then that this was really possible. Surprise, surprise, it began to happen. As we continued wrestling into early adolescence, things got a bit more violent. We were about equally strong, but I was still bigger, so when he would start to really get annoyed, I would just pin him to the ground and sit on him. He really hated it. Eventually I realized I was going to lose out in the end.

Natalie's report contains another element, the fact that as a boy her brother was enmeshed in a process of socialization that taught him "the rules of engagement" when it came to physical aggression in a way it did not teach her.

He could punch better and harder than I could. But because he was a boy and was raised well, he wouldn't punch me or anything as hard as he could, whereas I as a girl had almost no reservations about using my full strength to attack. Like I said, he could hit harder (he also was growing up in a neighborhood where boys learned to stand up for themselves and actually fight) while my main line of defense was merely my weight. We were incompatible. He was no match for my size, and I couldn't really match his strength to actually fight. So that's when we stopped wrestling and fighting. I finally got the message.

Again, traditionally most girls have gotten the message that physical aggression is a losing proposition sooner than most boys have. At every point after age four, boys on average have demonstrated more physical aggression than girls. Most girls have exceeded boys in learning socially acceptable ways to get what they want that don't include as much physical aggression. They have been taught by fighting with their brothers or peers that physical aggression is ineffective for them *and* that there are better ways to fight than with fists. They have learned to use social and emotional weapons. They have also been more likely to learn to value, appreciate, and obtain more positive physical affection, which waters the seeds of compassion. But all this does not preclude change in the way girls calculate the costs and benefits of aggression. If girls get stronger or at least think they are stronger, they may become more ready to use physical aggression. This may extend to technologies that augment physical strength. In the Old West the pistol was called the great equalizer because it enabled small men to be as dangerous as big men. It's reasonable to speculate that as guns become more permissible and available to girls, that will unleash more aggression in them because it will reduce their weakness relative to boys. As we shall see in Chapter 4, this may be already happening as the cultural images of girls presented in the mass media more and more come to include gun-toting heroines and villains who can give Rambo and the Terminator a run for their money.

All this is not to say that girls who do not move into this new nontraditional realm of physical aggression are nonaggressive. To use the current psychological terminology, when they have wanted to use force against others, girls mostly have moved from raw, blunt physical aggression to more subtle relational aggression. The larger spiritual issue lies in the fact that if all forms of aggression (physical and nonphysical) are counted equally, girls are just as aggressive as boys. In our socially toxic world this means that they need spiritual intervention as much as boys do to water the seeds of nonviolence and compassion, an issue to which we shall return in Chapter 8.

I think we can learn much about the dynamics of aggression among girls by focusing on issues of power. As we have seen already, the dynamics of power in the lives of girls play a significant role in moderating their inclination to display physical aggression. What is the role of power in the relational assault that has formed the backbone of female aggression traditionally? Researchers have found that other children recognize the power of relationally aggressive girls. The more relationally aggressive a girl is at the start of the school year (at least for third to ninth graders), the more popular she will be, on average, later that school year. The link was not observed for boys, however. Incidentally, granting relationally aggressive girls popularity doesn't mean that their peers like these girls. Popularity is about social power, and for girls that power is evident in the skillful application of relational aggression. Liking is something else, as many a physically aggressive boy has learned.

Everything we know tells us that the role of physical aggression in the lives of girls is subject to many influences. The point is not that all girls are destined to become just as physically aggressive as boys in childhood and adolescence after their initial equality in infancy. *The point is that girls can be and in fact are more physically aggressive than they were in the past and that this upward trend is continuing as the cultural and social changes that unleash and empower girls proceed.*

Tremblay's research warns us that we shouldn't assume that girls *can't* be as aggressive as boys. It simply tells us that they have not been in the past. Girls have been traditionally less physically aggressive than boys *not* because they lack the biological capacity to be physically aggressive but because they tend to give up physical aggression more readily and effectively than boys, because they more easily translate their aggressive impulses into relational and verbal aggression, and because they more readily learn and display nonaggressive strategies for resolving conflicts, gratifying impulses, and achieving their goals.

Traditionally girls and boys are set on different pathways, pathways that start at nearly the same point but begin to diverge early as a result of messages received from parents, peers, television, movies, teachers, grandparents, and others in the child's world. Historically most girls have been taught to give up hitting because it is not "ladylike," while most boys have been taught that aggression is "manly." Girls have been locked into a prison of femininity, but they are breaking out (even as some boys are rebelling against the constraints of narrow traditional masculinity). Girls have traditionally been less physically aggressive than boys, but like almost everything else in human development, this can change.

Why? It's because one of the most important lessons we learn from studying human development is that there are no guarantees that patterns observed in one time and place will always apply to others. As a result, few facts about aggression are fixed and forever unchanging. For example, it is taken as a given in America that "females attempt suicide more than males, but males actually kill themselves more often." This is not a fact in contemporary China, where females actually do kill themselves more often than men. It is testimony to the hard state of life for women in China. And it reflects the fact that the method of choice in rural women is ingesting insecticide, which is highly lethal in a setting with little emergency medical care, such as rural China, but less so in a more medically sophisticated setting—like the United States.

Context matters. Rarely does the process of cause and effect work universally. Rather, it operates in the context established by culture, gender, ethnicity, prior experience, and historical circumstance. This is the fundamental lesson we learn from scientific research on human development. When we look at the development of children and ask, "Does X cause Y?" the best scientific answer is always "It depends."

A few questions will serve to illustrate this important proposition. In their research Sarnoff Mednick and Elizabeth Kandel asked, "Does early neurological damage lead to violent delinquency?" They found that if babies with minor neurological damage were born into well-functioning families and communities, they were at no greater risk of violent delinquency in adolescence than were biologically normal babies. But if the same babies were born into dysfunctional families, they were four times more likely than biologically normal babies to end up as violent delinquent adolescents. Does early neurological damage predict later violent delinquency? It depends.

Does developing a chronic pattern of aggression and bad behavior, acting out, and violating the rights of others by age nine lead to becoming a serious violent delinquent in adolescence? It depends, in part, upon the neighborhood in which you live. Rolf Loeber and David Farrington report that although overall 30 percent of such nine-year-olds become seriously violent delinquents, in some neighborhoods the figure is 15 percent, while in others it is 60 percent. Does early trouble with antisocial behavior predict later trouble? It depends.

Here's another question. Is permissive parenting successful? A study by Percival Symonds in the 1920s found that permissive parents produced the most competent, happy, and successful children. But when Diana Baumrind repeated Symonds's study in the 1960s and 1970s, she found that permissive parenting was associated with producing the least successful, least happy children.

Why? One hypothesis is that when Symonds was doing his research on parenting in the 1920s, the world outside the home was highly structured, even authoritarian. In that time and place the big risk was that children would be "overcontrolled," and a permissive parent might be a breath of fresh air, so to speak. By the 1960s, however, Baumrind was studying parenting in a context in which the world outside the home was becoming more and more socially toxic and out of control, and in that setting the danger was that children would be "undercontrolled." Thus what children needed was an "authoritative" parent who could help instill the kind of self-discipline needed for them to navigate successfully the turbulent world around them.

This hypothesis, while untested empirically, is consistent with the findings from several studies by the child psychologist Al Baldwin and his colleagues. These studies report that parents raising children in dangerous inner-city neighborhoods need to be more controlling and powerful to protect their children and increase the odds of their success than do parents raising children in safer, less threatening communities, who can afford to be more "democratic." What kind of parenting works best? It depends.

It depends. It depends. It depends. That is one of the most important messages from modern developmental science, and it provides the foundation for the ecological perspective as laid out by my mentor, developmental psychologist Urie Bronfenbrenner, beginning in the 1960s. Urie's books *Two Worlds of Childhood* and *The Ecology of Human Development* pioneered in making the case for the paramount importance of context in shaping the workings of developmental influences, those that are found in the child's biology, the child's psychology, the child's family, the child's schools, the child's community, the child's society, and the child's culture.

A direct implication of this ecological perspective is the fact that rarely, if ever, does a single influence determine the course of a child's life, for better or for worse. Whether these influences are negative—risk factors—or positive—developmental assets—it is extremely rare that a single influence is decisive. Rather, it is the accumulation of risk factors and the accumulation of developmental assets that generally describe the level of social toxicity and social robustness, which, when coupled with the forces of human biology, tell the story of a child's development.

As we saw in Chapter 1, things are changing for girls when it comes to aggression, and many of the old research truths are changing as well. One of the clear themes in research on gender and aggression is that the more recent the research, the smaller the gap between girls and boys. For example, as I noted earlier, whereas in the 1960s research on the effects of televised violence on childhood aggression showed toxic effects for boys and not for girls, the same research now demonstrates that effects are present for girls. Our ecological perspective predicts this because it insists upon the fundamental truth that all research findings are subject to change if and when cultural and social conditions change. That now leads us to look at the changing cultural and social conditions that are shaping the development of girls, particularly with respect to getting physical in all its dimensions and ramifications.

Part Two

How Is Culture Changing the Lives of Girls ?

3

Girls Unleashed

When legendary anthropologist Margaret Mead decided she wanted to become a mother, she chose the most brilliant man she knew to be the father, psychiatrist Gregory Bateson. But where to raise this precious child? As Mead tells it in her autobiography, *Blackberry Winter*, the couple decided that if the baby were to be a boy, they would live in England (Bateson's home) because it was a great place for a boy to grow up. But if the child were a girl, they would reside in Mead's home country, the United States, because both believed America was a better place than England for a girl. Mead and Bateson made their decision in 1938. They had a girl, Mary Catherine Bateson, and she was raised in the United States.

America has long prided itself on being the land of the free. But even in America this freedom has historically been limited and imperfect for girls and women. The history of women's rights in America is a story well told by others and not the main focus of my analysis, but a few words are in order to set the stage for looking at the situation of contemporary girls.

In many concrete ways, females have long been second-class citizens. Not until 1920, when the Nineteenth Amendment granted women the right to vote, did females achieve any genuine political equality as citizens. The gender inequities and the political agitation that led to passage of the amendment did not stop with gaining the right to vote, of course. Both the inequities and the agitation for egalitarianism continued through the 1930s. During World War II so many men were away in the military that a compelling labor shortage temporarily trumped the bias against women in the workplace. Many women were accepted in jobs previously off limits to them. After the war ended in 1945, men in positions of leadership conspired to get women out of the workplace and send them back to their homes, reopening jobs for men returning from the armed forces. In retrospect, however, it seems clear that this was just a temporary setback for female liberation; the genie was out of the bottle and was never going back to stay.

Nonetheless, it took the civil rights movement that began in the 1950s to initiate wide-ranging changes in the rights of women, further advanced by a coherent women's liberation movement beginning in the 1960s. Technology played a role in stimulating and abetting these changes. The widespread availability of safe and effective methods of contraception in the 1960s, coupled with court cases and legislation establishing women's "reproductive rights," did much to liberate women from the burdens of unwanted pregnancies. But it was not until the 1970s that laws and legal practice began to revoke the right of a man to beat his wife that many husbands presumed came with the marriage license.

Only then did many females begin to achieve legal and social equity as spouses (which is not to say that wife beating has stopped, of course).

Although more and more economic opportunities have opened up to women since the 1980s, at present women still earn on average only about seventy cents for every dollar men earn. Viewed from a universal egalitarian perspective on human rights, America has not achieved full equality between men and women. But we have come a long way. Both from where we started and in contrast with many other societies, American women are liberated. But what has all this social change meant for girls? In one sense that's an easy question to answer: The result has been the unleashing of girls from the oppression of the old patriarchal values and social structures and the corresponding blossoming of opportunities of all kinds. That's what the New American Girl is all about.

Today the empowerment of girls and women is evident throughout our society in newly opened jobs, new athletic and artistic roles, expanded educational possibilities, and greater presence in public spheres than ever before. I relish the opportunities my daughter has before her in twenty-first-century America. I am delighted with the positive possibilities that await my five-year-old goddaughter. I am relieved that if I have a granddaughter, she will not face the limits and boundaries that my mother faced. Moreover, it is not just a matter of new roles opening to girls and women.

Research published in 1970 revealed that when asked to identify desirable traits in people, mental health professionals generated three lists that were really two lists. How could this be? The answer is that the "adult male" list and the "adult" list were essentially the same (including descriptions like "independent," "powerful," and "self-reliant") and different from the "adult female" list (including descriptions like "dependent" and "nurturing"). This is changing. The fact is that girls no longer have to choose between being "feminine" and being "human," as they did in the past. The whole range of human traits is open to them as never before. I relish the fact that the girls in my life are likely to embody a full range of human capacities and experience, not be limited to the traditionally feminine ones.

My pleasure is based upon more than just a personal feeling. It finds validation in research that assesses the capacity of children to bounce back from and overcome adversity (resilience, as it is usually called by psychologists). As compiled by psychologist Emmy Werner and others, research on resilience documents the fact that traditional girls who have only "feminine" characteristics are at a disadvantage when it comes to coping. They are less flexible and less likely to access social resources that can increase an individual's power to master challenges that the world may present. In contrast, the most resilient girls are likely those who combine in their repertoire of characteristics and skills such traditionally masculine traits as being autonomous and independent (rather than being passive and dependent) with their traditionally feminine traits, such as emotional expressivity, social perceptiveness, and nurturing.

The term *androgyny* refers to this human completeness. Put simply, androgyny enhances resilience. The same goes for boys, by the way; combining traditionally feminine traits with their masculine traits makes for greater resilience in boys. It's akin to saying that kids are more adaptable when they have both hands free than when they have one hand tied behind their backs, even if they are inclined to be right- or left-handed. Unleashing girls to be fully human rather than narrowly feminine promises to be a positive factor in their development, particularly considering the social toxins they must confront each day.

For example, there is tremendous competition for access to children as consumers, most notably through the medium of television. James McNeal, author of *The Kids Market: Myths and Realities,* is one of the leading experts on selling to children. Writing in *Mothering* magazine, Gary Ruskin reports that McNeal sees children "as economic resources to be mined." To show just how despicable this can be, Ruskin cites the work of Cheryl Idell, a consultant who has written about advertising strategy for corporate clients seeking to sell to children. According to Ruskin, Idell advocates that corporate clients capitalize upon nagging and whining by children to motivate parents to make purchases. "In other words, Idell's job is to make your life miserable," says Ruskin. This is business as usual in much of corporate America and the reason why some psychologists have sought action by the American Psychological Association to declare collaboration with this process a violation of ethical standards.

When it comes to adolescents, one of the primary messages employed by the medium to motivate kids to buy is delivered by linking sex and popularity. Only the most resilient girls can resist. In *Reviving Ophelia,* Mary Pipher illuminates the role of television (and other mass media) in linking together consumerism, sexuality, and popularity. As Pipher sees it, this has had an enormous negative impact on girls. The television watched by young girls is full of characters, real and fictional, that exquisitely combine sexuality with conspicuous affluence in a socially toxic brew.

Girls' independent access to the culture via television, and vice versa, puts them in the "care" of programmers whose allegiance is to advertising revenue and exposes them to cultural icons who degrade and debase and then offer affirmation for those who toe the line and conform to standardized images of sexual attractiveness. Think MTV. Think Britney Spears. Think Paris Hilton. Think Christina Aguilera. Think *Fear Factor.* Independent access to television is one of the principal vehicles for exposing young girls to the socially toxic elements of American society. And successfully dealing with social toxicity demands all the resources a resilient girl can muster. In the dog-eat-dog world of pop culture only the strong survive morally and emotionally.

Our goal as a society ought to be to offer girls cultural space in which to be physical and popular in a nonsexual and nonmaterialistic way. But the media's linking of consumerism, sex, and popularity forces girls to confront the discrepancy between themselves and the relentless parade of slim, busty, sensual pop divas like Britney Spears on a daily basis. One emerging danger is that the advertising industry will expropriate female athletes and sexualize them as a way to increase their hold on girls. This is already under way. Take tennis star Anna Kournikova. Here's the lead in *Hello! Magazine*'s profile of her: "In 2001, tennis star-turned-sex symbol Anna Kournikova took home £220,000 in tournament prize money. It was a sum overshadowed by the £7 million-plus she banked for endorsements, flashing that model smile for everything from Adidas to Charles Schwab investments. And the offers keep rolling in, though she's never won a major singles tennis title." If the industry were to accomplish such a takeover of female athletes, it would have succeeded in overriding the positive empowerment messages of girls in sports and transforming them into further messages of sexual subjugation.

The outcome of this cultural battle is unclear. At present it seems the advertising industry is mostly successful in its campaign to persuade girls that their worth as a person depends upon their ability to be Britney Spears. Only the most resilient girls can resist this toxic cultural onslaught; ordinary girls are often powerless to resist. They have bought into the toxic myth that you are what you wear, and this leaves them feeling anxiously empty inside. A visit to any mall will verify this as girls move from Old Navy to Abercrombie & Fitch in search of the right sexy look to fill the void inside.

Social historian Joan Brumberg sees further evidence of this toxic trend in her book *The Body Project*, an analysis of teenage girls' diaries and journals across the twentieth century. As Brumberg sees it, the most dramatic change is that girls used to write mostly about issues of character—for example, "Am I a good person who lives up to her highest values?"—and now they write mostly about body image, sexuality, and popularity: "Do I meet the grade as a sexy diva?" How could they not when they are awash in a sea of images that demand this of them daily? And how especially painful this is when the discrepancy between the ideal of the superslim but busty figure is at odds with increasing rates of adolescent obesity (which has tripled since the 1970s). Plus, it's a physiological rarity to be both slim and busty, one reason why growing numbers of girls and young women opt for plastic surgery to override biological probabilities. Today's culture liberates girls to be sexy, but in many cases it imprisons them in the requirement that they use their bodies as sexual bargaining chips in the competition for status and prestige among their peers.

Beyond the general effects of increasing resilience and providing a more positive social climate for females generally, how does the liberation of women translate into the experience of girls? I see two important themes that provide a starting point for this discussion: providing affirmation for girls who do not conform to traditional conceptions of being "ladylike" and promoting activities like sports that teach girls they can use their bodies powerfully for more than sexual purposes. Both of these have had demonstrably positive effects on girls, but as we shall see, each has a dark side as well.

Whereas it used to be "unladylike" for a girl to show assertiveness, it is now much more socially acceptable, even desirable. The consequence of this shift is higher self-esteem and resilience, but also the possibility of greater aggressiveness.

Culture is particularly important when it comes to gender. In his book *Listening to Prozac*, psychiatrist Peter Kramer offers a pertinent example. Prozac is part of a family of psychoactive drugs commonly prescribed to help people suppress some aspect of their behavior or personality that impairs their ability to be who they want to be. When it works well, Prozac helps shy people suppress their shyness and be more bold. Anxious people can be more calm and confident. Passive people can be more assertive. This latter point is particularly relevant to women.

Kramer points out that in nineteenth-century America there was a positive social role for passive females. Too timid to face the world directly, these women might find refuge as housekeepers in the homes of more assertive siblings, as companions of elderly persons, or as the wives of patriarchal husbands. Kramer's point is that in the America of the early nineteenth century there was nothing psychologically abnormal or pathological about such women. Quite the contrary. Their attributes were deemed desirable: feminine and ladylike. It was their brash, bold sisters who were thought to be unhealthy or abnormal. They were the ones who as little girls were constantly asked, "Why can't you be more ladylike?" and "Why can't you be more like your sister?" Eighteenth- and nineteenth-century literature is full of such sister pairings. Think Jo versus Meg and Beth in Louisa May Alcott's *Little Women*.

Today the situation is reversed. It is the passive female like Alcott's Beth who is likely to have difficulty finding a place for herself in the world. She might even be diagnosed as suffering from a psychological disorder and in fact be prescribed Prozac. Her assertive sister—like Jo—in contrast is likely to find that the modern world welcomes her with open arms. In a June 2004 issue of *Newsweek* Anna Quindlen wrote in her column entitled "To Hell with Being Well Behaved": "Recently a young mother asked for advice. What, she wanted to know, was she to do with a 7-year-old (daughter) who was obstreperous, outspoken and inconveniently willful? 'Keep her,' I replied. I have never been a fan of tractable women, having mostly experienced self-loathing when I tried to masquerade as one." *Little Women*'s Jo would find a home with Quindlen and many other modern parents.

Of course this is not to say that assertive women find the welcome mat out in all settings. There are even today social and cultural settings in which the "old" femininity is still the rule and the "new" femininity anathema. Many fundamentalist religious communities exemplify this, whether they be Christian, Jewish, or Muslim. These communities still abhor liberated and empowered women and would rather fetter girls than unleash them.

What is more, research by psychologist Madeline Heilman demonstrates that the bias against assertive women still exists in many people's hearts and minds when it comes to the workplace. Helman examined responses to profiles of women who succeed in business. She found that successful women in traditionally male-dominated fields (like engineering and finance) were more likely to be rated as unlikable, selfish, manipulative, and untrustworthy by their coworkers (male and female) than successful women in more traditional feminine fields (such as human resources). Coworkers rated men with the same performance in all these fields as pleasant and likable. This might be called the Martha Stewart syndrome: Successful women are now welcomed in the more traditionally feminine aspects of the business world but are still subject to bias when they take over traditionally masculine work in that world. But the bottom line is that even if their home communities and families do not welcome individual assertive females, as a group they have many options. This is good news. And it starts in childhood.

When I was in elementary school in the 1950s, many communities did not allow girls to wear pants to school, some making an exception for blizzards. Girls might be the class secretaries, but they were never class presidents. Any girl who showed interest in the activities reserved for boys had to contend with the derogatory label "tomboy." For the past twenty years, report after report from prestigious academic and educational institutions has documented the progress made in making the world of childhood and adolescence more emotionally safe for assertive and demanding girls and demands that this progress continue. That's girls unleashed. That's good news.

However, as girls are unleashed from the cultural straitjacket of traditional femininity, some will inevitably evince unbridled aggressiveness in a negative sense. After all, as Tremblay's research demonstrates, girls certainly have the capacity for aggression. This is evident in the case of relational aggression. Today's empowered queen bees documented by Rosalind Wiseman are truly an aggressive group. A visit to any high school will reveal a lot of girls who have obviously said good-bye to passivity and embraced aggressiveness.

Girls can be mean. There's no doubt of that, and there's no news there. Girls often express this meanness by asserting their dominance through relational violence. These power struggles are not new on the cultural landscape of girls. What is new and changing is that our toxic culture's glorification of "hot" girls gives them extra power to torment and hurt as the spirit of meanness moves them. Whereas once these girls were marginalized by "good girls," now they are the dominant force in the competition for power within peer groups. The toxic materialism feeds their meanness, and it hurts.

You can hear the pain of it in eighteen-year-old Jessica's account. She is resilient but nonetheless hurt by coming to terms with the effects of the toxic sexualized and materialistic culture in her peer group. In her account she speaks for many middle-class girls like her. She grew up in the suburbs of Philadelphia with two professional parents who struggled to find a middle ground between giving her what she thought she needed to be popular and what they remembered from their own childhood was "appropriate." Here's Jessica's account of how this played out in her high school:

My high school was filled with girls who lived for putting other girls down, making fun of what other girls wore, and embarrassing other girls. My school was filled with seemingly invisible acts that only girls could pick up on. Personally I experienced the aggression of girls when my closest circle of friends betrayed me. I had been best friends with a core group of girls for three years when they became fascinated with a new girl, Blair, who "dressed to impress," offered them concert tickets, and used her house to throw parties. She desperately tried to buy their friendship, and they did not seem to mind. I knew they were taken in by how "hot" she dressed and how "cool" she seemed, like a girl right out of a television program. I could not lower myself to be suckered into that type of behavior and found myself being ostracized by my best friends. They began to lie to me about where they were going and what they were doing, leaving me home on the weekends. On top of that, between classes in school they would huddle in a circle, and when I approached, they would abruptly stop talking and make me feel like an outcast. This came to a head after the homecoming rally. They all decided to go to a local bagel shop, and I started to follow them because they were still my friends. However, they began to whisper and laugh. Finally Blair, who seemed to make all the decisions, turned around and told me that I was not allowed in her car and proceeded to tell me that I was a "bitch" and that she hated me. I stood there unable to speak. I was in disbelief that she could be so crude. She had no reason to hate me, but she did. Girls hate any other girl who is competition or who can be competition. Girls can be truly mean. Three years of friendship ended one afternoon in the parking lot of the high school.

Jessica says, "I could not lower myself . . ." but it still hurts to be forced to choose between good values and peer popularity. In a sense, Jessica's story represents the worst of both worlds, the relational aggression of the old femininity coupled with the materialistic sexuality of the new toxic culture. But her resilience and the positive changes afoot for girls offer hope of a new way out of this cultural prison for girls. This new way out lies in unleashing girls from the patriarchal order of the old femininity and replacing it with the empowerment of the New American Girl's physicality. The hope that lies in the liberation of women is the unleashing of girls to have the psychological and social resources that flow from androgyny, from escaping cripplingly narrow sex roles.

Let's look at situations in which girls combine physical aggression against self with relational aggression as a form of coercion. Kim is a nineteen-year-old engineering major from Minneapolis who grew up with three brothers. Here's her account of how her girlfriend combined relational aggression with physical assault against the self to manipulate her parents:

> My sixteen-year-old close friend Kelly called me from the emergency room of our local hospital. She told me that she had gotten into another one of her "normal" arguments with her mother and stepfather and had been so angry that she punched a glass window. When I asked her why, she justified her action by replying, "I needed to make my mother understand how mad I really was." Two years later this same friend was rushed to the hospital after taking more than twenty Tylenol pills. This followed a confrontation with her mother after Kelly had been caught having a party at her grandmother's home without permission. When I asked her why she took the pills, she said, "I wanted to punish my mother, but I wasn't trying to kill myself." After she had convinced the psychiatrist at the hospital that she really wasn't suicidal, she was allowed to go home.

Some preadolescent girls seem unaware of how their aggressiveness is related to their "excessive" self-confidence. They just act. But adolescents like Kim's friend Kelly tend to be more aware. Kelly is quite aware of what she is doing. This does not mean that what she is doing is healthy, of course, just that as a teenager she is capable of articulating her tactics in a way that is more sophisticated than the naive self-understanding of prepubescent girls. But girls like Blair and Jessica are not free of the social toxicity of our culture. Instead, they are awash in it.

A study of adolescents in Finland found that popularity increased for aggressive girls and that girls with high self-esteem were more aggressive than those with lower self-esteem. That warns us against assuming that unleashing girls is simply a positive process. Remember from Chapter 2 that it is mostly the lack of power among girls, not some inherent inability to aggress physically, that has restrained their physical aggressiveness. Equalizing power between the genders can lead to higher self-esteem for females by unleashing them from the prison of traditional femininity if it is accompanied by character education that instills positive values. But this same higher self-esteem can be linked to aggression if it is not. Unleashing girls is only the first step in transformation. What matters is what else happens once the prison door is open.

I see three elements in the process of unleashing girls from passivity and directing them toward assertiveness that merit attention for their potential effects on physical aggression in girls. One is that the cultural imagery of girls increasingly emphasizes physical aggression as an attribute of assertive girls. This is clear in an increasing number of films and television shows, and we shall take a look at it in Chapter 4. We can see a second element in the way socialization practices that used to reinforce feminine passivity are being replaced with empowerment training; we return to this issue in Chapter 8. The third is the lack of socialization experiences in the lives of girls that commonly do the job of controlling and channeling aggression in boys (Richard Tremblay's play fighting and father/child wrestling), a topic that we examine in Chapter 9. But before we turn to those issues, there is another aspect of the unleashing of girls that demands attention— namely, the impact of participating in athletic activities.

Participation of teenage girls in competitive athletics and recreational sports has risen dramatically in recent decades, offering physical and psychological benefits that include the girls' seeing their physical power in domains beyond sexuality. But these experiences can also validate physical aggression in girls.

When I was in high school in the 1960s, boys played on the athletic teams; girls cheered them on. Very few girls played sports, and only a handful of boys cheered. This has changed dramatically; at least the girls playing sports part has. As I reported in Chapter 1, according to the National Federation of State High School Associations, in 1970 one in twenty-seven high school girls played a varsity sport. By 2002 it was one in three! In 1970, for every girl who played a varsity sport in high school there were thirty-five boys, a ratio of 35:1. In 2002 there were nearly three million girls playing varsity sports in high school and nearly four million boys. That means the ratio of girls to boys was 1:1.33. Now that's social and cultural change.

What does this mean for girls? It undoubtedly means that girls who would have been drawn to sports in an earlier era but who might have forgone the opportunity because of fear of being labeled negatively can now join teams without fearing that their participation in sports will compromise their femininity. What would have been a tomboy then is now just a girl who likes sports. In the bad old days tomboys were at best tolerated; in the new era girl athletes are celebrated.

It's hard to say with certainty what the overall effects of this on girls are, however. Because participation is mostly voluntary, you can't be sure that any differences you observe between athletic girls and nonathletic girls are due to their participation in sports or the reason behind that participation in the first place. Nonetheless, studies do at least document that playing sports in high school is associated with certain positive outcomes for girls. These include being 92 percent less likely to use drugs compared with nonathletic girls, being more likely to wait until they are at least seventeen to start being sexually active (54 percent versus 41 percent), being much less likely to have an unwanted pregnancy during high school (5 percent versus 11 percent), being three times more likely to graduate from high school, being less likely to have the kind of "hanging-out" time that is associated with getting into trouble, and having higher self-esteem and less depression.

All these findings are consistent with the idea that opening sports to girls is an effective way to help them cultivate physicality without limiting that physicality to sexuality and sensuality. It promises that girls' athletics can be a counterweight to social toxicity. Athletics teach a girl that there is more for her to do with her body than use it for sexual purposes. However, as I noted earlier, the socially toxic forces at work in our society do not give up easily, and efforts are afoot to expropriate female athletes for socially toxic purposes.

I am encouraged that the shift in the physicality of girls flowing from their experience with sports can stimulate change among boys as well. Previously, adolescent boys mostly got physical with adolescent girls in the back seat of the car or in the bedroom. Now they can share intense physical experiences with girls that are nonsexual, as playmates on the athletic field. That's a healthier climate for sexual politics. It may transform the sexual fascination males traditionally have had with physical aggression among females into a more wholesome appreciation. Traditionally a physical fight between two females is a "catfight," and few things have been more sexually provocative for a traditional male than a catfight (unless it is mud wrestling). This sexual fascination with female aggression is evident in the historical accounts of women boxing collected by Jennifer Hargreaves (and referred to in Chapter 1). As she reports of Victorian-era bouts, "women's boxing always attracted male voyeurs—not only working men, but also local dignitaries and businessmen. Its explicit sexuality (through bare breasts and ripping of clothes, the scope for male fantasies, and potential as a surrogate for male brutality against the 'weaker' sex) increased the entertainment value of women's boxing into the twentieth century."

But now more and more boys and men see more and more girls and women sweat in an athletic way. I certainly do at the gym where I work out. Certainly our more level playing field works against the toxic hypersexuality presented to girls as a normal self-image. Which is the stronger force, sexualized toxicity or athletic physicality? Some girls are overwhelmed by sexual social toxicity while others have been clearly liberated by athletic physicality. But overall the link between girls getting physical and boys getting sexual has declined, and it should decline even more in the years to come. This is the healthy fruition of many positive long-term trends, the arrival at a place where girls can be physical on terms that meet their needs for affirmation and dignity, as well as pleasure and sensual enjoyment. A twenty-two-year-old woman put it this way, after thinking over her experience as both an athlete and a sexually active teenager: "I think there is a common assumption throughout that sexuality is bad. In fact girls taking control of their sexuality is a good thing. Who says that girls shouldn't be able to express themselves with sex as well as with sports? The problem is with society's being too closed-minded in this area and not giving teens the information they need to have sex safely. Sex is a normal and healthy thing; it's society's fault for demonizing it." I am not unsympathetic to this view, with one big however:

For girls to play by these rules and not get hurt, they need to live in a world where the boys are "on the same page" when it comes to what it means for girls to get physical.

Thirty years ago I sat in a collegiate locker room listening to two male undergraduates talk about a girl both knew. "Is she liberated?" one asked. From the context it was very clear he was not asking if she believed women should have careers, receive equal pay, and hold public office. What he meant was, "Does she have sex on the first date?" "Oh, yeah," the second guy responded. I hear less of that these days. The new liberated boy is a much-improved version compared with the old one and a much better match for the New American Girl. That's good news.

So what's the bad news? There is no such thing as a free lunch. There are always side effects and unanticipated consequences of social change, even positive social change. When it comes to unleashing girls to be athletic, the costs mirror the benefits. Gone wrong, involving girls in sports carries the same risks as involving boys does: The cultivation of physicality will translate into physical aggression.

Participation in rough-and-tumble sports can increase aggressive behavior. When Jeffrey Goldstein wrote his encyclopedic review *Aggression and Crimes of Violence*, he concluded that participation in athletic activities has a measurable effect on aggressive behavior, increasing it in proportion to the level of aggression contained within the particular sport engaged in. Contact sports like hockey, football, basketball, rugby, and soccer pose a greater risk than noncontact sports like tennis and golf. *Aggression is contagious.* This has led to the constant debate within educational, mental health, and coaching circles about how to prevent this aggression in the first place or, if that fails, how to contain it when it does occur. As we shall see, the role of adults as coaches and parents in defining the meaning of athletic experience is critical. Indeed, much of my concern for negative consequences is linked to the degree to which toxic adults are brought into the lives of girls through their participation in sports.

I read about and hear more and more accounts of sports-related physical aggression among girls. In Texas a middle school field hockey tournament ended in a knock-down, drag-out fight involving girls from both teams. According to a news story from Chicago headlined GIRLS SUSPENDED FOR BRAWLING AFTER VOL-LEYBALL MATCH, fighting broke out after a hotly contested game when players from the losing team followed the winning team into the locker room and started punching and kicking them. And here's nineteen-year-old Tiffany's account of another incident. She tells of her experience as a high school athlete in her hometown, a suburban community just outside St. Louis.

> I was on the girls' varsity lacrosse team for three years. I guess when girls get aggressive, it's more personal than with boys. In our games the girls on the other teams used to go after our best players. My friend Jenny was one of the best players on our team. She used to get hit on the head at least three times each game— on purpose. The competition was less about the game and more about the individuals. The other team always did it when the referees weren't watching, so they wouldn't get penalties or get kicked out of the game. The girls did it because they wanted to hurt her. If she got hurt, she couldn't play, and she was our best player. I think they also did it because they were jealous of her. She was so good, and they weren't as good as she was.

Playing sports can bring out aggression. Most of this effect is psychological. The experience of rough-and-tumble sports models and reinforces physically aggressive behavior, such as crashing into people. That in turn tends to move to settings off the field, the court, and the diamond. That contagion seems clear. But more physiologically oriented researchers have also pointed to possible biological effects of sports. The links are complex, subtle, and somewhat controversial, but real nonetheless.

In a careful review of "Hormones and Sport: Behavior Effects of Androgen in Men and Women," published in the *Journal of Endocrinology*, neurobiologist K. Christiansen reviews the evidence linking athletics to testosterone and aggression: "In humans, testosterone cannot elicit violence. It can only alter the probability that aggression is shown in a particular situation under a specific combination of external and internal cues." This is consistent with our own ecological perspective. If the question is, "Does testosterone cause increased aggression?," the answer is, of course, "It depends."

Second, high levels of testosterone in childhood are found to be associated with "physical aggressiveness and intense energy expenditures (vigorous play) but not verbal aggression," and these childhood patterns show up in adolescence. Whether or not this early pattern of rough-and-tumble play becomes the pathway to physical aggressiveness depends upon how it is received in the social environment of the child.

Third, "Regardless of the kind of sport, maximal or submaximal exercise (5–30 min) normally results in significant increases in testosterone levels. . . ." Involving kids in athletics engages them in this kind of exercise, with corresponding effects on hormone production and metabolism.

Finally, "several studies have shown that assertive or aggressive behavior followed by a rise in status levels leads to an increase in testosterone levels." Also, "The experience of winning and a rise in status even seems to maintain an already elevated level, sustaining the winner's activation and readiness to enter subsequent competition for higher status." It would appear from these studies that the more the athletic experience is tied to competition, the more likely it is to produce the testosterone-aggression link. As girls participate more in competitive athletic activities, their testosterone will rise, and thus they will become more likely to resort to aggression when they become aroused by anger or frustration "in the heat of the game."

Here's twenty-year-old Latisha's account of her experience with athletic aggression. She writes as a college psychology major who can't wait to finish classes each afternoon to get out on the rugby field:

> Growing up, most girls have less exposure to contact sports than boys do. But that can change. Take rugby. It's a contact sport; frankly it's violent, a bit like soccer and football combined. It's played without pads and going into a rugby game, you know you are going to get tackled, pushed aside, possibly stepped on, and your goal is to do it to the members of the opposing team. It's close to hand-to-hand combat. Girls come out to play this game. Just one look at the bright eyes and smiles on the rookies' faces when they are told, "Today you are going to learn to hit," is enough to know that protecting females from contact sports is not something all of them appreciate. And watching the veterans play the game proves girls can be ferocious on the field. Before you dismiss this as a minority of girls, let me reassure you that these girls are "normal" and are no different from my friends outside the team.

Latisha's last observation is particularly interesting and very much to the point. A generation ago girls who played rugby would have been an extreme anomaly, and in all likelihood they would have been seen as very different from what Latisha calls normal; today they really are "no different from my friends outside the team." That's a sign of just how much things have changed with respect to girls' participating in competitive, aggressive sports.

But the potential links between competition and aggression are troubling, particularly in a social climate in which much of the athletic experience of girls is more and more organized around competition and winning. It's not too big a stretch to assert that cooperation breeds kindness; competition breeds hostility. This is part of what Thich Nhat Hanh means when he speaks of experiences that water the seeds of compassion versus those of violence. It takes enlightened adult supervision and leadership to water the seeds of compassion on the playing field. Evidence is this is in short supply in our society.

Consider the June 7, 2004, issue of *U.S. News & World Report*. The cover story is entitled "Rescuing Children's Games from Crazed Coaches and Parents." And who is on the cover? A little girl in a baseball uniform, playing the infield, her expression one of intense resolve.

The article chronicles the toxicity of today's organized sports for kids. These include violent parental behavior toward children, coaches, or officials; 84 percent of parents said they had witnessed this. They include kids' being called names, yelled at, or insulted while playing; 45 percent of kids reported this. They include kids' being hit, kicked, or slapped while participating; 18 percent of kids reported this. There are also reports of rising numbers of sports-related injuries among children. Of course all this is happening in the lives of children in counterpoint with the bad behavior of professional athletes as watched by children on television, which includes everything from televised brawls during basketball, football, hockey, and baseball games to widespread steroid abuse.

There is also evidence of more and more intense competition starting earlier and earlier, with the rise of "traveling teams" that select the cream of the crop of children as young as eight for enhanced competition. The intensity of all this competitiveness is mirrored by the rise of a positive backlash, most notably in the form of the National Alliance for Youth Sports founded by Fred Engh (author of *Why Johnny Hates Sports*) and by the Women's Sports Foundation. Competition in athletics is a risky business, as Christiansen's review of the neurobiological evidence makes clear. I think the overall effect of girls in sports is overwhelmingly positive. But this does not mean we can or should ignore the physiological and the psychological risks. By acknowledging them, we can deal with them.

Here's what one high school coach told me about his experience of all this on the front lines:

I have been coaching and teaching physical education for nearly twenty years. In that time I have had the opportunity to work with kids in many different settings and at many different ages. The primary difference I have seen as a coach and an educator in the past ten years comes from the attitudes of the parents. I believe the pressures the girls are feeling are more in line with what the boys have felt forever. In years past, for women, the biggest talk of the Olympics was girls' gymnastics. That isn't so anymore. With the girls' soccer team winning the World Cup and the U.S. women's softball team having total domination for the past twelve years, I believe it changed our entire attitude about women in sports. In Mia Hamm they saw a very beautiful world champion in a sport that everybody's daughter plays. Add to that the growth in the LPGA and the WNBA. Parents started having professional dreams and aspirations for their daughters as well as their sons. Parents see sports as a way to pay for a child's college education. Rightfully so! Since the early 1980s Title IX has been making colleges move toward gender equity, so many universities started adding girls' sports. Since this trend has come into effect, it is amazing how many opportunities there are for girls to attend college on athletic scholarships. Which brings me to the current trend in women and the growing violence. Imagine the pressure to succeed that we place on our children. Like the guys who have been pushed all their lives and told how far they are going to go in athletics, I would imagine the seeds of inadequacy are planted in girls too. I wish I had a dollar for every time I heard a parent tell me his or her daughter was going to be a division I ballplayer. The children's failures to meet these expectations and the resulting parental disappointment must weigh heavily on these children. Many of our girls have been pushed to be great, and by the time they hit high school and begin developing as women they have to start making big decisions. Many decide not to be involved in sports anymore because they can't take the pressure. Some rebel, and now that they have been trained as physical competitors instead of as princesses they have the same capabilities to do battle as do the boys. And they do. I see more and more of it.

Girls are not immune to the aggressive contagion effect of competitive sports. The biology of competition and aggression knows no absolute gender boundaries. Certainly their traditional roles and attitudes have shielded girls from these links historically, but that is changing. It's up to coaches and parents to minimize the toxic side effects of physical competition. How? By using athletics as a vehicle for teaching character. The best coaches and parents have always done this.

So what's the bottom line when it comes to the benefits and costs of unleashing girls from traditional "feminine" attitudes toward physical aggression? The new freedom and assertiveness experienced by girls can boost self-esteem and self-confidence. It can replace traditional problems of depression and self-doubt with buoyant confidence. It can offer girls who are different a positive way to be so. It can displace self-destruction to more healthy forms of coping. These all are positive changes, and we should welcome them.

At the same time we know that these positive changes are not the only changes, and we know that while they may be beneficial for most girls most of the time, there is a potential dark side to all this. We need to worry about what happens when girls are un-leashed from the strictures of traditional femininity but are left to deal with social toxicity without experiences and training that prepare them to be sufficiently resilient. We can see this dark side in the increasingly toxic nature of the media experience of Amer-ican girls today, the topic for Chapter 4.

4

From Powder Puff to Powerpuff Girls: How Pop Culture Celebrates Aggressive Girls

have known Sally since she was born five years ago. My wife and I often babysat for her when she was an infant, and this relationship has continued to the present. Her parents are friends, and I know them to be loving, kind, and gentle. Before Sally started kindergarten, she attended the nursery school program that has its outdoor play space in sight of my office window. As a result, I have been able to watch Sally play with other children as well as see her at home with her parents. What do I see? In addition to being an apple of my eye, Sally is a very aggressive child. Although she is not as aggressive as some of the boys in her class, I have seen her push other kids down to the ground, hit other children, and even slap her father. In all this, Sally's behavior in no way seems surprising or shocking, though a generation ago it would have been.

It's also not surprising that Sally loves watching television and does so every day after she comes home from kindergarten, much of it without direct adult supervision. In that she is not unique or even special. One of the earliest and most enduring findings about television concerns this empowerment of children—at the expense of their parents.

Researchers in the 1950s consistently reported that parents didn't know how much television their children were watching, and that continues to this day. Early on, researchers found that children were exercising heavy influence in the choice of what to watch. By 1969 more than 25 percent of households in the United States contained two or more television sets. Today most households do. The possibilities for children to have independent access to the culture available on television without parental mediation multiply with each additional set in the home. Television opens girls to a host of influences that parents might not choose if they could more closely control what their daughters watch. This is not necessarily because those parents are oppressive and patriarchal. It can be and is because parents have as their motivation the best interests of their children, not simply the profit motive that guides much of what appears on the screen.

Like most children of her age in America, Sally spends an average of three or more hours per day watching television. Children spend more time with media than on any other activity besides school and sleeping. One study reported that 25 percent of sixth graders watch more than forty hours per week of television. This is more time than they spend in school. According to one study, at ten on any Saturday morning, about 60 percent of the six- to eleven-year-olds in America are watching television.

Why is all this significant? Evidence from a half century of research demonstrates that television viewing stimulates and validates physical aggression for children. For boys, this effect has been evident since this research began. The premier long-term study of the effects of television on children's aggression, led by psychologists Leonard Eron and L. Rowell Huesmann, began reporting in the 1960s that their research was revealing effects for boys but not for girls. The more boys watched television as children, the more physically aggressive they became, even after other influences, like parenting, social class, and temperament, were taken into account.

That was then. Now Eron and Huesmann's research shows the same effects of television on the behavior of girls as it does for boys, and has done so starting with girls raised in the 1970s and 1980s in comparison with the girls raised in the 1950s and 1960s. This is consistent with another of their studies, which looked at Israeli children growing up in a suburb versus a communal settlement (kibbutz). For the children raised on the kibbutz there was no relation between TV violence viewing and aggression, but for those growing up in the suburb there was. Why? The authors speculate that in the kibbutz there is a strong ideological stance against violence with the group and that this miniculture overrides the toxic effects of television violence.

Sound familiar? This could also explain why effects for American girls appear to be much stronger among females growing up in the seventies and eighties than for girls growing up in the fifties and early sixties. That's a dramatic and important change in the cultural and psychological life of girls. Consider the significance of this for a moment: For the first two decades of television viewing in America, girls were mostly immune to its toxic effects with respect to aggression, but in the last two decades that immunity has ended.

Among the findings from Eron and Huesmann's research was this: "Females who were high-volume viewers of violent shows as young children were more than twice as likely as other young women to have thrown something at their spouse and more than four times as likely as other young women to have punched, beaten, or choked another adult." These findings hold for girls regardless of how initially aggressive they were, how smart they were, how well educated or affluent their parents were, and how they were parented, including whether or not their parents used corporal punishment.

A study conducted in Canada in the early 1960s compared the level of aggression in children in a community after TV began to broadcast there with that in children in two similar communities that had no television reception. It found a 50 percent increase in aggressive behavior among four- and five-year-olds in the community that was exposed to television in comparison with the two communities that were not. Another study found that rates of larceny went up in American cities that had TV reception in comparison with communities that didn't. Also, there is Robert Centerwall's study, in which he reported that fifteen years after television broadcasting had begun in three different societies—South Africa, Canada, and the United States—there was a dramatic increase in serious violence.

Speculates Huesmann: "It's possible that the feminist movement of the late '60s and '70s has made females less inhibited about expressing aggression. Also, there has been an increase in aggressive female role models on TV and in the movies." That's for sure, and Sally is a living example of how this shift in aggressive female role models has translated into the lives of real girls.

One of Sally's favorite programs is *Powerpuff Girls* on the Cartoon Network. She also likes the books that accompany the series. The Powerpuff Girls are a group of three cartoon figures, Buttercup, Bubbles, and Blossom. Each has a particular personality; all are physically aggressive. Each episode contains one or more of the characters' taking some physically aggressive action, usually for prosocial purposes (to protect someone, to help someone, to foil an evildoer).

Consider the episode titled "Bubble Trouble" in the book version (and "Bubble-Vicious" in the televised cartoon version). It tells the story of Bubbles's struggle to gain the respect of her sisters, Buttercup and Blossom. The story opens with Buttercup on a rampage: "Hey, this Powerpuff sure can pummel! Slam! Bang! Thwop!"

"Man, Buttercup, you're HARD-CORE," Bubbles squeaked.

At first Bubbles is not up to the aggressive standards of her sisters, but over the course of the story she makes the grade. After she pummels the villain (Mojo), leaving him battered, "YOU'RE HARD-CORE!" her sisters shout. The message is clear and unambiguous: Girls who hit are hard-core and praised for it. Indeed. Of course *Powerpuff Girls* is not the only program Sally watches. Like most girls, she watches more than three hours a day (the national average is between three and four hours), and by doing so, she is watching many programs with aggressive and violent characters.

Numerous content analyses of television have shown that violence is presented frequently and in ways that can readily contaminate kids' thinking, feeling, and behavior. One study reported that there are about five incidents of violence per hour in prime time. Saturday morning programming for kids has even higher levels because of its disproportionate use of violent cartoons. This exposure adds up. One study found that over the course of her childhood a typical girl watching the "normal" amount of "regular" television will have witnessed 180,000 murders, rapes, armed robberies, and assaults—10,000 murders, rapes and aggravated assaults per year on television. These figures were lower when television began broadcasting on a widespread basis in the 1950s, but the trend was up to a plateau in the 1970s that continues to this day. This means that the end of girls' immunity coincided with television's achieving its current toxic level with respect to violence.

What does all this aggression mean in the context of the plots and characters? For a start, on television about a third of the violence is justified and socially acceptable. It reflects justice and morality by the fact that it is the good guys and gals doing it. This normalizes violence and increases the contaminating effects of such programming because a child does not have to choose between being violent and being good. The effect increases because in more than half the cases there is no apparent consequence associated with a violent act—no immediate pain (58 percent), no immediate observable harm (52 percent), and no long-term suffering (87 percent), none of the emotional signals that might dissuade sensitive and moral children from using violence to meet their objectives, be they prosocial or antisocial.

What is more, when compared with adult programming, children's programs are particularly likely to contain violence (69 percent), and less likely to show long-term consequences. The study conducted by Eron and Huesmann mentioned earlier revealed that the more kids accept all this violence as real, the more likely they are to act out aggressively in the future. As Huesmann puts it, "We also found that greater identification with same-sex aggressive characters and a stronger belief that violent shows 'tell it like it is' predicted violent adult behavior."

This last point is particularly important. Why are girls now showing the same effects of viewing violent TV as boys traditionally have? One reason is that there are more and more "same-sex aggressive characters" for girls to relate to on the television and movie screens that they watch. What's more, the increase in female physical aggression offscreen contributes to a self-validating upward spiral. The more girls hit, the more likely it is that girls watching girls hit on television will rightly conclude that these violent shows do indeed "tell it like it is," because they do. This strengthens girls' aggressive tendencies and undermines the traditional process of giving up physical aggression. Remember, girls start out about as physically aggressive as boys, so if the process of unlearning aggression erodes, there is every reason to think girls will hold on to their aggression the way boys do.

Moreover, in assessing the impact of these televised images, we must always remember that most of them are being received by children without benefit of adult interpretation. Kids watch a lot of television alone or with their peers and siblings, not with their parents. One reason is that most children live in homes with more than one TV. In fact children are less likely to live in a home with just one television than in a house with five or more. Also, for the most part it is kids who decide what they will watch on these televisions. Half the children surveyed in one study did not have any parental rules limiting their time in front of the television or the kinds of programs they could watch. For children eight and older, 61 percent said they watch what they want when they want. With the proliferation of cable television channels that offer a constant diet of films, that goes for movies too. What children see there amplifies the messages they receive from conventional made-for-TV programming.

I played hooky from the office one warm day in spring 2004 to see the film *Mean Girls* (based upon Rosalind Wiseman's book *Queen Bees and Wannabes*). The book and the screenplay by *Saturday Night Live*'s Tina Fey are a tour de force on the topic of relational aggression by adolescent girls. But what struck me about the movie was not the relational aggression that is the movie's primary focus, but the role of physical aggression in the lives of these girls.

Two images capture this. The first involves the heroine, Cady (a newcomer to North Shore High School). For a time she buys into the relational bullying perpetrated by the queen bee (Regina) and her minions, but as Cady comes to her senses, she begins to imagine physically aggressive responses to the pain and frustration produced by Regina. However, it is only after she breaks through the web spun of popularity and relational aggression that Cady's fantasies of physical aggression actually come to fruition—Regina is hit by a bus—while her breakthrough in dealing with relational aggression is mirrored by her female classmates, a brawl in the school's gymnasium. As has been the case in countless boys' movies over the years, this act of collective physical aggression is cleansing and restorative to the group. But this is not the only cleansing and restorative act of physical aggression in the movie. After Queen Bee Regina has been deposed, she finds solace in becoming a highly aggressive lacrosse player. The movie closes with the image of her running down the field whacking opposing players with her stick, an image of strength, healing, and acceptance. Finally, her fellow players mob her enthusiastically to celebrate her physical power. She "scores" on the lacrosse field in a manner that is presented as morally, emotionally, and socially superior to her former strategy for scoring in the sexual politics of her high school's web of relational aggression. She comes of age through physical aggression and becomes an exemplar of the New American Girl.

These images are important because they symbolize an important reality about girls who hit. First, images of aggression are not foreign to girls, even conventionally feminine girls. Indeed, psychologist Larry Aber and his colleagues reported in their study of eleven thousand school-age kids that at age twelve, girls actually had higher levels of aggressive fantasies than boys of the same age. Second, relational aggression can give way to physical aggression, and it can appear to serve a positive function, at least as a transition from the prison of relational aggression to a more healthy way of being, as it does for Regina.

Physical aggression may be a social problem, but many clinicians suggest that it is healthier to be physically aggressive toward others in a "socially acceptable" way than to engage in violent behaviors directed against oneself or to engage in passive aggression in the form of psychological violence against others. As we shall see in later chapters, however, this transition is not always smooth.

Remember the young female witch Hermione's punching out of the bully Malfoy in the movie *Harry Potter and the Prisoner of Azkaban*, mentioned in Chapter 1? Hermione's aggressive response to the bully is actually consistent with the overall presentation of kids in the mass media: Prosocial aggressive behavior rules. A content analysis of television completed by researcher Kathleen Heintz-Knowles for the advocacy group Children Now found that while prosocial behavior is more common than antisocial behavior by children on television and is more likely to be effective than antisocial behavior, there is one major exception: TV teaches children that *aggression works*. Children Now reports:

- Seventy percent of child characters on fictional shows engage in prosocial acts, while 40 percent engage in antisocial acts. (Many characters display more than one kind of behavior.)

- Prosocial behaviors are most likely to be seen as effective in meeting the child's goals, while antisocial behaviors are more likely to be shown as ineffective. Sixty-one percent of prosocial behaviors were effective, while antisocial behaviors were effective just 34 percent of the time.

- Although most antisocial behaviors do not pay off for the children on television, physical aggression is effective in meeting the child's goal most of the time.

Remember, physical aggression is not presented as antisocial behavior in the context of American culture as it is represented on television. The Children Now study reveals that physical aggression is rewarded more often (53 percent of the time) than affection (46 percent), explaining feelings (45 percent), and performing responsibilities (32 percent), though less frequently than cooperating (91 percent) and helping (73 percent), both of which do not rule out aggression. Of great interest for our purposes here, verbal aggression is rewarded less often than physical aggression (only 16 percent of the time versus the aforementioned 53 percent of the time). Girls represent about half the child characters on television but are twice as likely to show affection and 40 percent less likely to demonstrate physical aggression than boys. They are thus generally less effective than boys.

Given the importance of power in the lives of children, this is a significant finding. Girls want to be powerful. It has only been because they were strongly discouraged from physical aggression that they have traditionally forsworn it in the past. But if cultural change opens the door for girls, they will walk through it and choose power over ineffectiveness. Who wouldn't? This sends a clear message to girls who are inclined to adopt the more traditionally feminine forms of verbal and relational aggression: Cross the bridge to the twenty-first century, get physical! The shifting patterns of behavior in "real life" suggest that girls are taking note that the traditional boys' strategy is more rewarded and effective than the girls' strategy. And they are implementing that recognition in the form of more physical aggression.

Here's one teenage girl's account. It comes from eighteen-year-old Anna. She's an engaging girl, a good student, an athlete, and a singer. She grew up in a blue-collar neighborhood of Chicago with two very traditional parents. But early on she found her own way through the maze of gender politics in childhood. She says:

> Why should boys have all the fun? That's what I want to know! Even when I was a little girl, I thought it was unfair that the boys got to do what they wanted and the girls had to be little ladies. I'd watch TV and see the boys were always in charge, doing things, fighting, being strong, whatever. All I saw the girls do was have tea parties and play with their dolls. And be nice to the boys. In school it was the same thing all over again: The boys were strong; the girls were weak. Back then I felt like I was the odd one because I took on the boys and didn't give an inch. But now things are different. I see more and more girls on television and in the movies taking action. Like Lara Croft. It's about time. I know I'm ready. Now when I go to the movies, I am looking for girls like me, strong girls who can kick ass.

Here's one of the principal changes in mass media over the last three decades: Whereas once the "good guys" and the "bad guys" could be differentiated on the basis of their level of physical aggression, now that is not true. The good guys are as violent as the bad guys (and in some cases, even more violent). The male heroes of the 1950s look quaint and almost feminine in their physical restraint, in comparison with today's manly men and even today's manly but sexy women like Lara Croft, the high-powered spy/adventurer of movie and video game fame.

How does the imagery of aggression fit into this mix? When girls are unleashed from the ties that bind them, what is the significance of new female aggressive images in the mass media? Answering these questions requires a more general understanding of the effects of television on aggression.

Concern about the impact of television began early, when in 1936 a British social psychologist named T. H. Pear raised the question of effects, asking, "What differences will television make to our habits and mental attitudes?" The area of influence most systematically studied since then has been the effect of television in transmitting and stimulating aggression in children. In 1972 a report to the surgeon general of the United States entitled *Television and Growing Up: The Impact of Televised Violence* surveyed hundreds of research reports and focused almost exclusively on this topic. The report cautioned that the common denominator of the existing research was a growing concern that there were negative effects of televised violence on behavior and attitudes of children. The toxicity of televised violence was becoming apparent.

In the 1990s the American Psychological Association examined thousands of studies and concluded that there is a direct link between viewing violence on television and increased aggression by children and youth. The American Academy of Pediatrics and other child-related organizations have joined the psychologists in warning of such effects. The pediatricians went so far as to urge parents to prevent all TV watching for the first three years of a child's life.

In 2004 the results of a new report requested by the surgeon general and the National Institute of Mental Health were published (not by the government but rather in an academic journal because of pressure from media lobbyists to compromise the study's science in favor of more industry-friendly conclusions). Compiled by a veritable who's who of research on aggression and the mass media, the report validated and extended earlier reports: There is a causal link between violence on television and aggressive acts committed by children. What is more, it found that negative effects from childhood can extend into adulthood and that although kids more prone to aggressive behavior for other reasons are a bit more susceptible to the effects of television violence in producing aggressive behavior, even kids at low risk of aggression for other reasons are also affected.

By now it is clear to most unbiased expert observers, in fact to anyone without an ax to grind who takes the time to look at the research, that the effect of televised violence is to increase aggressive behavior in boys and girls. How big is the effect? The American Psychological Association's 2001 report concluded that by itself TV violence accounts for about 10 to 15 percent of the variation in children's aggressive behavior when the most recent research is used to make this calculation.

Fifteen percent. Is that a big or a small effect? When something so important as aggression and violence by children is at stake, that's a big effect. As a point of comparison consider that this effect is as big as the average effect of smoking on the development of lung cancer. It is bigger than the effects of many other important public issues of health and development, such as those of exposure to lead on children's IQ scores, calcium intake on bone mass, asbestos exposure on laryngeal cancer, the nicotine patch on smoking cessation, self-examination on the extent of breast cancer, and secondhand smoke at work on the development of lung cancer.

Most people who smoke don't get lung cancer, but even the most addicted smokers now realize that their habit increases the risk significantly. Moreover, unlike the genetic factors at work in who gets cancer and who doesn't, the links between TV violence and aggression by children is a psychological effect and thus something we can control socially. The knowledge linking smoking and lung cancer is the basis for the massive public health campaign aimed at reducing smoking. This includes laws governing when and where adults may smoke and a ban on cigarette sales to kids. Yet we have few restrictions on television, even though its contaminating effect is probably more "pure" than the effect of smoking on cancer. How many people even consider TV a public health issue? The reasons for their reluctance are multiple and include popular cynicism about psychological research, the indirect nature of the effects, the fact that so many people enjoy watching violence, and the deliberate efforts of the media industry to obscure the reality of the science involved.

Most of the research on the effects of aggressive contagion from the mass media deals with television, but I think we can generalize to other visual media in the lives of kids today: movies, music videos, and video games. If you look at the voluminous research on the role of the mass media on aggressive behavior by children, three themes emerge: absorbing aggressive attitudes and behaviors; emotional desensitization toward real-world violence; and increased fear of being victimized by violence. All three can affect the way girls think, feel, and act. All three can promote a more negative view of the world and increase a predisposition to act self-protectively and with mistrust.

Girls saturated with toxic media violence absorb cultural validation for physical aggression, or to put it in Thich Nhat Hanh's terms, they water the seeds of violence. That undermines the traditional basis for their immunity to violence relative to boys. It is a spiritual as well as psychological assault because it starves the seeds of compassion. Girls saturated with media violence adjust their standards toward violence. They become less and less sensitive. They must do so to survive emotionally in the face of the repeated images of violence that confront them on the television, movie, and computer screens of their world. Girls saturated with media violence alter their worldviews, their social maps, to incorporate the messages of threat and danger that infuse those media images.

In short, confidence is displaced by fear. How do girls deal with their fear? Traditionally they might withdraw in passive terror. But the New American Girl is taught to fight back when she is afraid. Each of the effects of being immersed in media violence compounds the others. The effects multiply and magnify. Television and movies feed the world of video games, and vice versa.

Video games are a new area of concern for those who worry about the development of our children because of their disproportionately violent content. Among the most popular games, violence is the norm. Think Grand Theft Auto, in which the player is rewarded for a campaign of violence that includes murdering a prostitute after having sex. In one study, 80 percent of the games required physical aggression as part of the strategy for winning. While overall 67 percent of households with children have video game systems, girls have been less likely than boys to play these games (in one study, 37 percent of girls did not play versus 12 percent of boys). This is changing as the cultural landscape of aggression changes for girls.

Several studies have tested the effects of children playing violent or nonviolent video games. Most found that when kids played violent video games and then were given an opportunity to act aggressively, those who played violent games were more aggressive as measured by actual physical aggression toward another child as well as in a laboratory setting in which they delivered electric shocks to someone who provoked them or to punish someone who had violated a rule. The effects of playing the violent games were about the same for males and females. Overall the effects of playing violent video games have been demonstrated for all the components of aggression: feelings, thoughts, physiological arousal, and behavior. As with all the effects of media aggression on child aggression, the effects of video games are relatively small but are significant (accounting for about 9 percent of the variation in child aggression).

The technology of images in the media of television, movies, and video games has advanced. They have become more and more visually explicit in their treatment of violence and horror. With this increasing realism, another concern has arisen alongside the contaminating effect of violent images. This is the issue of media-induced trauma. Trauma is the experience of being simultaneously overpowered by unmanageable negative feelings (overwhelming negative arousal) and having your idea of the world blown away by horror (overwhelming negative cognition). With the power of contemporary special effects, coupled with the no-holds-barred approach to subject matter to which children are exposed, it is little wonder that the potentially traumatic impact of television and the movies is now an issue as never before.

I should note that if violent and sexualized material is presented visually, it can have more powerful effects than if the same material is presented only orally. Psychiatrist Lenore Terr notes in her book *Unchained Memories* her findings that young children who only hear about horrific events do not have the same traumatic responses as children who witness them visually. Think of all the horrific images in traditional fairy tales. In *The Three Little Pigs* houses are blown down, childlike piglets are terrorized, and eventually the predatory wolf falls into a pot of boiling water. Imagine if that same material were to be presented with today's state-of-the-art visual technology. Imagine the wolf boiling to death in slow motion with screams of agony.

Joanne Cantor and her colleagues have also offered some very disturbing research on this issue. They find that young children are frightened by what they see on the screen. Preschool children are more likely to be frightened by the appearance of a creature or person even if it's not harmful. But school-age children are likely to be frightened by the extent to which characters do scary things that seem real.

In one of their studies, Cantor and her colleagues asked adolescents and young adults of the 1990s to recall childhood fright reactions to the mass media, including the news. About 90 percent recollected such reactions. More than 25 percent reported that the fright reaction had lasted at least a year. More than half told of reactions that included difficulty in sleeping or eating. More than 20 percent reported "subsequent mental preoccupation with the frightening aspects of the stimulus." Movies like *Jaws* (sharks) and *Halloween* (mass murder) were associated with the most severe symptoms.

The findings of the traumatic impact of mass media images have been validated by other studies, including one that asked parents to identify their children's responses and learned that the reports of children and parents coincided in documenting traumatic responses. For me it echoes the findings from Kuwait after the Gulf War in the early 1990s, where researchers found evidence of posttraumatic stress disorder among children who had been exposed to videos of the atrocities committed against Kuwaitis by the Iraqi occupying forces. What are so many of the television, movie, and video game programs girls and boys watch but vivid presentations of atrocities? This may be one area of particular concern as more and more of the popular music environment of girls (and boys) has become both sexually violent in its lyrics and visually explicit through the domination of music videos as the vehicle for presenting that content. Girls have traditionally been taught to respond to terror with emotional withdrawal and passivity. The New American Girl is taught to fight back.

The combination of aggressive role models and traumatic imagery in the mass media is a powerful cultural force at work in our society, a force that now has important psychological ramifications for girls. Are these images provoking more emotional disconnection (what psychologists and psychiatrists call dissociation)? Some studies answer in the affirmative. For example, watching violent video games was associated with less helping behavior in one study. Why? Studies have demonstrated that as kids watch violent media, their physiological reactions become stunted, and this can decrease their inclination to help victims of aggression. We as a society have long relied upon the empathic and sympathetic impulses of girls and women to "tame" our patriarchal society. If girls are being desensitized by their increased exposure to violent images, then one of the important defenses against social toxicity is being eroded.

Are the violent images kids confront provoking strong impulses to become aggressive as a defense against a hostile world? While definitive answers to these issues of long-term effect must await the passage of time and the next generation of research, I believe there is cause for concern.

The media experience of girls is saturated with violent images. Consider music videos. I saw my first music video in a hotel room in Iowa two decades ago. Bored and a bit frazzled from traveling, I turned on the television and began to flip through the channels until I was stopped cold by Michael Jackson's "Thriller." Wow! This was amazing. Of course, compared with today's music videos, "Thriller" is actually quite tame. Its sexuality and violence are muted by today's standards.

A study conducted by Michael Rich and his colleagues looked at "Aggressors or Victims: Gender and Race in Music Video Violence." The researchers focused on MTV, which is watched by 78 percent of girls between the ages of twelve and nineteen (and 73 percent of boys). Females are 22 percent of the aggressors in these violent interactions (males 78 percent) and 46 percent of the victims. MTV is one of the principal vehicles for popularizing music and artists via music videos. And as others have found with respect to the links between TV violence and aggressive behavior, Donald Roberts, Peter Christenson, and Douglas Gentile found a positive correlation between amount of MTV watching and physical fights among third- through fifth-grade children. In addition, frequent MTV watchers were rated by peers as more verbally aggressive, more relationally aggressive, and more physically aggressive than other children. Teachers rated them as more relationally aggressive, more physically aggressive, and less helpful.

The linking of sexuality, material wealth, and aggression in these videos is a powerful common theme. Are there any limits? The answer is technically yes, but realistically no. Consider the case of Madonna's offering "What It Feels Like for a Girl." During the course of the video Madonna rams her car into a car full of young men who have been ogling her. She "Tasers" a man at an ATM, runs down a group of boys, blows up a gas station, and eventually ends her life in a murder-suicide. MTV declined to run this video after an initial airing. But this hardly indicates some sense of propriety on the part of MTV decision makers.

Pop music critic Eden Miller highlighted this in a piece written in 2000: "Sure, Madonna's spree of criminal and anti-social behavior isn't the best example for impressionable viewers, but since when has MTV been concerned with that? They may put on a socially conscious face, but many of the network's popular videos contain violent or questionable content, from Eminem's video for 'Stan,' where the Stan character drives his car off a bridge (with his pregnant girlfriend in the trunk, no less) to Robbie Williams' vulgar 'Rock DJ,' where he strips his skin off in graphic detail."

The Country Music TV channel reported that the Dixie Chicks' song "Goodbye Earl" (about planning and executing the murder of an abusive husband after a two-week marriage) was the most requested video of that particular season. Of course, women like the Dixie Chicks and Madonna still represent a minority of the violent images purveyed by the mass media. Males continue to dominate the images. Children Now's ongoing content analysis of television characters indicates that for many years males have outnumbered females in prime time, about two to one. But this does not guarantee that girls have therefore lacked aggressive role models in the mass media, because unlike boys, girls will model their behavior on the opposite sex. Why? I think it is partly because many girls have had a sense that the freedom and power available to boys are desirable. Few boys grow up thinking, I wish I were a girl, but it has not been uncommon for girls to "aspire" to masculinity.

Perhaps this identification with male role models has fed the aggressive fantasies of girls. But it is only as the cultural restraints on aggressive behavior on the part of girls have subsided that the impact of girls' identification with male role models has been evident in aggressive behavior. The available evidence tells us that girls are looking to male role models for psychological and cultural "inspiration," and this may magnify the impact of male violence on female fantasies, attitudes, and behavior. Asked to choose three roles with which they identified, just 25 percent of the girls chose only females (as opposed to 47 percent of the boys who chose only males); 57 percent of the girls chose at least one male, and 16 percent chose only males. In *My Fair Lady*, Professor Henry Higgins asks, "Why can't a woman be more like a man?" Well, maybe she thinks she can.

Girls are accessing male role models more and more. As a result, are they tapping into traditionally masculine approaches to aggression and thus being more and more open to influence by mass media images of violence? I think so. This account from a teenage girl certainly sounds like something an aggressive boy would do. The respondent is nineteen-year-old Annie, who grew up in a suburban neighborhood outside the upstate New York city of Utica:

In tenth grade, as I sat in my friend's car in the school parking lot, waiting for my lunch period to end and the next class to begin, I witnessed an accident. My friend Sally was driving through the lot when she was blindsided by Ryan Thompson, a senior on the football team, who was driving the wrong way down the one-way lane in the parking lot. After plowing into a parked car, Sally got out of her car crying hysterically. No more than a few seconds after Ryan stepped out of his car Sally attacked him. She tried punching him in the face several times and hitting his car several times. Although in the wrong in the situation, Ryan handled the attack pretty well and kept his cool. Sally, on the other hand, could not contain her frustration.

And here's eighteen-year-old Natasha's story. There's nothing special about Natasha. She blends in with the other students in her freshman psychology class. But her account sounds a lot like the way boys have used physical aggression to vent frustration and test their loved ones:

> Most of my aggression has always been toward objects: I often throw items in a fit of rage. Once, when I was in an argument with my boyfriend, out of frustration I just punched a wall. I don't really recall why I did it, but it didn't hurt too much, and in a way it relieved a lot of the tension running through other parts of my body. I have always had a rather high pain tolerance, so at the time I thought I had found my way of letting go of frustration and I did it again. My boyfriend stopped me, and then it was almost as if, since he cared enough to stop me, punching a wall could be a way to test if someone else still cared. Ultimately, the next day, when the bruise was so bad that it hurt to take notes, I really regretted it.

Hers is a modern story, a story emblematic of the aggressive culture that teenage boys have long inhabited, but that girls are now moving into in ever-larger numbers. Pop culture celebrates aggression. Girls are immersed in pop culture. It appears from the research of the last fifty years that girls were once somewhat immune to the influences of this immersion. Traditional femininity with all its restrictions, limitations, and powerful messages buffered the effect of media violence on girls, just as traditional masculinity amplified those effects for boys. All that is changing.

Girls are falling under the contaminating influence of TV as once only boys did, and their aggressive behavior is increasing. Images and behavior work together in a self-reinforcing system, escalating as time passes. As a result, the traditional differences between boys and girls in terms of aggressive behavior are diminishing.

As one scholarly examination of the psychological research put it, "Recent reviews find fewer sex differences with respect to aggression. In 1974, Maccoby and Jacklin held the opinion that aggression was the area in which perhaps the most clear sex difference could be found, but more recent studies do not agree." This same recent review of the evidence reported that only 5 percent of the differences in aggression by kids could now be explained by whether the children were girls or boys. Ninety-five percent of the difference is attributable to other factors in the child's background and development.

How are we to understand this 5 percent figure? As I noted earlier, television accounts for 15 percent of the variation in aggressive behavior, just as smoking accounts for about 15 percent in lung cancer. Each of these phenomena is caused by an accumulation of risk factors. The same is true when it comes to the role of gender in aggression. Where once gender may have been a highly significant factor in predicting which children would exhibit physical aggression and which would not, this is less and less the case. Rather, in today's world, most of the "causes" of physically aggressive behavior lie in factors that affect boys and girls nearly equally: their exposure to media images, their family backgrounds, the ways they think about conflict, their intelligence, their emotional sensitivity, and so on. After all these factors are taken into account, there is very little left to explain by gender. For the most part, it's a new ball game when it comes to physical aggression in girls. We can no longer assume they are immune to the factors that stimulate aggression in boys. As we shall see in Chapters 8 and 9, this has important implications for the policies and practices of parents and everyone else who cares for children.

The process of female liberation and equalization is nearly complete when it comes to aggression, and the mass media have provided one of the most important vehicles for achieving that dubious transformation. If Tremblay's finding that infant girls and boys start out equally aggressive turns the theoretical world upside down, then Eron and Huesmann's finding that girls used to be immune to the effects of TV violence but no longer are turns the social world of kids upside down. When it comes to the role of gender in the culture of violence, it truly is a new ball game, and we all are going to have to learn some new rules for playing. We can see one consequence of this in the way the traditional forms of relational aggression in girls have themselves become more aggressive, the topic of the next chapter.

5

The Evolution of Mean:
The New Language
of Girl Violence

As I wait my turn to merge left at a road construction site in my hometown, a car cuts in front of the SUV ahead of me. The driver leans out the window and shouts, "Wait your turn, motherf***er!" I am driving on the interstate and pass a car that is traveling too slowly for my taste. As I drive alongside and begin to pass, I glance over; the driver gives me the finger. Driving through town on a sunny Saturday, I pull up to a red light and notice that the car in front of me has a bumper sticker that reads, "Girls kick ass." All the drivers in these incidents were young girls, maybe seventeen years old. Point taken.

My wife and I sit in our favorite local café. A friend of a friend at the next table is talking about one of his daughter's telephone conversations with her friends that he overheard inadvertently the night before. "They were talking about anal sex, for God's sake," he tells us. "It's all 'fuck this' and 'fuck that,'" he says, bewildered at the language his sweet child uses with her friends. His daughter is twelve years old. I've met her. She *looks* like the twelve-year-olds of my youth. But what comes out of her mouth is quite different.

Traditionally, when girls want to hurt people, they do so by manipulating relationships, which researchers have come to call relational aggression. Of course the reality of day-to-day life among kids is that the lines between relational and verbal aggression often blur. For example, hard-core teasing that stigmatizes a child or an adolescent can be a form of relational aggression. Intent and consequence are often complex; some teasing is done in a way that bonds kids (particularly boys) together, but some either seeks to isolate and humiliate or unintentionally has that effect. And even if an individual is not scarred by teasing, if the content is toxic, it can have a corrupting effect on everyone involved that may not be observed until later. As we'll see in more detail shortly, it boils down to the issue of whether or not verbal aggression becomes part of a larger pattern of psychological maltreatment. It starts with the fact that girls generally are more adept than boys with words, and their verbal aggression thus can more readily be used in the service of relational aggression than that of their verbally clumsier male counterparts.

These findings are repeated in study after study, as psychologist John Archer's encyclopedic review makes clear. Socialization and biology speak with one voice on this matter. Little girls develop interpersonal skills more rapidly than little boys, and this is one reason they are able to switch from physical aggression to relational aggression earlier and more smoothly than boys. There may well be a biological basis for girls' ability and inclination to do this; girls may be primed for verbal behavior more than boys.

Researcher Eleanor Maccoby conducted a study in the 1960s demonstrating that for girls (but not for males) the amount of babbling in infancy predicted IQ at age five. Put this together with the fact that in utero the jawbone of the female fetus develops and begins to move before the jawbone of the male, and you have to think that there is something going on regarding the role of verbal behavior in the development of girls versus boys. It seems words play a bigger role in the development of girls than of boys (who end up equally smart but presumably take a different pathway, a nonverbal pathway, to get there).

On average, in comparison with their male peers, girls are better with words. It should come as no surprise then that traditionally, when girls have gotten aggressive, they have used words as their weapons more than they have fists. This verbal aggression often is integrated into relational aggression by virtue of the way words are used to hurt through manipulating relationships. However, the two forms of aggression are neither mutually exclusive nor necessarily uncorrelated.

In this sense, verbal and relational aggression can be a dangerous complement to physical aggression and may even provide a bridge to cross over from words to hitting, particularly in the settings that have always elicited the most intense aggressive responses from girls, conflict in the family and competition for the attention of boys. Here's Tina's account. A college freshman majoring in English, she comes from a two-parent family living in a Boston suburb: "One Sunday night when I was fourteen, my older brother was supposed to pick me up from my youth group meeting. This posed a special problem for me because I was embarrassed to be seen in his 1950s Mustang. He pulled up during the closing prayer and proceeded to rev up the unmuffled engine repeatedly while honking the horn. The racket was quite audible in the muted sanctuary. When I stepped outside, I marched right to his car, opened the door, slapped him across the face with all the strength I could muster, and screamed, 'Fuck you!' "

We can start with the fact that traditional patterns of verbal aggression not only remain in force for girls but may actually be escalating as result of the increasing social toxicity of adolescent culture, notably the vulgar hypersexualization of girls in public life. As we saw in Chapter 4, the mass media do much to shape and validate the way kids think, talk, and act. The fact that pop culture has come to validate ever more verbally sexually aggressive and degrading language plays a critical role in enhancing the nastiness of verbal aggression. Powerful nasty words abound in contemporary girl culture, and they hurt.

But doesn't the repeated use of these words actually cause them to lose some of their power? The term for the process by which repeated exposure to initially upsetting images leads to a decrease in their effect is *desensitization*. Does the prevalence of nasty words lead to desensitization? This may actually be the case in some respects. To listen to some of today's kids throw around the *F* word, you have to believe it has become so casual they really are desensitized to it. But the flip side of this desensitization is that as the process proceeds, two other things happen. First, it takes more and more vicious language to produce an effect—i.e., to really make a point, it's necessary to call another girl a bitch rather than to say she is mean. Second, the very process of desensitization leads to degrading the humanity of the other person (depersonalization it's called), and this itself facilitates all forms of aggression. What's more, as the nastiness of the language escalates, the consequences of making a mistake (by exposing an undesensitized girl to intensely nasty words) increase.

I hear this risky amalgam of verbal, relational, and physical aggression in Marsha's middle school recollection. Now a nineteen-year-old majoring in economics, she grew up in Dallas, with her parents and two siblings. Asked about observations of aggression when she was a teenager, she offered this:

> In eighth grade there were two Stefanies at my middle school. One of them was extremely popular and pretty, and one was not as pretty (and not as popular). Unfortunately, neither of the girls was very nice. They often said mean things about each other behind their backs—like "she's an ugly bitch" and "she's a cocksucking whore," really bad stuff like that. One time the pretty, popular Stefanie reported to a teacher some of the things that the other Stefanie had said. The uglier Stefanie was sent to the principal and received an in-school suspension. The very next morning we all were seated on the bleachers in the gym. This was where we were supposed to sit before the first bell rang. Popular Stefanie was standing right in front of me, talking to a group of students, when I saw the other Stefanie enter the gym. She scanned the room, saw pretty Stefanie, and made a very angry beeline straight for her. I could not believe what happened next. Uglier Stefanie grabbed the other Stefanie by the hair, and in seconds both Stefanies were on the ground. Popular Stefanie just cried as the other Stefanie screamed, scratched, and beat her head into the gym floor while holding on to her hair. Finally a few teachers were needed to pull one Stefanie from the other.

As I pointed out in Chapter 4, technology can provide new toxic influences on the development of aggression—for example, the dark "opportunities" provided by video games. But new media can also provide new venues for the expression of verbal and relational aggression and for the toxicity of these forms of aggression to flourish. Consider the emergence of girls' involvement in Internet chat rooms. One evening I was signing copies of my book *And Words Can Hurt Forever* (written with my colleague Ellen de Lara) after giving a talk to parents at a middle school in a small upstate New York community. A mother handed over a printout of her thirteen-year-old daughter's "conversation" in an Internet chat room. Here's an excerpt (complete with the online nicknames, slang, and verbal shortcuts that dominate kids' Internet communications, but with a little translation where needed):

> **Dogs8emmi:** who's this?
> **Neversaythat33:** Someone. When are u gunna fucking move? So I hear that u bitch at my crew?
> **Dogs8emmi:** w/e [whatever]
> **Neversaythat33:** don't w/e me u dyke
> **Dogs8emmi:** fine bitch
> **Neversaythat33:** ill kick ur ugly dirty lil ass fucker

And later:

> **Dogs8emmi:** what do you care about making me feel bad when you obviously have a sad life already
> **Neversaythat33:** cuz umm u fuck with her ill mess u up bitch. GO FUCK UR DOG AND HORSES SOME MORE U DYKE
> **Dogs8emmi:** I know who you r
> **Neversaythat33:** who am I bitch?
> **Dogs8emmi:** that's right . . . your just a bitch who is jealous of me.
> **Neversaythat33:** jealus of u? umm no way. whoa id kill myself if I looked like you and acted like you.

These are suburban middle-class girls. They are what would ordinarily be thought of as "nice" girls. It's unlikely they hear this kind of language at home. But they do hear it in the music they listen to and the movies they watch—and from their peers. These girls, like many of their male counterparts, are steeped in the violent imagery of the music they listen to. As the transcript makes clear, these girls also go beyond listening. They absorb this imagery and incorporate its coarse language and nastiness into their daily chat room discourse.

There is a contaminating effect of being awash in this verbal cesspool. For example, a set of five studies conducted by psychologists Anderson, Carnagey, and Eubanks provides clear evidence that songs with violent lyrics increase aggressive thoughts and feelings. As is always the case in this type of research, the observed effects were small. But these effects do accumulate and compound their impact as girls are exposed to the same violent images in music, in movies, on television, in video games, and in music videos. As a footnote to this, I might add that the National Center on Lost Children estimates that many kids engaging in sexual themes in Internet chat rooms are vulnerable to being solicited by sex offenders.

The kind of aggressive nastiness captured by the mother in her thirteen-year-old's chat room goes on every day and night in virtually every community in America. Girls are online, aggressing against other girls in a nasty blending of the traditional form of girl violence—name-calling, social comparison, and rumormongering—and the modern penchant for what we used to call obscene language. The relative anonymity of the Internet chat room accelerates and exacerbates the process and the content of these exchanges. The process feeds back into the face-to-face interaction of girls in "real life." Several incidents have

The Evolution of Mean

occurred in which girls have either killed their online tormentors or killed themselves to escape the shame and humiliation.

Spend some time in the hallways, locker rooms, cafeterias, buses, and bathrooms of American middle, junior, and senior high schools, and you will know that sexualized verbal aggression is not confined to chat rooms. It is woven into the fabric of girls' lives in our toxic youth culture. Some girls are deeply hurt by it. Why? Because this verbal and relational aggression constitutes psychological maltreatment, which is the most potent form of assault there is, short of murder or physical mutilation.

I have been interested in psychological maltreatment for a long time because human development takes place in the mind and spirit of the child, and these are where the most grievous injuries are suffered, those that produce the most lasting effects on behavior and development. I believe there are at least four forms of psychological maltreatment involved in nonphysical aggression among girls: rejection, terrorizing, isolating, and corrupting. I laid these out first in reference to parents' treatment of children in my 1986 book *The Psychologically Battered Child*, but the effects when coming from peers are just as devastating.

Rejection is about actions that send the message "You are not good" and thereby offer a negative definition of self to a child. As anthropologist Ronald Rohner documented in his 1975 book *They Love Me, They Love Me Not*, rejection is universally a psychological malignancy, an emotional cancer that disrupts development and distorts behavior. Read Rachel Simmons's book *Odd Girl Out*, and you will see that the relational aggression that forms the traditional backbone of girls' assaults on each other is steeped in rejection.

Where does rejection fit into the culture of today's girls? I think my visit with Ann makes it clear:

Seventeen-year-old Ann opens her backpack and pulls out a dog-eared notebook. "This is it," she announces. The cover simply says, "Slam." She opens it and thumbs through some pages. "Here," she says, handing it over for me to inspect. At the top of the page is the heading "Kaitlin." Ten lines follow, each written in a different hand and including the following: "Dresses like a boy." "Dyke." "Dorky." "Not cool."

"'Does she know about this?" I ask.

"Oh, yeah," replies Ann, "we showed it around in the cafeteria last week."

"Has Kaitlin seen this?" I ask.

"Yeah," Ann responds with a smirk. "We showed it to her too."

"How did she respond?" I ask.

Ann smiles. "At first she said nothing, but then she got all teary and stuff."

"Why did you do it?" I ask.

Ann responds quickly. "She pushed one of our friends in gym class the day before, and we wanted to let her know she couldn't get away with that shit. Now nobody will talk to her. Even the girl jocks are afraid to be seen with her."

Rejection is a powerful emotional stimulus. It can readily escalate into physical aggression. Here is Nina's insightful account of how her rejection sensitivity precipitated physical aggression. Having grown up in a small town outside Toledo, Nina felt rooted in her neighborhood, her school, and her community. Her loving parents provided her, an only child, with a strong sense of her own worth and value. All this did not blunt the hurt she felt when exposed to rejection:

"No, you can't play with us right now. Why don't you go eat another doughnut or something?" These words hurt, especially coming from Amanda, one of my best friends in third grade. I guess it doesn't justify pushing her on the playground, but I did, and I pushed her with all the force and aggression my body could muster. We all know that "Sticks and stones can break your bones"; all hurt, but words can hurt forever. Words are actually more significantly disturbing, especially to a young and very sensitive girl such as myself at the age of eight. When Amanda made a derogatory comment about my eating habits, I was beside myself. She knew, as did most, that I was extremely insecure about my slight pudginess. Therefore I was not only offended by her words but by the fact that she used these words to hurt me. Amanda knew very well that I would be offended and feel rejected by this comment, yet she said it anyway. She *wanted* me to feel upset. In addition, my act of violence was triggered by jealousy. Amanda was playing a game with my *very best friend*, Katie. I use the term *best friend* significantly, because to girls, the term *best friend* is more than just a concept; it's a title and an honor (that implies making friendship bracelets and having regularly scheduled play dates). Granted, this concept is much more extreme for younger girls. However, it is highly valued at any age. Since Katie and Amanda were playing together, I felt like the excluded third, the "crowd." This was not a justified reason to hit Amanda, by any means, but perhaps this possessive jealousy is what drove me to be aggressive.

Rejection is perhaps the most important and most fundamentally destructive form of psychological maltreatment there is, but it is not the only form. Terrorizing, using fear to torment, punish, and manipulate, is also an important element of bullying and harassment in adolescent girl culture. Perpetrators use the fear they incite in the victim to achieve dominance and thus gain power. Here's one girl's experience with terrorizing.

Jeanne is a nineteen-year-old psychology major. The younger of two sisters, a very strong-willed but sensitive girl, she told me this story of her encounter with childhood terrorizing:

I was about nine. I had just moved from a small town to a metropolitan suburb. I entered fourth grade in a new school, and everything was going fine until I was promoted to the fifth grade the following January, doing two years in one. That would have been fine except that I was now the youngest in my class, and the tallest, oldest girl in my class was twelve and mean. I remember the terror she instilled in all of us younger classmates. As I look back on it, I realize she was probably in the opposite situation to mine—she must have been redoing fifth grade—seeing how most of the other students in my group were about eleven. This twelve-year-old towering dark-haired girl had the unfortunate reputation of being from the toughest neighborhood, and she let us know it. She ruled us with an iron fist, which she didn't hesitate to use after class to threaten and beat up whoever had challenged her authority or inadvertently discontented her that day. I was one of those girls. I can't recall whether it was for having defended myself or a classmate (I did tend to be an advocate for the downtrodden even that far back), but one afternoon she let me know that she was expecting me in her chamber of tortures, alias the open field across from school. I was utterly petrified. I heard nothing all afternoon but the pounding of my own heart. I was a wreck. At three-fifteen, resigned to be beaten up, I made my way to the open field. I don't know why, but I didn't think I had a choice to run away or tell my teachers to defend me. I just went. She belittled me in front of the watching crowd, forcing me into verbal submission that she was the queen bee and that I was to do as told from then on. I agreed. I never forgot her power over me and over all of us, for that matter, or the terror she instilled in me. After her, I made a point of keeping to myself more. The anxiety of that experience, magnified by the innocence of my youth, left a definite imprint on my consciousness.

Another element of psychological maltreatment is isolation. Human beings are social creatures, and to feel right about themselves, they need to be in relationships. This seems to be particularly true of girls, who tend to be more affiliative than boys. This is the core insight of Rachel Simmons's book *Odd Girl Out*, and it is the touchstone of the power that relationally aggressive bullies use to torment their victims. Being alone is a powerful threat to the traditional girl's sense of self-worth, and threatening a girl with isolation is in some ways the worst threat of all. As a form of psychological violence, isolating involves cutting girls off from essential peer relationships.

I should point out that the "wrongness" of each form of psychological maltreatment is its violation of kids' basic human right to be treated with dignity. This is not to say, however, that the effects of psychological maltreatment are automatically and always only destructive. As is the case with all human experiences, the consequences depend to some extent upon the individual. For example, some kids who are isolated respond in ways that can actually produce especially creative characters. This may be especially true in the case of particularly creative people, whose tortured pasts may become the basis for creative resolutions. Examples are found in the characters in Chaim Potok's *The Chosen*, one of whom, a genius, is deliberately psychologically maltreated by his father in order to build empathy in his brilliant son, and in the work of Eudora Welty, who drew upon her own suffering as a result of being socially isolated to cultivate a very sympathetic attitude toward society's downtrodden. While suffering can be the impetus to enhanced development, its more typical effect is to harden the heart of the victim and instigate a cycle of emotional violence.

There are many bases for being isolated—wearing what the leading crowd decides are the "wrong" clothes, having the "wrong" hair, or listening to the "wrong" music, for example. Once isolated, girls can easily become disconnected from the moderating forces of mainstream society and susceptible to strange thoughts and feelings. Ironically, this state of isolation may bring together pairs of kids who link up in their estrangement from the larger group and begin to develop odd and sometimes dangerous ways of thinking about themselves and their lives. This appears to have been a feature of the awful process that led Eric Harris and Dylan Klebold to undertake their assault on Columbine High School in 1999. And consider this example offered by my colleague Ellen de Lara in our book *And Words Can Hurt Forever: How to Protect Adolescents from Bullying, Harassment, and Emotional Violence*:

Michelle feels very isolated and lonely at school. She is a marginal student, at best, who sees herself as never intentionally hurting anyone. Much of the time she is neglected, her basic emotional needs being ignored by her peers. When she is not being neglected she is being rejected. She doesn't understand why she is picked on to the extent that she is. At the beginning of the school year she had a best friend but that relationship fell apart, and she is clearly unhappy and confused. Despite her best efforts, she cannot figure out what went wrong and now just wants to get out of school. Her words give us a direct view into the school day of many students like her.

I ask her, "Do you like school?" She replies: "Not really. I like the classes, but not the people. If I could be home schooled, that would probably be better. The people in school pick on you all the time. Right now, I have a problem with people spreading rumors around about me. I don't really like it. Most days I don't want to even come here. The teachers and guidance— they just know I'm here and that's all they really care about. People say that I'm, like, fat, which I know I am but they don't need to be picking on me about it. They spread it around that I'm pregnant and I'm not. Just dumb things. My ex-friend, she used to be my good friend but then a couple of weeks ago she started spreading rumors. So now she's not my friend no more."

Ellen notes that Michelle's isolation and exclusion from friends and peers are, unfortunately, the experience of many, many girls on a typical schoolday. These children rarely report what is happening to them to a parent or to any adult. They suffer terribly and in silence most of the time. In our study of "The Secret Lives of Teenagers," conducted with students at Cornell University, we found that most girls (67 percent) said they felt humiliated at school, and nearly half (40 percent) said their parents didn't know. Also, a majority of girls (61 percent) reported having been afraid of other kids at their high schools, and about a third (28 percent) said their parents never knew. This is all the more striking considering that in order to be admitted to a prestigious Ivy League university like Cornell, these students have to be high achievers in their high schools. If these elite students felt such a high level of emotional assault and deprivation in high school, we can only wonder what most students feel!

Yet another form of psychological maltreatment is corrupting. Corrupting means learning ways of thinking, speaking, and acting that make a child increasingly unfit for "normal" or healthy experiences. Many parents have been shocked to hear their previously sweet children begin to spout angry and obscene language as they move into the world of adolescent peer groups. Research shows that this negative language has an effect on behavior.

Researchers studying the behavioral effects of this peer contamination process report that when peers laugh at and make fun of positive activities and endorse negative activities, previously positive-minded kids start to slide toward antisocial behavior. This is one reason why girls (and boys) in groups usually behave worse than kids alone. The group's norms drift toward the foulest, nastiest end of the spectrum represented by the group, as the average slips lower and lower. The lowest common denominator rules in most cases. As we shall see in Chapter 6, there are always some girls who enter adolescence predisposed to antisocial and self-destructive behavior. Thus there are always negative influences available in the middle and high school to set in motion the process of corrupting. This has always been true, but in the world of today's girls, the magnitude of corruption available to be spread by the peer process is as never before.

Consider the case of Karin. She incorporates the worst of this corrupting process in the context of a socially toxic culture. What's particularly striking about her case is that she comes from a "good" family: two involved parents, a father who works as a local police officer and a mother who works as a real estate agent. The parents have worked hard to spend time with Karin and pro-

vide a positive climate in the home. As a child she played baseball and was the apple of her father's eye.

If there is one thing that Karin's parents might be faulted for
it is that they reduced their level of supervision as their daughter
entered middle school, something that seemed to flow naturally
from their own busy work lives. Her childhood had been unremarkable in most ways, and she seemed to want the freedom
they were inclined to offer. But as she moved into adolescence,
Karin fell prey to the social toxicity of her sexualized peer group:
Sixteen-year-old Karin sits on her bed, surrounded by the stuffed
animals of her childhood. She sounds weary as she reflects on her
life "in the old days"—when she was fourteen.

> When I entered high school, I started hanging out with some
> girls who were different from my friends in middle school. These
> were really cool girls. They dressed really hot, and I guess I was
> flattered that they wanted me to be their friend. I wanted to be
> part of their group, and looking back on it, I was willing to do
> almost anything to get their approval. Before long I was dressing
> like them and talking like them too. They talked really tough and
> dirty, you know, "fuck this" and "fuck that" and "shit" and "you
> bitch and you cocksucker." Stuff like that. We really put down
> girls who were goody-goody and enjoyed shocking adults with
> what came out of our mouths. And before long I was fucking
> boys just like them. We would go to parties just to show off how
> sexy we were. We'd brag about the hot older boys we fucked and
> the sex games we played, like on the Playboy Channel. Some-
> times we would have sex with four or five different guys in one
> night in one of the bedrooms at the party. All kinds of sex, you
> know, oral sex and anal sex and regular sex. At first I was grossed
> out by it, but eventually I just accepted that it was what "we" did.

This went on for about a year and a half until I got sick and was out of school for a month. When I came back to school, it seemed like I didn't fit into the group anymore. For a while I was really lonely. Then I made some new friends, and life changed, but I still feel dirty sometimes when I think of how I was back then. I guess you can't go back.

Where does the "old" aggression of verbal and relational violence fit into the lives of girls amid an increase in the "new" aggression of physical violence? For one thing, by degrading "the other" through verbal assault, girls create a fertile climate for physical assault. Dehumanizing and depersonalizing the other are one way to lower the psychological and emotional standard for hitting. Girls can tell themselves that they are still morally OK. They can justify themselves by saying, in effect, "I attack only people who are lower forms of life than I am." This is one way in which the increasingly toxic verbal aggression of girls may set the stage for increasing physical aggression. Boys have been doing this for a long, long time, but it has a newfound place in the culture of girls.

Compare the traditional "you're not nice" with the contemporary "you're a f***ing bitch" for their dehumanizing and depersonalizing content. The first is a judgment of character; the second is a statement of dehumanizing contempt. There *is* a correlation between verbal violence and physical aggression. The more girls verbally degrade and demean one another and the more they isolate and reject one another, the more they set the stage for depersonalization and dehumanization. The other conditions for physical assault are increasingly met for girls because of changing cultural messages and reduced social controls. The link between attacking with words and attacking with fists grows stronger.

The more girls depersonalize and dehumanize other girls, the more they set the stage for physical assault. This is why the issues of verbal and relational aggression and the issues of physical aggression are not distinct and separate issues. Rather, they are psychologically linked processes and merit attention together in the world of girls.

One commonly noted difference between girls and boys is that overt aggression seems more likely to end relationships between girls than boys. Simmons noted this in her book *Odd Girl Out*, and I hear it in the stories girls tell. Boys often report returning to friendship, even initiating friendship in the wake of physical aggression. But girls usually speak of physical aggression as the end of relationships. Literature and life are full of boys who have had physical fights and thereby "cleared the air" in their friendships. I recall such experiences from my own childhood. But girls typically had different experiences.

Sandra is an eighteen-year-old history major. She sings in the college choir and plays on the women's basketball team. She was raised by her single mother in a suburb of Atlanta, and her story chronicles the way verbal aggression leads to physical aggression when girls are released from the traditional taboos:

> My ex-best friend and I lived around the corner from each other and grew up together. We spent every day side by side until sixth grade. Throughout our friendship I noticed that she would often make derisive remarks and nasty comments. Afraid to stand up for myself, I would never tell her how I felt about her condescending undertones or hurtful words. At one particular incident, however I decided that I had had enough. We had been fighting for quite some time, about what I could not remember. She started saying hurtful things about me and my family, and

we began to shout at each other. At one point she slapped me across my face. I was shocked. I could not believe that someone I considered my best friend could do something so violent and aggressive. Not knowing what else to do, I grabbed her and forcefully pushed her away from me. Under normal circumstances I could never have laid a finger on her, but I felt that if I did not respond to her, she would continue to torment me. Unfortunately it took that episode for me to realize that my friend was no friend at all.

What's striking to me about this story is that because physical aggression was so alien to the relationship between these two girls, they had no common physical language to resolve their conflict in a way that many boys would have had.

One place where physical and verbal aggression come together increasingly is in the actions of female bullies. These girls often move smoothly between verbal and physical assault. Listen to Allison's story. Raised in Boston, with very strict and traditional parents, Allison was sent to parochial school starting in kindergarten. She was always a leader, on her girls' soccer team and in the classroom. Her encounter with a female bully at school left her feeling shocked:

Attending an all-girls' high school provided me with plenty of situations where physical aggression was present. A particular example comes to mind. Every day this one girl would ask a very naive girl for money for lunch. The girl being bullied came from a broken home where money was always tight. However, because the classmate asked her in a way that was hard to answer no to, the girl would reluctantly hand over whatever money she had to the bully. After a few weeks of this, I felt that it would be beneficial to stand up for this girl and tell the bully that this girl's situation was not good and would she please just remember her money for lunch in the morning (she came from a very well-off family) instead of asking this other girl. This was when the aggression started. Instead of handling the situation like a young adult, she started with verbal abuse. She called me names that were really nasty. After some time of this she escalated into downright anger. She threatened to throw me down the stairs and said that I had better watch my back when I was walking. If it hadn't been for the intervention of my friends, there was no doubt in my mind that she would have charged at me right there and then. Because I had confronted her about her bullying, she decided I deserved to be attacked verbally and maybe physically hurt.

Bullying is widespread among girls. It usually takes the form of relational aggression, however. Stephanie's account is illustrative. Now a nineteen-year-old sociology major in college, she was an astute observer of the social scene growing up:

Starting in seventh grade, a group of rude, obnoxious girls began forming a clique in my middle school. Anna, the leader of the clique, despised me. I was studious and well liked by all my teachers, and I actively participated in class. Anna was the opposite. She was a below-average student who often caused distraction and trouble in class. Soon I became the object of her aggression. When the teacher wasn't looking, she would throw spitballs in my hair, and so would her followers. Sometimes she sat behind me and pulled my hair. Other times she would take the pencils off my desk and break them in half. In gym class she would "accidentally" hurl balls at me. She even threatened to beat me up a few times. She seemed to find pleasure in seeing me cry whenever she did something mean. I never spoke up to Anna because I feared that she and her friends would gang up on me. I stopped participating in class, hoping not to draw Anna's attention toward me. Instead she gained power from my submission. She continued to be mean, bossing me around, stealing my belongings, and putting me down. Meanwhile many other girls either joined her group or befriended her to avoid her cruel treatment. The misery did not stop until I moved away the summer before starting high school.

Are girls meaner than they were in the past? There's no evidence of that. What is clear is that the intensity of the meanness has shifted, becoming more overtly and aggressively sexual in nature. How could it not? Astute observers like psychologist Mary Pipher (*Reviving Ophelia*) and historian Joan Brumberg (*The Body Project*) have documented this insidious process. Whereas once it was relatively easy for a girl to have a relatively nonsexualized cultural space in which to be a teenager, now that is much more difficult, almost to the point of impossibility in some schools and communities. The language they speak, the clothing they wear, the music they listen to, the movies and television programs they watch, and the magazines they read all immerse girls in sexuality, much of it blatant. Either you join or you face being ostracized. It's very difficult to avoid breathing in an atmosphere of aggressive sexuality. While this may convey certain advantages compared with the passive sexuality of the past, it also forces girls to deal with issues of sexuality earlier than they might have done so in the past.

Here's Erica's story. It saddened me to hear the bitterness and the pain in her voice as she recalled her confrontation with toxic sexuality in early adolescence:

Upon hearing the term *young girl,* one often thinks of the stereotyped image of the innocent, sweet, and heaven-sent little angel in the frilly pink dress with golden curls and ribbons in her hair. That was me in elementary school. But it didn't last. Take the innocent fourteen-year-old, put her in low-cut tight jeans below her belly button and a shirt that stops just below her breasts, and you have today's girl. That's what I faced when I arrived in high school. The pressure to look like the sexy girls was awesome. It was too much for me, that's for sure. I wasn't ready for it and all the attention I got from the older boys. Looking back on it, I wish there had been some other way to be cool.

There is an aggressive edge to this sexuality. It validates aggressive impulses and the linking of sex and violence in girls' minds and hearts. And boys are often quite willing to collaborate in this, fed as they are by media images of "bad girls." What is more, this hypersexualization intensifies and accelerates competition among girls. Competition for what? Competition for boys (or for other girls in the case of lesbian youths), first or all. Even after all the shifts toward female liberation and empowerment, boys are still equated with prestige and power for many girls. Psychologists studying aggression between girls report that it is most likely to arise in situations of competition for boys and that it reflects our evolutionary past, one element of survival of the female fittest was the ability to attract and hold the most valuable males.

Girl after girl tells some version of the same story. Marti is a nineteen-year-old premed student majoring in human development who grew up in Minneapolis:

When I was a junior in high school, the worst fight I witnessed was between my friend Heather and another girl in the school. Heather had been dating this guy for a long time but hadn't slept with him yet. It seems the other girl was trying to steal him away from her, and her way of doing it was to offer more sex than Heather was willing to give. When Heather found out, she became very angry and told this girl to back off. However, the girl ignored her warning and spread bad rumors about Heather, saying she was a slut and slept around. When Heather found out about the rumors, she became furious. One day Heather walked up to this girl in the back of the math classroom and slapped her in the face. She yelled and physically abused the girl. The girl fought back, and soon it was a real brawl. They were scratching and pulling on each other's hair. Eventually other kids intervened to separate the two girls.

Reports increase of girls physically assaulting peers because of jealousy, often prompted by one girl's having sex (hooking up) with another's "man" (who may be all of sixteen years of age). Female gang wannabes are engaging in ever more violent behavior to gain the acceptance of their aggressive male peers. As always, the links between sexuality and aggression are most clearly seen at the extremes of behavior. The toxicity of the verbal and relational aggression so common among girls supports and fuels these physical assaults.

Alongside the positive features of liberating girls to be more aggressive, there has been an increase of abusive meanness in girls. It flows from the dangerous mixture of traditional themes of verbal and relational aggression coupled with the toxicity of the aggressively hypersexualized world in which today's girls live. Bad language fuels bad behavior, and the potential for damaging psychological maltreatment among girls (and between boys and girls) grows as a result.

We have seen that there is more than one aspect to this New American Girl. Side by side with the positive unleashing from the bonds of traditional femininity and patriarchy is the infusion of social toxicity into the inherent aggressive impulses and behavior that come as standard equipment for children, girls and boys alike. I have long believed that the most serious effects of social toxicity are to be seen in the most vulnerable kids exposed to it. This brings us to a look at the most troubled girls, among whom delinquency, aggressive behavioral problems, and self-destructive assaults have been on the rise.

Part Three

When Things Go from
Bad to Worse
for Girls,
Then and
Now

6

Cinderella Strikes Back:
Girls Who Are Sad,
Mad, and Hurt

The story of Cinderella is a traditional story of child abuse and neglect. The motherless girl is emotionally abandoned by her father and then hurt by her mean stepmother and stepsisters. But her sweet nature and the intervention of her fairy godmother save her, transforming her sadness into joy and love. In the end she even welcomes her former tormentors into her life with the charming prince. End of story. Literature is full of other stories of abused and neglected girls who are rescued, who suffer in noble silence, or who even respond benevolently to their tormentors.

But court records are full of different stories about maltreated girls. They offer a different set of narrative patterns. These stories often turn out badly. The sad and hurt girl gets mad at someone. Cinderella gets even. Traditionally this meant hurting herself or allowing others to hurt her. But increasingly it means acting against others directly through assault. Here's what Tanya had to say about such an abused and troubled girl. Coming of age on the Southside of Chicago in the 1990s, Tanya was no stranger to violence. The poverty and the social deprivation around her scarred many young lives. Tanya was one of the fortunate ones, however. Smart, energetic, attractive, athletic, and blessed with two loving parents, she parlayed her strengths into a scholarship to an Ivy League university. However, she hasn't forgotten the many kids left behind in her neighborhood. She recalls one in particular, a girl who came to school with welts and bruises from the whippings she got at home when her abusive father was drunk. Here's Tanya's account:

There was this one girl in my junior high school who would always cut the entire lunch line. Her name was Tainesha. No one ever said anything to her because everyone was simply afraid of her tall, muscular appearance. I didn't know much about her, but other kids said she had a terrible home life: Her mother had died when she was six, and her father was mean to her. One day my friends and I strolled into the cafeteria, sat down, then got on line for lunch. As soon as I was about to devour my chicken sandwich and potato puffs, I heard a loud crack and a bunch of screams. All of us at my lunch table stood up on the surrounding chairs to see what the cause of the commotion was. Sure enough, it was Tainesha. Apparently a girl had been sitting in her usual seat. Tainesha demanded that the girl find another seat, but the girl had refused. Tainesha took her lunch tray and cracked it in half right on top of the girl's head. Her scalp was split open by the impact. The situation was a bloody mess, and the girl had to be rushed to the hospital. All Tainesha had to say was "She shoulda moved." Tainesha got suspended for a month, but no-

body messed with her after that. A few years later she dropped
out of school, and I heard she got arrested for assault and went
to jail.

A troubled girl often hurts others. She expresses her rage in
ever more frequent physical assaults that may afford her a
temporary sense of relief, no matter what the long-term consequences. This same trend toward physicality finds expression in
the forms of self-assault chosen by today's troubled girls. If she
hurts herself, today's troubled girl is more likely than before to do
so in the physically aggressive form of cutting. Like the troubled
girls who assault others, girls who cut themselves often say it
makes them feel better in the short run. Nineteen-year-old Mary,
a biology major from Phoenix, offers this account of how her
cousin's troubles were expressed through physical self assault:

> My uncle and his girlfriend had my cousin Elizabeth when
> they were quite young. Once she was born the two of them split
> up, and neither of them had the most stable living conditions, so
> Elizabeth spent a lot of time with my family. We liked her, and
> she seemed to be a sunny, easygoing child when she was living
> with us. About two years ago Elizabeth changed. Her dad re-
> married, and because he was now considered to have more sta-
> ble living conditions, Elizabeth moved in with him and his new
> wife. Unfortunately the stereotypical evil stepmother situation
> ensued. It appeared that her stepmother was treating Elizabeth
> more as a chore than as a daughter. We thought it was abusive.
> Things went from bad to worse, and Elizabeth started cutting
> herself on her arms and legs. She said it made her feel better. She
> was admitted to the hospital and then sent to a residential cen-

ter for kids with her problem. She is out now, and we see her during summer vacation. She no longer seems comfortable with herself, and we rarely hear her laugh. I miss the old Elizabeth.

Many studies have linked such early experiences of child maltreatment—physical, psychological, and sexual—with later aggressive and antisocial behavior. In particular, abused children (girls and boys) are more likely to develop a chronic pattern of aggression, bad behavior, acting out, and violating the rights of others. If these children develop this pattern by age ten and come to the attention of mental health professionals, they are likely to be diagnosed with conduct disorder (CD). However, I should note here, before we go any further, that the criteria used for diagnosing conduct disorder don't seem to fit the way girls experience it as well as they do boys, and as a result, girls are less likely to be accurately identified if they are having this sort of developmental difficulty. This problem is being addressed but makes it difficult to make confident statements about historical differences in rates of conduct disorder for girls versus boys.

It does seem clear, however, that if girls do develop a negative pattern of aggressive antisocial behavior by age ten, they are on the fast track to serious violent delinquency in adolescence. As I mentioned in Chapter 1, about 30 percent of ten-year-olds diagnosed with conduct disorder end up as serious violent delinquents in adolescence, and a majority end up troubled, if not in trouble, in psychiatric facilities and rehabilitation hospitals, if not in prison.

Not all maltreated girls turn out badly. In fact, most do not. Why? Why do some abused girls walk this path while others do not? And why do some children who are not abused and neglected in the first place develop this pattern? Put most simply, what makes a child turn to conduct disorder is risky thinking about social relations. It is because of the link between being an abused child and developing this pattern of risky thinking that there is a link between child abuse and conduct disorder in the first place. This risky thinking is evident in the child's internal map of the social environment, her social map.

The social map is the child's rendering of what the social world looks like and how its various parts relate to each other. It is like any other map in that it is drawn from a particular perspective and thus subject to bias resulting from where that perspective is centered. If we start with the objective of facilitating child development and producing an adult who is competent and prosocial, the need is for a social map that finds an effective balance of being realistic and positive. To be effective, a girl's social map must contain enough positive elements to sustain her emotionally and enough realistic elements to equip her to avoid making major mistakes in her relationships with other people.

Psychologist Daniel Goleman has offered the concept of emotional intelligence as a way of describing the key to a successful and responsible life. This concept is very much in line with the idea of social maps' being positive and realistic. In Goleman's view, the essence of emotional intelligence is having the skills and motivations that lead a person to understand, care about, and work effectively with the feelings of others, live productively within society's norms, control impulses, and manage her inner life in a way that harmonizes inner needs and outer social realities.

One source of the images of the world displayed in a girl's social map is her intellectual competence (knowing the world in the scientific sense of objective, empirical fact). Another element is her moral and emotional inclinations. Both intellectual competence and emotional inclinations are the product and the cause of experience. How a girl sees the world affects how she acts, and how she acts affects how the world treats her. It is a cycle, for better or worse. Negative social maps breed emotional disability and distorted thinking; emotional disability and distorted thinking lead to negative social maps.

In early childhood, the outlines of these social maps begin to emerge. It starts with what we commonly call attachment. Knowing your caregiver and having expectations for how that caregiver will treat you are your first social map. It reflects an understanding of the lay of the land emotionally and socially, the infant's social environment in terms of its responsiveness and security.

Because it provides a secure base of human operations, a secure homeland in the social map, secure attachment provides a foundation for exploration, physically and emotionally, and ultimately a positive pathway for the child. Without this starting point in attachment, the child—girl or boy—is psychologically homeless. Thus the child's social map begins to emerge without appropriate boundaries, allies, and orientation to the emotional lay of the land.

Psychologists studying attachment have discovered that secure attachments are mostly consistent and uniform for girls and boys and are associated with positive, healthy development. About 65 percent of American infants show secure attachment. Conversely, insecure (unhealthy) attachments take several distinct forms and are associated with problems in development. They arise from some combination of ineffective, abusive, or neglectful parenting and response patterns in the child that steer its reaction to the parents' behavior. For example, while research shows that in general "sensitive caregiving" is most likely to produce secure attachment, this effect is particularly important for distress-prone infants who are more likely to develop insecure attachment than other babies.

To the point here, troubled children and youths are disproportionately likely to evidence insecure attachments. What is more, girls and boys tend to differ in what kinds of attachment problems they have, a fact that has important implications for understanding aggression against self and others.

One negative pattern is anxious-preoccupied attachment. Here the child is "unable to anticipate whether her attachment figure (typically a parent) will consistently respond, and if she does whether her continued availability can be depended upon." Where does this pattern come from? Mostly it comes from the child's "normal" efforts to make sense of an erratic and unpredictable parent. The parent's inconsistency teaches the child to be wary and hypervigilant, unsure and on guard. Of course, some infants, particularly distress-prone infants, are more likely to respond this way than others.

In one study of troubled kids conducted by Marlene Moretti and her colleagues, 40 percent of the troubled girls were classified as "preoccupied" as compared with 15 percent of the troubled boys. Sixteen-year-old Mandy says: "I never know what my mom is going to do, which mom it's going to be when I go home, the angry one that hurts me or the nice one that bakes cookies."

A second type of insecure attachment is dismissing avoidant, in which the children have given up on attachment and "seem uninterested in attachment relationships with others, satisfied with their sense of self worth and competence to manage in the world, and somewhat oblivious to their feelings and needs of others." Why? Kids develop this pattern as a defense against neglect and emotional abandonment by parents. It seems to flow from a self-protective lowering of expectations on the child's part. Given that girls are more generally oriented to emotional connection, it is not surprising that they are less ready to give up attachment. Boys are primed for independence, so it is not surprising that disengagement in response to abandonment plays a larger role in the lives of troubled boys than in troubled girls. In the same study of troubled kids by Moretti cited earlier, only 6 percent of the troubled girls fell into this pattern, as compared with 31 percent of the troubled boys. Seventeen-year-old Tom says: "My parents? Fuck them. I couldn't care less whether they live or die."

For the third type of insecure attachment—fearful or anxious/ambivalent—troubled girls and boys were about equally represented (42 percent of the girls and 35 percent of the boys). This pattern seems to evolve in families where parents are themselves impaired, and children develop an attitude of watchful caring with an overtone of worry. Sixteen-year-old Janice says: "I am always worrying about whether my mother will be OK, you know? I mean she is such a basket case I never know if she is going to make it."

Research shows that whether the expression of aggression in behavior is toward others or self is related to the connection between gender and attachment types (notably the fact that girls are more likely to develop an insecure-preoccupied instead of a dismissive-avoidant attachment pattern). This means that it is the differences in the type of attachment difficulty girls and boys experience rather than the consequences of gender itself that affect the form aggression takes in the lives of troubled kids. As in so many other cases, there is an intermediary influence between being a girl and behavior, and the changes in these intermediary influences are responsible for many of the potential and actual differences between traditional girls and more and more girls to-day. The biology of being a girl has not changed, only the social, cultural, and psychological forces that surround and interact with that biology.

The variations in insecure attachment type exhibited by kids are important because they bear on the amount, type, and target of aggression shown by girls and boys who are troubled. Remember that aggression can be "expressive," in the sense that it is mostly about expressing powerful emotional states, or "instrumental," in the sense that it is mostly about using force in a calculating way to achieve concrete objectives. The insecure-preoccupied group of kids showed most aggression against others with whom they were in a relationship and they feared would abandon them (expressive aggression). Eighteen-year-old Rhoda says this: "When my boyfriend seems cool or distant, it freaks me out! And when I get agitated, the slightest thing can set me off against him. That's when I want to hit somebody. That's when we fight. I know he cares when I can get him to fight with me."

The insecure-dismissive group was most likely to commit acts of aggression against others to achieve dominance or gain access to resources (instrumental aggression). Sixteen-year-old Bertha offers this account: "No girl is going to mess with me. No way. Some girl tries to put me down or take my stuff she is going to pay the price. I'll slap her as soon as look at her before I let someone take me on."

The insecure-fearful group was mostly aggressive toward self (expressive aggression). Here's eighteen-year-old Natalie's account of how this works for her: "I cut myself. It calms me down when I am feeling alone and sad. I know it's crazy, but it does help. And it helps people around me know they have to take me seriously."

In a very real sense, childhood social maps emerge from early experiences with infant attachment, but they develop in response to experience and emerging capacities during a girl's childhood and into her adolescence. What is more, her social map more and more becomes the cause of her experience. By the time she enters adolescence a girl is likely to be acting consistently upon the basis of the information contained within her social map. Her childhood social map comes to fruition in adolescence.

As sixteen-year-old Martha said while she awaited a family court ruling on whether or not she would get to keep her baby: "When I meet someone new, right away I do something bad, so I know where I stand with them." Martha's social map predisposes her for crisis, violence, exploitation, anger, and rejection because she broadcasts negativity in her behavior, which nearly guarantees negativity in response from the world around her. All this strengthens her negative social map, which she formed during the years she spent with her abusive mother. Now a teenage mother herself, she is dangerously at risk for repeating that abusive treatment toward her own child; her social map must be changed if she is to find a new path and not simply travel the route she and her own mother traveled that has brought Martha to this point.

The girl whose map renders her as an insignificant speck stuck off in a corner or as a beleaguered city-state surrounded by enemies accrues more and more negative experiences. In contrast, the girl whose map contains allies and expectations of acceptance acts confidently and securely and increasingly finds the positive places in life.

Is a girl's social map positive? Does it say: "Adults are to be trusted because they know what they are doing," "People will generally treat you well and meet your needs," "School is a safe place," "I am a valued member of my society," "The future looks bright to me." Or is it negative? Does it broadcast: "Strangers are dangerous," "Take what you need because no one is going to help you," "Get them before they get you," "Always expect betrayal." The most important message contained within a girl's social map is whether it speaks of acceptance or rejection. Why? Because, as we saw in Chapter 5, children have a universal craving for acceptance, a need to be included, and rejection is a psychological malignancy.

Psychologist Geraldine Downey and her colleagues have explored the concept of rejection sensitivity, a social map that leads girls (and some boys for that matter) "to anxiously expect, readily perceive, and overreact to rejection." Like many other aspects of a girl's social map, rejection sensitivity readily stimulates a vicious cycle: "[w]hen faced with mild or ambiguous negative experiences with others the child with rejection sensitivity sees rejection and responds with 'over-reactions,' especially those involving hostility and aggression, which are likely to elicit actual rejection by others." This applies to both boys and girls but is a special concern for girls.

I hear it in Amanda's story. A nineteen-year-old who left college during her first semester because of a suicide attempt and has now returned to college, Amanda grew up in Seattle, in a middle-class neighborhood, her divorced mother a full-time stay-at-home mom, her absent father a pilot for United Airlines. For her, like many other sensitive girls, rejection stimulated self-destructive behavior:

> It was in high school that I faced depression and suicidal thoughts. As I've gotten older, my thoughts about committing suicide have increased. Sometimes it doesn't feel like a con-

scious thought but is more of a yearning to take an impulsive action. This is a point I feel many people do not understand. When I have suicidal thoughts, it is not about a plan to go to a better place. Suicide for me has little to do with getting somewhere else and more to do with leaving the present place. Often what spurs my suicidal thought is a failure. Whether it is large or small, when I mess up, I hate myself and see no future success as possible. I begin to hate myself and do not see why anyone else would like me. I often have an urge to jump off a cliff or drive my car into a tree. What usually spurs my emotional rage is a fault or failure on my part. I hate to be embarrassed or look incompetent, anything that I feel will lead people to reject me. Stress about being perfect in other people's eyes drives me to hate who I am. I can't stand the feeling that they will not accept me unless I am perfect.

Amanda believes that if she is not perfect, she will face rejection. Not being perfect, she feels rejected. This feeling stimulates her self-destructive behavior. What does she mean by being perfect? Here's what she has to say to that: "Perfect? I mean being pretty and sexy and popular and successful with boys and joining a good sorority and doing well in school and pleasing my parents. You know, everything."

Traditional culture heightens the problem of rejection sensitivity for girls. For one thing, girls are more likely to experience rejection because of the male bias in the culture. Recall from Chapter 1 that researchers found traditionally most people regard "masculine" as synonymous with "adult" and distinct from "feminine." Consider the traditional difference between the terms *sissy* (a boy who is like a girl) and *tomboy* (a girl who is like a boy). The former is negative because a boy is "lowering" himself to femininity. The latter is negative because a girl is seeking to claim an elevated status to which she is not entitled. Neither term would have such connotation in an egalitarian society, and the fact that *tomboy* has lost some of its negative connotation is a measure of progress.

Here's Josephina's story. Raised in a very traditional family, with two brothers and two sisters, in a blue-collar neighborhood in Detroit, Josephina learned in her childhood some powerful lessons about what it means to be a girl in traditional patriarchal culture: "In my family it was pretty clear that the boys came first and the girls came second. It started with my mom and dad. Dad was the boss; Mom was a second-class citizen in comparison with him. The same thing went for my brothers and me. They got to do what they wanted. I had to do what I was told to do. They were the bosses of me even when I knew better. When I was five, I announced at dinner one night that I was going to be a man when I grew up. They all laughed, and one of my brothers told me I was stupid and that I was stuck with being a girl, like it or not."

What is more, girls traditionally depend much more than boys on being popular and attractive rather than competent and talented. They have been taught to look to those with whom they have relationships for validation (and thus acceptance) rather than to their own power. Most girls feel strong pressures to be perfect in ways that put them at the mercy of others for reassurance of their worth. Many of the traditional sources of success for girls are "subjective," in the sense that they require other people to validate them. Boys traditionally get validation for things that are more "objective," in the sense that they exist apart from what other people think. For example, a girl can be pretty only in the eyes of others (subjective) while a boy who can throw a ball has a positive attribute that is mostly true regardless of who he is in the eyes of other people (objective). Traditionally, a girl's experience of these subjective evaluations builds up, and with it the validation that goes a long way toward defining her social map. That goes far as well toward defining the sources of her strength and vulnerability, including rejection sensitivity and insecure attachment.

But the New American Girl increasingly plays by a new set of rules. Here's Jennifer's illuminating account of how this works. The only child of two college professors, Jennifer is the New American Girl par excellence. She speaks as a boy might about how her athletic competence provides a foundation for her self-esteem, one that is not open to negotiation in the traditional system of girls' peer groups:

> I play lacrosse, and I'm good at it. When I started at my new school, that was the one thing I could hold on to when I started to feel strange and out of place. On the field it didn't matter how I looked or what clothes I wore, not to the real players. Of course some of the girls were not serious about playing. They were just coming out for the team because they thought it would be cool. At first they looked down on me because I am not the conventional idea of good-looking. The first time they saw me score a goal in a scrimmage that began to change. They saw what I could do, and they had to respect that. Even some of the boys noticed me then. It was cool.

The forces shaping social maps are internal and external to the girl. They include her culture. Does it value and affirm girls or subordinate and denigrate them? They include her temperament. Is she born active or passive, impulsive or reflective, easily soothed or irascible? They include experiences of being nurtured versus neglected, accepted versus being rejected. Is she consistently loved versus being jerked around emotionally?

The traditional expression of physical aggression in girls has been focused on people with whom they have relationships, people close to them, people with whom they have emotional bonds. Why? One reason is that a girl's power is more likely to be greater in intimate situations because of who she is in relation to the other people in that setting—an older sister, a girlfriend, a mother—than in more impersonal social situations in which her status is linked more to what she is allowed to do according to traditional sex-typed roles and restrictions. And greater power means greater willingness to take the risk of aggressing physically. As girls' power increases, their physical aggressiveness increases as well.

Another reason for the traditional focusing of girls' aggression in intimate rather than public settings is that girls have traditionally been largely confined to these settings rather than invited into the larger world. This made for girls who were highly oriented to intimacy, relationships, and social connection and focused the impulses for power and dominance on the "small world" of relationships rather than the "big" world. Traditionally a girl's aggression is therefore more likely to arise as an expression of her intense anger in situations that threaten to cut her off from emotional bonds. It's worth noting, however, that as the process of unleashing girls proceeds and girls change, the targets of aggression change as well. I believe we are seeing more and more of this, as girls exhibit aggression for reasons other than rejection—for example, for the sheer pleasure of power and to gain access to resources.

It is not surprising that traditional research has found that depression and aggression have been much more strongly linked in girls and women than in boys and men. This seems to be because threats to intimate relationships tend to bring out overwhelming feelings of despair and helplessness in girls and thus aggression, sometimes against self, sometimes against others. It is not surprising that most of this aggression takes place in the intimate settings that give rise to despair, depression, and rage when girls' relationships are threatened.

But there is a new theme to girls' aggression. Recall child development researcher Eleanor Maccoby's classic summary of the research on this matter: "Boys are more concerned with competition and dominance, with establishing and protecting turf, with proving their toughness, and to these ends they are more given to confronting other boys directly, taking risks, issuing or accepting dares, making ego displays, and concealing weakness. . . . Girls, though of course concerned with achieving their own individual objectives, are more concerned than boys with maintaining group cohesion and cooperative, mutually supportive friendships. Their relationships are more intimate than those of boys." But is this still true?

It may be true that in the past girls were more oriented toward group cohesion and intimacy, but as even Maccoby's assessment indicates ("Girls, though of course concerned with achieving their own individual objectives"), it is not that girls uniformly and exclusively eschew power. Rather, it is that in the past their best chance of experiencing power was in the context of intimate relationships where "maintaining group cohesion and cooperative, mutually supportive friendships" was the norm and relational and verbal aggression was the weapon at hand to demonstrate power.

This is changing, even as double standards continue. Today's girls can seek power more directly outside the context of intimate relationships, but they may still experience disapproval when they do. Girls can more and more take on the world directly in a manner that once was defined as masculine and un-feminine, but they still may find that their assertiveness is less welcome than it would be if they were boys. As the social domain for girls grows, so does the range of settings in which they can seek to meet their needs for power. Competition thus becomes less risky for girls as they are welcomed into settings (like athletics) where it is the norm, even though there remain restrictions (like no hitting in girls' ice hockey).

As the prohibition against physical aggression by girls diminishes, they are freed to use physical aggression more openly in all settings as a vehicle for expressing power. This includes the intimate relationships that have been their traditional setting for assertion of power.

I see this in Marjorie's memoir. An eighteen-year-old majoring in environmental studies, Marjorie grew up in Miami, in an upper-middle-class suburb with her lawyer parents and her older brother and younger sister:

> When I was in seventh grade, a group of three boys constantly used to make fun of and pick on me. We all had been friends in sixth grade, and then, after the summer, they started being cruel to me. They would say or do anything to hurt me, and I tended to ignore them when they did this if I could. At the end of seventh grade a friend of mine decided to have a party to celebrate the end of the school year. The boys who had taunted me came to the party uninvited and were being unpleasant to several people who had been invited. One of the boys started picking on me, including spraying me a with a water gun, and this finally forced my anger with him to burst out. I began by pushing him, and this ultimately resulted in the two of us getting into a physical fight that included pushing, hitting, and kicking.

> After this fight I went home feeling horrified that I had done
> something that would make me an outcast. But looking back on
> it, I can see that it actually made kids respect me more. Those
> boys never picked on me again.

Marjorie was a girl caught between the old and new cultures
of girls. She feared her physical aggression would make her an
outcast. That fear is the voice of the traditional past, not the
future. Now, six years later, she sees that her fears were un-
founded. More and more, Marjorie's behavior finds peer acceptance, even admiration. Her physical aggression is defined as
legitimate power assertion without the gender discrimination of
the past being invoked to stifle her.

Unfortunately, one form of physical aggression among girls
that appears to be increasing is physical assault against their own
bodies in the form of self-mutilation, cutting. How does this
form of physical aggression by girls fit into the larger picture? For
one thing, in contrast with males, whose physical assaults against
self are usually tied up with difficulties in managing aggression
generally (for example, punching a wall or breaking a window),
females' assaults on themselves traditionally are tied up with efforts to manage anxiety and depression.

According to most researchers and clinicians, cutting is not
usually a precursor to suicide (any more than most forms of
physical assault against others are simply a precursor to murder).
Moreover, like other forms of physical aggression, assault against
oneself sometimes feels better than what appear to be the available alternatives to a child or teenager struggling with inner pain.

For me, the most moving and revealing explanation of cutting
came from one of my best students. Elaine was always in the

front row in class, a look of interested intelligence in her eyes. Her written work was excellent; her class participation insightful and well grounded. I had met her parents and seen the affectionate way they embraced her on parents' weekend. There was nothing overt about her that prepared me for her story:

Cutting has become a bigger trend among unhappy adolescents. Those on the outside looking in at this phenomenon may be confused and shocked because they have no idea how someone could do something of that nature. I can speak from firsthand experience as I myself used to cut. Depression is a disorder that hurts you from the inside. It's a war with yourself that nobody else can truly understand. Depression is a battle you fight with yourself every moment of every day. The pain you feel comes from inside, something no ibuprofen or soothing hugs can heal. It's a pain with no feasible solution. That's why so many depressed people make their own kind of pain—a new pain. Cutting creates a new sensation, a new outlet and a new way of experiencing pain, a type of pain that you alone have control over. You hurt yourself on the outside to get rid of the pain afflicting you from the inside. As strange as it may seem, when you're depressed, you feel dead on the inside, and watching your own blood fall from your wrists somehow reminds you that you are still alive. Having a physical pain takes your mind off just that, your mind. It's something real that you can focus on that has nothing to do with the issues you struggle with in your head. Though obviously self-destructive, many depressed people use cutting as a form of self-medication, much the way some others turn to alcohol or drugs. The truth is, however, that this only makes the situation worse.

Cutting and burning offer some respite for troubled girls to distract attention from what they experience as unbearable feelings. For these girls, the physical pain actually is preferable to the negative feelings it replaces. There is a physiological basis for this belief. Self-assault of this type often does provide temporary relief because there is an increase of chemicals in the bloodstream (endorphins) that result in a feeling of pleasure or at least numbness. Cutting is about using physical assault in a desperate effort to find a way to live.

Other assaults against self are suicidal in nature. These acts are attempts to murder the self, not to buy it some respite through the sensations of cutting or burning. For this reason, I shall postpone a discussion of self-assault in the form of suicide until the next chapter, where I look more generally at lethal assaults, against self and others. Here let's return to the world of assaults linked to generally troubled behavior, to conduct disorder.

Assaults against others form the foundation for the diagnosis of conduct disorder that is strongly linked to the experience of child maltreatment. What is it about the social maps of girls who have been maltreated that leads them to develop conduct disorder? Generally they are negative and unrealistic.

Remember that the social environment is always broadcasting messages, some positive, some negative. A girl filters all these "data" through the social map of attachment and rejection sensitivity and then digests them through her thinking processes (social cognition). Psychologist Kenneth Dodge and his colleagues have found that children differ in how they receive and organize social information, and the results of these differences go a long way toward explaining how conduct disorder arises and flourishes in some abused children and not in others.

Dodge and his colleagues found that the odds that an abused girl (or boy) will develop conduct disorder increase if the child's thinking about social information is characterized by four distinct patterns in her or his social mapping process: being hypersensitive to negative social cues, being oblivious of positive social cues, having a narrow repertoire of responses to being aroused, and drawing the conclusion that aggression is successful in social relations.

The first two patterns push a girl's social map toward negativity. Under normal circumstances most of us receive both positive and negative social information, and this keeps our social maps balanced, a realistic mix of the positive and the negative. This person is smiling, but that one is frowning. This one has a positive tone of voice, but that one has a threatening tone. This one is kind, but that one is mean.

Some kids receive only the positive, and this skews their social map in an unrealistically positive direction—what might be called Pollyanna syndrome—but this is actually more functional than its opposite. The kids Dodge was concerned about suffer from this opposite problem: They receive only the negative and thus see the world in increasingly negative terms. They experience an unrelentingly negative pattern that we might call the war zone mentality, in which the perception of threat increases and the defensive inclination to hit first and ask questions later arises.

What is more, some of these children are at heightened risk for translating the experience of being the victim of child abuse into the experience of being the perpetrator of conduct disorder because their understanding of how the world works is also unrealistically skewed. Mark Twain wrote that if the only tool you have is a hammer, you are likely to define every problem as a nail.

The reverse is true as well: If you define every problem as a nail, the only tool you need is a hammer. Kids at risk for aggression suffer from a similar limitation. Their answer to every question is aggression. What to do if afraid? Hit. What to do if confused? Hit. What to do if frustrated? Hit. It is as if they had a road map that had only north on it. All roads lead to aggression; it is the only direction they know.

Whether this "hitting" takes the form of relational or physical aggression is a matter decided on a daily basis as children assess the cultural and social messages they receive. Because of the messages they have received about physical aggression's being a no-no, girls have traditionally tended to implement this skewed thinking by hitting with words, while traditional boys have tended to hit with fists.

There is more. The problem with these kids is that they have gone beyond simply possessing and demonstrating a narrow range of responses to being angry, afraid, frustrated, and covetous (namely, physical aggression). They have taken the next step and actually believe that aggression is successful. It is not surprising that this is a tempting possibility for a child living in an abusive family. Like a little anthropologist, the child observes and records in the notebook of the social map: Mom and Dad are arguing. Dad hits Mom in the face, and she shuts up. Note to self: Hitting works well (at least if you are a boy who can identify with father). Baby brother is whining for ice cream. Mom slaps him, and he shuts up. Note to self: Slapping is effective (particularly if you are bigger and more powerful than the target of your aggression). I take Joey's toy. He starts to complain to the teacher. I hit him in the stomach. He shuts up. Note to self: Hitting in the stomach stops kids from complaining to teacher if you hit hard enough (but also remember that there may be smarter ways to hurt Joey that will not be noticed and punished by the teacher. Girls, take note).

The bottom line in all this? Dodge reports that if abused children develop the four risky patterns of thinking (that is, focusing on the negative, ignoring the positive, being limited to aggressive responses, and believing aggression is successful), they are eight times more likely to develop conduct disorder than abused children who don't. Abused children who *don't* develop these risky patterns of thinking are no more likely than nonabused children to develop conduct disorder. But of course that raises some questions. Why do some abused children develop risky thinking while others don't? Why have boys historically developed conduct disorder at a higher rate than girls? Why do nonabused children develop conduct disorder at all? All three questions invite answers that involve human biology.

The question of which abused children develop risky thinking and why finds a provocative answer in the work of Avshalom Caspi, Terrie Moffitt, and their colleagues. Their study grew out of research with animals showing that when there was a deficiency of certain chemicals in the brain (neurotransmitters), the affected animals were more aggressive, particularly when put in stressful situations. Why? Because the chemicals involved affect the brain's response to threat and stress. When there is a deficiency of these chemicals, the brain has trouble processing social information effectively in ways that are the animal equivalent of what Dodge and his colleagues demonstrated with children, and these problems lead to more aggressive responses.

The crucial chemicals in the brain are under the control of an enzyme linked to a specific gene (monoamine oxidase A—the MAOA gene), and Caspi and Moffitt set out to trace the impact of all this on child development. Through its effect on the enzyme, the gene can turn the important neurotransmitters off, causing the deficiency, or on, leading to the normal levels of these chemicals. When the MAOA gene is off, the child does not have the same level of activity in the important neurotransmitters of norepinephrine, serotonin, and dopamine than when it is on. The result is that the child with the MAOA gene off is less able to deal with stressful information and more prone to overreact to potentially threatening situations.

Does this sound familiar? It should. These are exactly the issues Dodge identified in his study of why some abused children develop conduct disorder while others do not do so. Sure enough, the results of Caspi and Moffitt's study shed light on the unanswered question in Dodge's research—namely, why do some abused kids develop risky thinking (and thus become prone to conduct disorder) while others do not?

If abused children have the MAOA gene turned off, about 85 percent develop conduct disorder. If they are abused and have the gene turned on, the figure is about 40 percent. If the MAOA gene is turned off and the child is not abused, the rate of conduct disorder is about 20 percent. And the rate is 20 percent if the gene is on and there is no abuse. Although this is only one study, it is consistent with the research on animals mentioned before and with other preliminary studies of the links between neurotransmitters and aggression in humans, so it is worth taking seriously even if it isn't definitive.

That having been said, several things are clear from Caspi and Moffitt's results. First, when a child faces the combination of being abused and having the MAOA genetic vulnerability, the likelihood of negative outcome is extremely high (85 percent). Second, most kids who are abused and don't have the MAOA vulnerability avoid the negative path of conduct disorder (60 percent). Third, if children are not abused, the relevance of the MAOA vulnerability evaporates (conduct disorder rates of 20 percent in both groups). Remember, it is the accumulation of risk factors, risk factors in context, that determines their outcome. Few risk factors have much effect when they stand alone.

This all applies to childhood and adolescence, but does the combination of early maltreatment and MAOA vulnerability lead to an adult life dominated by negativity? Our ecological perspective would predict that the answer is "It depends," and the data say as much. The effects of the childhood double whammy (that is, being abused and having the MAOA gene off) are much less dramatic when the researchers look at whether or not an individual is convicted of a violent crime (32 percent) and whether or not the individual demonstrates symptoms of antisocial personality disorder in adulthood. Caspi and Moffitt's results indicate that while the pathway into conduct disorder in childhood is almost a given for children who get the double whammy of being abused and having the MAOA vulnerability, the pathway from there into an antisocial life in adulthood is subject to other influences, such as whether or not there is therapeutic intervention, whom the individual hangs out with and marries, what school the individual attends, and so on.

That's a point worth remembering. In support of this idea, research compiled by criminologists Rolf Loeber and David Farrington reveals that the odds that a child with conduct disorder will become a seriously violent delinquent in adolescence depends upon a variety of social factors. For example, while overall 30 percent of kids with childhood conduct disorder move on to serious violent delinquency, in some neighborhoods the figure is 15 percent while in others it is 60 percent.

How does all this research relate to girls? The starting point is the fact that the important MAOA gene is located on the X chromosome. Thus, if boys get the off gene on their one X chromosome, they experience its effects because their other chromosome is the Y, which is nearly empty (twenty-five genes versus five thousand genes for the X chromosome). In other words, the Y chromosome does little more than determine gender. As my mentor Urie Bronfenbrenner used to put it, "The Y won't do much for you, but at least it will make a man out of you."

The off MAOA gene is relatively rare, so if females have it on one of their X chromosomes, they are likely to have the on gene on the other, shielding them from its effects. As Caspi and Moffitt put it, "Because MAOA is an X-linked gene, affected males . . . produce no MAOA enzyme—effectively, a human knockout." Thus girls may well have a genetic protection against the development of risky thinking in response to being abused. But this protection is not absolute, and the link between being maltreated and developing conduct disorder still exists for girls.

Why? One clue lies in the Caspi-Moffitt data themselves. Among kids with the MAOA gene turned on who were abused, the rate of conduct disorder was about 40 percent. This means having the MAOA vulnerability is not a necessary condition for developing conduct disorder in response to being abused. Abuse can have its negative effects even in "normal" children. Second, about 20 percent of the kids studied who neither were abused nor had the MAOA vulnerability developed conduct disorder. Both these findings point to the open door for girls to develop conduct disorder and start out on the path to serious criminal aggression.

What is more, many kids with conduct disorder were not abused at all. How does this happen? How and why do nonabused girls develop conduct disorder? Researchers point to a variety of conditions that increase the risk:

- The emotional effects of rejection sensitivity and insecure attachment predispose troubled girls to aggression in all its forms, including conduct disorder. Not all bad outcomes are the result of child maltreatment; abuse and neglect are not the only causes of developing insecure attachment and rejection sensitivity. Nonmaltreated girls can become troubled girls who can learn aggression from the mass media (as the research in Chapter 4 demonstrated) and from associating with aggressive peers.

- Poverty and racism increase stress on girls, disorganize child-rearing efforts, and increase the odds of sexual victimization and violent assault that traumatize girls and set them on the road to troubled behavior. All these social risks increase the odds that a girl will be drawn to aggression as a way of dealing with the difficult world she faces around her and inside her. They disrupt the process of unlearning aggression just as they disrupt the processes of learning to read, do arithmetic, and spell.

- Family disruption undermines the discipline and focus children need to develop good habits of mind and behavior, which, when replaced with bad habits, can evolve into conduct disorder. Some cases of conduct disorder do evolve gradually as the accumulation of bad habits in response to ineffectual parenting. In these cases it is often hard to see how many small mistakes accumulate in the form of socially ineffective behavior, but a fine-grained behavioral analysis often demonstrates that this is precisely what has happened. Long the province of clinicians and researchers, this understanding has been brought to pop culture through television programs like *Supernanny* and *Nanny 911*.

- Difficult temperament that puts the child at odds with others can open the door for learning negative behavior. Some children are easy from the start: They sleep well, they soothe easily, and their bodies process the environment smoothly. Other children are difficult from the start: They sleep erratically, they cry easily and are difficult to soothe, and their bodies have trouble adjusting to the environment. Temperamentally easy children are easy to teach positive behaviors, whether it be reading, table manners, or controlling aggressive impulses. With temperamentally difficult children all these tasks are more complicated and less readily accomplished. A classic study found that by elementary school only 10 percent of children who had been easy babies had developed significant adjustment problems versus 70 percent of those who had been difficult babies. The resulting hostility, anger, and disaffection can set the stage for a girl to hold on to aggression rather than give it up.

• Negative influences in a girl's immediate social environment outside the family can shape her response to aggression. Peers play an important role, directly, as she encounters them in school and in the neighborhood, and indirectly, as she encounters them via the mass media. Few girls are totally immune to these negative influences.

These last three merit some additional explanation. With regard to family disruption, parents who provide inconsistent discipline and who accede to a girl's aggressive demands may inadvertently reinforce aggressive behavior and sow the seeds of conduct disorder rather than persuade her to give up aggression. Psychologist Gerald Patterson's meticulous observations of parents dealing with demanding children has shown how this happens. The child's negative behavior (whining, crying, tantrums) seems to stop only when the parent gives in to the child. This relief is highly reinforcing to the parent (increasing the likelihood of giving in again in the future) and is highly reinforcing to the child (teaching the lesson that aggressive negativity is rewarded).

This is the foundation for the parenting adage "Don't give in to terrorists, no matter how little they are."

Most children engage in temper tantrums before the age of five. Most have learned to give them up by age nine. The combination of children's becoming more adept at meeting their needs through less aversive tactics and parents' finding ways to discourage children using tantrums does the job most of the time. But sometimes the "natural" experiences of childhood are not enough to terminate these tantrums (through some combination of difficult temperament on the child's part and unwitting behavior on the parents'). A long-term study conducted several decades ago revealed that girls who had not given up temper tantrums by age nine were more likely to have conflicted and unsatisfying marriages, to have reduced financial success, and to be seen by their own children as irritable and difficult. Now, with the unleashing of girls to be physically aggressive and assertive, the emergence of conduct disorder is one outcome of this process. The cultural messages about aggression for girls are changing so dramatically that it can no longer be assumed that girls, particularly troubled girls, will see aggression as unfeminine.

Beyond the subtle parent-child interactions that lead to trouble in temperamentally difficult children stands the fact that some children are just so difficult that they don't respond to the normal methods of socialization. Ross Greene has studied children whose temperaments are so difficult they are termed explosive. For these children, because of their neurological vulnerabilities, life is like having someone scrape their fingernails on a blackboard twenty-four hours a day. Their daily experience is filled with overwhelming arousal and stress. It is little wonder that they are irascible and prone to develop a pattern of aggression, bad behavior, acting out, and violating the rights of others.

Finally, when it comes to the child's immediate social environment, it is important to look at the school as an influence. Historically this has been evident for boys. For example, Sheppard Kellam found that if a boy predisposed to aggression is assigned to a first-grade classroom with a "weak" teacher, by sixth grade that child might be twenty times more aggressive than if he had been assigned to a first-grade classroom with a "strong" teacher or if he is exposed to an intervention program called the Good Behavior Game (which we shall examine in Chapter 8). Why? Because in the weak teacher's classroom aggressive peer groups form and amplify the aggressive behavior and attitudes of the children who join them. In the strong teacher's classroom or in the classroom with the Good Behavior Game, in contrast, such aggressive peer groups are not allowed to form, and the boy's predisposition to aggression is blunted rather than enabled. Just as the latest research on the effects of TV violence now includes girls among the affected, we can expect that research will document the increasing relevance of classroom climate and the effects of the Good Behavior Game on girls as well as boys. In the new world of empowerment, what's true of boys is more and more true of girls, for better and for worse.

With all the diverse and changing forces at work in causing and reducing aggressive, antisocial, and out-of-control behavior in children, it's hard to come up with an exact number for how many girls develop conduct disorder and how this compares with boys. Like counting anything else about children, estimating the numbers for diagnosis of conduct disorder takes place in a social and cultural context, and consequently our ecological perspective tells us that if we ask, "How much conduct disorder is there?" the best answer is "It depends."

This is the major reason why published estimates of conduct disorder run from the 85 percent of boys in the double whammy situation in the Caspi-Moffitt study to 1 percent (a figure given for middle-class girls on average by the National Center on Mental Health in the 1970s). Specific groups lie somewhere between these two extremes, with the average rate for boys historically being set at somewhere between 6 and 16 percent and for girls at 2 and 9 percent. Of course, as I noted earlier, there have been problems in the diagnosing of conduct disorder in girls because of difficulty in seeing their aggressive behavior. These problems in diagnosis make it difficult to make gender comparisons with complete confidence.

The variations in these numbers depend upon who is being studied, where they are being studied, and when they are being studied. The figures differ from social group to social group, from historical period to historical period, from culture to culture, and from boys to girls. There is some evidence that they are increasing. This makes sense in the context of research by psychologist Tom Achenbach that reported a near doubling of the proportion of American kids troubled enough to need professional mental health intervention, from 10 percent in 1974 to 18.2 percent in 1989. With more kids in general growing up troubled it should not be surprising that conduct disorder is increasing.

Of course our principal interest lies with the gender differences, as they have existed in the past, how they have been changing, and how they may exist in the future. What lies ahead? I think we can expect to see increasing rates of conduct disorder for troubled girls. We may even see increasing numbers of the most troubled girls crossing the final line from assault to homicide. Here's a sampling of the reasons why.

- Although boys are traditionally diagnosed with conduct disorder more than girls, the gap between girls and boys narrows in adolescence (presumably because of the powerful sexual challenges posed to girls in adolescence that push vulnerable female teenagers over the line into serious behavior disorder). We can expect it to narrow still further.

- Traditionally, physically aggressive girls stop short of lethal violence; in 2001 girls accounted for 23 percent of arrests for aggravated assault, but only 10 percent of arrests for homicide. This too may change as the processes of changed learning about aggression intensify for coming generations of girls.

- Services for troubled girls traditionally lag behind services for troubled boys, but adolescent girls end up with more severe treatment (incarceration) than boys with comparable records. There are signs of new interest in gender-specific programming for troubled girls, but these are in their infancy.

- Traditionally, conduct disorder in teenage girls is more likely to be associated with self-destructive behavior and depression than among teenage boys. For example, in one study of troubled teenagers, 64 percent of the girls had attempted suicide versus 3 percent of the boys. This gap also may narrow in response to the general trends we are observing in the development of girls and boys, including more and more troubled girls' choosing more lethal methods when they try to kill themselves.

Girls have always been victimized by parental abuse and neglect and by peer violence and sexual assault. When they have not been resilient enough to overcome traumatic attacks, their responses have traditionally been mostly passively self-destructive in nature: internalized suffering and accepting further victimization. The forces of biology and culture have dictated this in the past. The MAOA gene and all it represents buffered girls' thinking in ways that led them away from conduct disorder. Traditional femininity cultivated passivity and prohibited physically aggressive responses.

However, while the biology is constant, the culture is changing. The social toxicity of the culture coupled with the unleashing of girls from the traditional prison of femininity places hurt and sad troubled girls at risk for becoming aggressive troubled girls. Conduct disorder can and does arise in children with the MAOA gene turned on.

We began Chapter 1 with the startling finding that the gap between boys and girls in assault has decreased dramatically (from ten boys for every one girl a generation ago to only four boys for every girl now). Now we can see how this finding fits into the larger patterns of shifting culture and experience in the life of the New American Girl. But how does this process affect the extremes of murder and suicide?

7

Girls Who Kill . . .
Themselves or Others

S ome girls do more than hit. Some girls kill. It's a small number overall, but it nonetheless means a great deal. Lethal
assault, against self and others, is a terrible thing. It challenges
us all, intellectually, emotionally, and spiritually, to know that
children can and do manifest the ultimate forms of physical
aggression. But it is something we must understand.

Although the numbers fluctuate a bit, and there are some
long-term trends, these days, on average, juveniles commit about
two thousand murders per year. That is about 12 percent of the
total number of murders committed each year overall in the
United States. Female juveniles commit about 10 percent of
these juvenile murders—a bit more than two hundred. That's a
small proportion of the American total, but let's remember that
the rate at which American girls commit murder is actually

higher than the rate for *boys* in some other societies—Austria and Japan, for example.

The available evidence tells us that there has long been a pattern of differences between female and male murderers. These different patterns boil down to two things:

- Females are more likely to kill in the context of a relationship than as part of another more impersonal crime.

- Female killers are more likely to suffer from overt depression.

This should sound familiar because these are two of the same differences found between female and male assault in general. We can see these traditional patterns in the following two examples.

> Seventeen-year-old Janette killed her twenty-one-year-old boyfriend, Fred. The two had been on the rocks for months, arguing, separating, getting back together, then repeating the process again a few weeks later. Friends reported that Janette was alternating between periods of intense happiness and intense sadness, paralleling the ups and downs of her relationship with Fred. Three days before his death Fred told Janette, "This is it, the end. I can't take this anymore. It's time to move on with my life." Janette waited for Fred outside his apartment and shot him when he stepped out of the car. She made no effort to escape, instead simply waited for the police to arrive and take her into custody.

And this:

Sixteen-year-old Marsha told police that she had killed her four-month-old baby because he would not stop crying. "I'm a bad mother," she said. "I couldn't make him stop crying. He didn't love me. That's all I wanted, was for him to love me." The girl was alone in her parents' apartment at the time of the baby's death. Her parents had gone out for the evening and Marsha expected them back by ten. They were late arriving, and when they did so, they found their daughter sitting on the couch, holding the dead baby in her arms.

Most of the murders that girls commit take place as part of a relationship. Like the girls in these two examples, female murderers typically kill their parents, their lovers, their children, their rivals, or their friends. Most of the girls who do the killing are very sad, often because of the threats to their relationships that figure in their murderous behavior. But there is another kind of lethal violence by girls that concerns us and, although the numbers are still small, seems to be on the rise. Here the violence seems to take a more impersonal form, one we have long associated with boys. Again, here are two examples:

GIRL, 12, CHARGED WITH KILLING 4-YEAR-OLD

BALTIMORE (AP)—*A 12-year-old girl has been charged in the beating death of a 4-year-old family friend, according to police documents. The girl, whose name was not released, was arrested Friday in the death of Randy Allen Weeks, who died Oct. 19, according to police documents obtained by The [Baltimore] Sun. Police refused to release details about the case, which was one of more than 30 youth homicides in Baltimore this year. At least nine victims have been younger than 10 years old. "Our prosecutors are confronted with the raw emo-*

tion of these tragedies day after day," said Margaret T. Burns, a spokeswoman for the state's attorney's office. "They are weary from the grief that is shared by the families in our community. They wonder 'Are we losing this battle?'" Baltimore Health Commissioner Peter Beilenson, who leads a panel that reviews unexpected child deaths, said he cannot remember any other recent deaths in which the suspect was a girl. "However, it does point out that girls are unquestionably becoming more violent," he said, noting charges against several women and girls earlier this year in the brutal beating of a 12-year-old girl at a birthday party.

And a colleague who works in the Maryland prison system offered this example.

Robin, a twenty-two-year-old white female, is currently serving a seven-year sentence for manslaughter. She is a first-time offender housed in the adult system because of the nature of her crime. She was locked up at age eighteen while she was still in high school. Robin maintains that she was raised in a loving environment by her single mother. Obviously the mother was out of the home a lot in order to provide for the family. Robin has older brothers. During her teen years Robin began to stay out late, skip school, and party with her friends. She also began to drink heavily. On the night of her offense Robin was drinking with three young men and driving around the neighborhood. According to police reports of the crime, an older man flicked his cigarette butt to the street, and it hit the male driver of the car in which Robin was riding. Robin and the boys jumped from the car and beat the man to death with a baseball bat and by kicking him about the head and body.

What Robin did seems indistinguishable from the pattern commonly found in young males who engage in extreme violence. There is no relationship here between the perpetrator and the victim. This is not retribution for serious harm done to the perpetrator by the victim or someone whom the victim represents. There is no profound sadness. There is instead a warped concept of "honor."

I prepared for my book *Lost Boys* by listening to boys who killed. I was struck by how often they explained their actions as a response to disrespect. "He disrespected me" was the message, whether they used the word or not. I thus came to see one of the underlying issues as one of "honor."

There is a long history linking honor and violence in our country and around the world. In many traditional and tribal societies dishonor meant death. In feudal Japan it was customary for defeated warriors to kill themselves or invite execution to avoid the dishonor of defeat. In Pakistan and other countries even today a girl or woman can be killed because she has "dishonored" her family (by associating with an inappropriate sexual partner or even by having been sexually victimized through no fault of her own). As chronicled by Fox Butterfield in his book *All God's Children*, the "culture of honor" is one reason why the American South has experienced higher homicide rates than the rest of the country for more than three hundred years. Those differences continue to this day in populations with southern roots.

What is the culture of honor? It is the belief that one's reputation in the community and sense of positive personal integrity are of the most important value, something more valuable than life itself. Its positive side causes people to act with integrity in the face of temptation and threat. But it also leads to action to maintain honor that subordinates other virtues like compassion, compromise, humility, and forgiveness. It is what led nineteenth-century South Carolina Senator John Calhoun's mother to tell him that if someone were to insult him or his family and he were to do anything but kill that person or die trying, she would disown him. Honor above all else.

In today's world honor continues to be a force to be reckoned with. It is the source of so many street killings in which one young man insults another and the wronged party responds with lethal violence, often saying, "I did what I had to do."

In traditional cultures honor is principally a masculine value, attribute, and expectation. It is common for men steeped in many traditional cultures to argue that "women have no honor" except through their relationships with the important men in their lives—fathers, brothers, husbands, sons. What men often meant by this statement was that females would accept insult without retaliation and, to avoid bloodshed, would argue for compromise even if it meant accepting a measure of insult. Naturally, this has exacerbated the victimization of women, but that is not its only effect.

Traditionally, the social trade-off for the female lack of honor was that in situations of conflict, girls and women could be relied upon to defuse potential violence by seeking compromises and deescalations. They are precisely the kinds of situations in which society has traditionally relied upon girls to be a restraining, civilizing influence on honorable boys flooded with insult-fueled rage. It's a common theme in scenes that recur in the mass media and on the streets: "Come on, Bobby! Let him go! Come on, honey. Let's just go back to the party!" From what I am seeing and hearing, however, this is changing. Why? I think one place to look is in the way the culture of feminine role models and messages is changing. We saw that in Chapters 3 and 4. There are two new messages for girls to replace the old one of restraint and caring: "Girls kick ass!" and "I will fight for my honor!" The new feminine hero is an action figure, a person of aggressive honor. It's unclear where that will lead the next generation of potential female killers. We can see glimmers of where it could take us in the two reports cited earlier: Girls may amplify aggressive behavior rather than inhibit it.

Of course murders are not the only killings that teenagers do. There is also suicide, self-murder. Fewer than three thousand kids kill themselves each year, but this figure is more than the one for those who kill others. Of these, about 30 percent are girls. By the late 1990s the rate for girls was about 12 per million, and for boys about 41 per million. From 1981 to 1998 the suicide rate for girls increased 7 percent while for boys it increased 23 percent. Many more—many more girls as well as boys—attempt suicide.

I think understanding girls who kill themselves is part of our larger need to understand physical aggression in girls, particularly because, as we shall see, there are changes afoot in the patterns of lethal self-assault. Traditionally, girls have been subject to higher levels of depression, which in turn leads to suicidal behavior. Of course some have argued (I think persuasively) that the male-female gap in depression is smaller than it appears because males are prone to mask their sadness and perhaps transform it into something else—addictive behavior, for example. Terrence Real's book *I Don't Want to Talk About It* does a good job of exploring this phenomenon. When we add male covert depression to the picture, males and females would appear to be equally depressed. But more males act out aggressively with others when depressed, as I discovered in the work that led to my book *Lost Boys.* For all the reasons discussed in earlier chapters it is not surprising that girls have been more likely to respond to their depression by acting on it. What is changing, however, is the level of physical aggressiveness with which girls are acting against themselves.

Here's a typical account:

> Laura was seventeen when she died. Never a particularly outgoing girl, she had seemed increasingly sad and distant in the weeks prior to her death. Never a very popular child, she had few friends and none who considered her their "best friend." Laura had dated a boy named Darryl for four months before he dumped her for one of her friends three weeks before the junior prom. That was seven weeks before she killed herself with her dad's gun. When her mother found her in her bedroom, there was a short note that simply said, "I'm sorry. I just couldn't take the pain anymore. Please forgive me. Love, Laura."

For both suicides and murders, gender differences in methods of assault play a role in the ultimate fatality rates. Traditionally, boys have used guns in a higher proportion of assaults against self and others than have girls. One recent report indicates that a new method, hanging, is on the rise. Certainly the method affects the outcome. By the end of the 1990s girls had used guns in less than 40 percent of the murders they committed while males had in more than 70 percent of their murders. In the case of suicides, girls, like Laura, used guns about 50 percent of the time versus about 60 percent for boys. Using a gun increases the lethality of any assault. Anything that affects the social acceptability of using firearms may ultimately affect the lethality of assaults committed by kids. The proportion of girls using guns in deadly assaults has increased and represents a shift from their traditional methods.

That's one reason why images of aggression by girls in the mass media are so important and why real girls using guns can set off a chain reaction of changing norms that can ultimately affect the social realities of female aggression. If girls see girls using guns, it normalizes using guns; that in turn increases the odds of a troubled girl's using a gun, particularly in a society like ours where guns are so readily accessible to kids. When I asked eight-year-old kids in a Chicago suburb if they had access to guns, a third said yes and explained to me how they would get one. In one study, a majority of teenagers reported that they could get a gun in a few hours if they thought they needed one.

It truly is a vicious cycle. What is more, we know from research on a variety of destructive behaviors (like drug, alcohol, and tobacco use) that kids tend to overestimate the frequency with which peers are doing these things. Kids routinely overestimate the proportion of their peers who are taking drugs, drinking, and smoking. The same may be true as the vicious cycle of gun imagery for girls increases, with the mass media amplifying reality and reality imitating mass media imagery. Time will tell.

In the grand scheme of statistical things the number of girls who kill themselves or others is small, hundreds of individuals in a society of three hundred million people. But each killing is a disaster for the people involved and brings sadness to the whole community. Each is a commentary on the state of affairs in our society as a whole. Each speaks volumes about despair, anger, sadness, and spiritual emptiness. Moreover, these killings shed light on larger issues and trends in child development in our society. Each killing says something about the many other kids who commit acts of potentially lethal assault, the shooting, stabbing, cutting, starving, and beating that do not result in a dead body.

It doesn't take a lot of death to affect kids' sense of safety and appreciation for life. In the worst war zones I have visited—the former Yugoslavia, Guatemala, Mozambique, Kuwait, Cambodia,

Iraq, and Israel-Palestine—the killing was still sporadic, and the proportion of the people killed or injured statistically small. Most days in most war zones are quiet. The same is true of cities. When I lived in Chicago at the height of the "youth violence epidemic" of the early 1990s, most days were without shooting incidents. But it takes shots being fired only once every few weeks, injuries once a month, and deaths a few times a year to create the war zone mentality for kids and adults alike. It won't take much killing by girls to change everyone's perception about female murder and suicide. The psychological consequences of fear operate at low levels of statistical reality. One need only track the culture of fear in America after 9/11 to know the truth of this statement.

While the current situation of kids killing themselves and others is a sad state of affairs, let's remember that it is not completely new in our history, at least with respect to lethal boys. It is hard to get a picture of teen suicide prior to 1960 because of overwhelming problems with the records. Most that did occur were inadvertently mislabeled or were covered up to reduce stigma. But there is historical information that speaks to juvenile homicide as a fact of life in the United States well before the twentieth century.

A century and a half ago a *New York Times* editorial bemoaned the fact that "the number of boy burglars, boy robbers and boy murderers is so astoundingly large as to alarm all good men." A child psychiatrist working in Manhattan for the juvenile court in the 1950s said, "At first it comes as a shock to meet youngsters under 16 who rob at the point of a gun, push dope, rape and kill. I've seen boys of seven so small they could barely clear the desk who had sold themselves to sex perverts. Others had shot out kids' eyes or had clubbed or knifed them, just for the fun of it." In the mid-nineteenth century the governor of New York had to call out the militia to deal with rampant youth gangs in New York City, as the recent Martin Scorsese film *Gangs of New York* vividly dramatized. In *Kansas Charley*, her case study of fifteen-year-old Charley Miller, who was executed in 1892, social historian Joan Brumberg has documented numerous cases of juveniles upon whom the death penalty was imposed in the nineteenth century, kids who would not be out of place on Court TV today. But one striking aspect of all these historical accounts is the virtual absence of girls.

Beyond the near absence of girls in accounts of killers in the past, there are other features of the contemporary situation that are distinctive. For one thing, we must recognize that the size of the problem is different today. There was a sevenfold increase in per capita aggravated assault rates among youths in the United States from 1956 to 1996. And although most studies have shown a decline since the mid-1990s for boys, the numbers for girls involved continues to increase. From 1980 to 1997, the rate of criminal activity for female adolescents rose 69 percent while for males the increase was 26 percent. From 1980 to 1999 the proportion of girls arrested for aggravated assault went from 15 to 22 percent of the total, an increase of nearly 50 percent.

One other historical trend is worth noting. Following the reinstitution of the death penalty in the United States in 1975, kids were being tried and incarcerated as adults in record numbers, in what seems like a macabre return to the medieval concepts of children as simply small adults. It was not until 2005 that the two hundred individuals who committed murders when they were under the age of eighteen were spared death sentences because of the Supreme Court's ruling that capital punishment for minors is unconstitutional. Virtually all these individuals are boys. But even these numbers are not the whole story.

Americans are compulsively attuned to numbers when it comes to social issues. Maybe it is our fascination with the stock market, where every little numerical up and down is big news. But this fascination with the short-term statistical ups and downs of death draws us into an analytical world much more complex than it appears at the outset. It might seem that murder and suicide death rates are a simple matter—i.e, did someone kill somebody or not? But in fact there are many complexities that can obscure underlying realities. For example, it is important to remember that homicide rates provide only an imprecise indicator of the overall problem of violence in the lives of American children and youths. Behind each murder stand many nonlethal assaults on others, just as behind each suicide stand many nonlethal assaults on the self. This ratio increases as medical trauma technology improves, preventing assaults from becoming homicides, and it decreases as the weapons used in assaults become more lethal.

The FBI has documented that the homicide rate dropped during the late 1990s in part because of improved medical trauma technology, which rushes emergency medical technicians to victims of violence, offers them much more effective emergency intervention on-site than has ever been possible before, and speeds the victims to hospitals where they receive much more sophisticated surgical treatment than could have been imagined even a few decades ago. One study concluded that without these advances in medical care, the homicide rate since 1960 would have been five times higher than it actually was! Compared with 1931, the murder rate was little changed, but the rate of aggravated assault by the end of the twentieth century was *seven and a half times higher* than at the start of that century.

As I noted before, the same complex interplay of technologies producing changing outcomes for assaults against others is at work for suicides. In America it is taken as a fact that females attempt suicide more than males but kill themselves less often. But in contemporary China females actually do kill themselves more often than males, in large part because the method of choice (self-poisoning through the ingestion of insecticide) is highly lethal in rural China, where the benefits of modern emergency medicine are largely absent. In the United States, girls commit suicide via poison at a rate much higher than boys (25 percent for girls compared with 6 percent for boys). But in the context of our highly sophisticated system of emergency medicine, poisoning is a very inefficient tactic of self-assault, and many, many poisonings do not result in death. One statewide study (in Oregon) found that 78 percent of suicide attempts involved self-poisoning, and few were fatal. Conversely, almost all the suicide attempts involving firearms were fatal.

Overall about 3 percent of high school girls report attempting suicide, compared with about 2 percent of high school boys. Not surprisingly, some experts estimate the true number of attempts to be much higher, with many undetected attempts for every completed suicide. Our own study of the "secret lives of teenagers" asked students at Cornell University in confidence to look back on their time in high school and report on whether they had ever seriously contemplated suicide or ever attempted suicide. This was a highly select and accomplished group of young people attending an elite Ivy League university, disproportionately student leaders, star athletes, scholastic exemplars, and activity mavens. Nonetheless, 32 percent of the young women said that at some point in high school they were so depressed that they had seriously considered killing themselves (compared with 18 percent of the male students). We found that 4 percent of the female students said they had actually attempted suicide (compared with 1 percent of the male students). Of course it is possible that the high achievement orientation (verging on perfectionism in some cases) of these students has inflated their suicide orientation. Still, it is a sobering revelation.

One indicator of why it is so hard to come by reliable data on suicide attempts is that when we asked these students if their parents were aware of what they had done, the overwhelming majority said no. Nearly 90 percent of the young women who said they had seriously contemplated suicide said their parents did not know, and nearly half the students who actually had attempted suicide said their parents didn't know.

Whether it is suicide or murder, behind all these statistical findings are real girls (and boys), each of whom has a story to tell. The first murder case in which I served as an expert witness took place in Milwaukee more than a decade ago. Felicia Morgan was then a fifteen-year-old girl facing murder charges, in adult court, for shooting another teenager on the street. Why? The obvious answer was "for her jacket." A fifteen-year-old shoots and kills another teen on the street to get the other kid's jacket! Except for the fact that she was a girl, and most kids who kill are boys, this case represented everything America feared about poor minority youth and street crime at its worst—just as the suicides of smart, well-educated, affluent kids represent our greatest fears about middle-class life for kids.

But Felicia was represented by a smart, tough, bighearted lawyer, Robin Shellow. Robin's big heart reached out to Felicia. She saw in her more than a street monster. She saw a hurting child inside a scary teenager's body. And so she called me. At the time I was starting to do lectures and publish articles about how family abuse and neglect mixed with life in violent inner-city war zones pushed kids toward a war zone mentality. Robin saw in this work a way to make sense of Felicia and her actions and cast her as more than a violent monster who could take the life of another kid with cavalier bravado.

The key to Robin's defense of Felicia was that the combination of family abuse and neglect with the socially toxic influences of violent inner-city life had created in Felicia a way of thinking and feeling that made acts of insane violence sensible to her. The press latched on to this and began to call this the urban psychosis defense. It was their term, not Robin's—or mine, for that matter.

Robin asked if I would come to Milwaukee and testify in Felicia's defense, in an attempt to get the jury and judge to see what this troubled fifteen-year-old did as rooted in her traumatically abusive and devastatingly neglectful family in combination with her life on the streets in an urban war zone. The prosecution objected to my testifying, arguing that what I might have to say would be irrelevant to the case. At that time my focus on the developmental pathways to lethal youth violence was alien to the court's way of looking at these kids.

In a hearing before the judge, while the jury was out of the room, I was asked to outline this developmental pathway. Looking back on it now, more than a decade of additional experience in courtrooms and several books on youth violence later, I see how relatively crude and vague my analysis was. Nonetheless, I think that my testimony was relevant because girls like Felicia *are* shaped in important ways by the multiplication of family abuse by neighborhood violence.

Felicia had been the victim of numerous significant traumatic events in her life: physical and sexual abuse, physical and emotional harm on the streets. In recent decades we have learned more and more about how these kinds of experiences shape the thinking and feeling, and thus the behavior, of children and teenagers. The more we know, the more compelling becomes the argument that we must understand all this to make sense of what these kids do at their worst. We must see these dangerous kids as untreated traumatized children inside scary adolescent bodies.

The judge did not agree and instead accepted the prosecution's arguments that what I had to say was irrelevant to the guilt or innocence of Felicia. I was sent packing, back on the train to Chicago. It was the first time I had been rejected by a court as an expert witness in a murder trial, but it was not the last.

There are two pieces of follow-up information worth noting. For one thing, it would appear that despite ruling out my testimony, the judge did hear some of the message. He sentenced Felicia to a relatively short term (twelve years out of the life sentence available to him). Second, Robin appealed the judge's decision not to allow me to testify. At the state supreme court level two of the three judges sided with the trial judge, one agreeing with him that the testimony was irrelevant, one disagreeing, and the third thinking it was relevant but affirming the judge's authority to make the decision about admitting it. However, years later the case made its way to the U.S. Supreme Court and was reversed. At that time Robin Shellow negotiated a deal with the prosecution to have Felicia released on the basis of the time she had served in the interim, while the case was on appeal.

Other cases followed, cases in which I was allowed to testify before the jury, cases in which the testimony sometimes seemed to make a difference in the outcome (usually a life sentence instead of the death penalty sought by the prosecution). All but one involved young boys or men who killed. The one exception was Marilyn, a young Hispanic woman, mother of two children in Chicago, who was part of a double murder when she was eighteen. Interestingly, in her social history was mention of her being a "tomboy" as a child and a lone sister in a household of aggressive brothers, so perhaps it is not surprising that she went down a more typically masculine path when she lost her way. Her story was full of abuse and disrupted relationships, all set within the context of gang violence in her neighborhood (all her brothers were at that time in jail, one for murder).

An interesting feature of her case was that she had been sexually abused by her maternal uncle. Initially she refused to disclose that fact in court because of the effect it would have on her mother to learn that her brother had sexually abused his niece, her daughter. Eventually she agreed to make the disclosure after I impressed upon her the fact that this bit of information was most likely to elicit some sympathy from members of the jury and spare her life. As it turned out, that was exactly what happened. When I testified about the abuse and its impact, I could see sympathetic looks on the faces of several jurors, some of the women in particular. Sympathetic looks directed at defendants are rare indeed in courtrooms in which juries or judges are making decisions about the death penalty. The jury rejected the prosecutor's demand for a death sentence; she was given life in prison.

Over these years I have heard so many stories with the same themes, with only the gender of the perpetrator and the circumstantial particulars changing: who abused the child, what kind of abuse it was, what the child's injuries were, how soon the child began to come unraveled, what form the breakdown took, how deeply violence was integrated into the child's strategies for dealing with the world that had dealt a raw deal. But the cases of these two girls stuck with me, because they were gender exceptions and I wanted to understand them better. Indeed, they were one of the inspirations for this book. I now see that Felicia and Marilyn may not have been simply psychological curiosities by virtue of their gender. Rather, they may have been harbingers of the future if the trend continues for abused and troubled girls to act out rather than act in. As always, preventing child maltreatment and reforming sexual politics are two of the more reliable ways to prevent subsequent violence in all its forms.

Virtually all my court cases are characterized by a history of child maltreatment in the background of the perpetrator. This is not to say that all murders are committed by youths who have been abused and neglected. I am called as an expert witness only when issues of maltreatment and trauma are factors in the perpetrator's personal history. But that is not to say that "my" cases are all that unusual either. As we saw in Chapter 6, studies reveal that childhood experience with traumatic maltreatment is a common thread in most murders committed by kids who first develop conduct disorder and then move down the violent path that may end in murder. Probably 80 percent of murder cases involve perpetrators who were scarred by early traumatic maltreatment and whose lives were seriously sidetracked in the lost zone where so much of the worst violence occurs and is experienced. Why is that?

I think the reason is that most murders are committed as the culmination of a long pattern of aggressive antisocial behavior that starts in childhood and that experiences of traumatic maltreatment are the most likely human events to set a child in motion on the pathway that leads to killing another person. I have called the males who commit these acts lost boys. But what about lost girls? Are they any different from murderous boys? What is known about the characteristics of girls who murder when contrasted with their male counterparts?

Girls who kill are mostly like boys who kill, untreated traumatically maltreated children who inhabit the bodies of teenagers or adults. As the cultural shifts we saw in Chapters 3 and 4 continue, we can only expect that more and more of these troubled girls will express themselves though violent assault of the kind that has become routine for lost boys. It's already happening in the rise of violent girl gangs. Reports proliferate of gang-related violence involving girls as perpetrators.

But as is the case with boys, there are girls who kill whose lives seem to contradict the general pattern that links early abuse to conduct disorder as the launching pad for lethal violence. There are girls whose lethal violence seems to come from nowhere psychologically. These girls, like their male counterparts, are particularly troubling because it is harder to understand where they are coming from developmentally. Consider this case: Seventeen-year-old Amy seemed indistinguishable from other girls in her high school. She was neither a student leader nor a social isolate. She was neither an excellent student nor an academic failure. She was neither pretty nor ugly. Her home life was by all reports unremarkable. "Average" seemed to describe her in every way. She was the kind of girl who does not stand out from any crowd. Why then did she kill her former boyfriend and then herself? After the fact we might point to some genetic basis for depression that Amy hid from everyone. In retrospect we might assume that she reached her limit for acting OK when she was not OK. But why did she kill? Honestly, we don't really know and may never. But we can speculate from what we have learned so far.

Amy may well have been a worst-case scenario, in the sense that all the trends I have been exploring came to a boiling point in her life. Perhaps she was a very sensitive child who suffered disproportionately from the hurts of childhood. Perhaps she hoarded these little emotional cuts and bruises. Perhaps she felt trapped between the rock of her growing sadness and the hard place of what the people around her expected of her. Perhaps as she struggled to formulate a strategy to get through her life, she was exposed to the new violent female images available in the mass media of her generation—violent music videos, violent movies and television programs, violent video games. Whatever the mix of images, perhaps they fitted together in Amy's troubled consciousness. I fear there are more girls like Amy coming along.

The culture of girls is shifting away from the stifled femininity of the past toward a more egalitarian social reality in the present and the future. This is happening both at the top, where talented girls are now free and empowered to achieve in traditionally male domains (sports, for example), and at the bottom, among the victimized, angry, traumatized, and troubled girls who are looking for a fight and are willing to deliver the ultimate blow against anyone who gets in their way or pushes their buttons. Unless we see the trends emerging in the thinking and feeling of the new girl, the empowered girl, the unfettered girl, we shall not see her as she is. When she is good, she is very, very good. But when she is bad, she can be lethal.

Part Four

What
Now
?

8

Lifelines and Safety Nets:
Helping Girls Get Physical
Without Getting Hurt
or Hurting Other People

How do we support the positive elements of unleashing girls physically without allowing this liberation from the bonds of traditional femininity to translate into problematic physical aggression? We face two big challenges in accomplishing this. First, the unleashing of girls is taking place in the context of rising social toxicity. This social toxicity undermines the supports girls need to grow with character: a positive identity, a sense of being rooted, and spiritual connection and depth. Programs must address the elements of social toxicity I have outlined in earlier chapters. Second, the process of peer influence is powerful in girls' lives and is often—perhaps usually—a negative influence. This is why declining benevolent adult involvement in the lives of girls is a social problem in its own right, particularly when coupled with the multiple elements of social toxicity.

With these two issues in mind, I see four programmatic elements needed for girls lest they suffer from the dark side of unleashing them from traditional femininity into the world of assertive physicality. First, we need to build the developmental assets that reduce aggressive behavior and promote good character. Second, we need to look at the various efforts to empower girls and be sure they are not neglecting the need to channel assertiveness and are thus inadvertently encouraging violence. Third, we need to look at the various programs currently dealing with relational aggression in girls and see how well suited they are to deal with physical aggression. Fourth, we have to look at the various intervention and treatment programs for violent boys and make sure they are suited to the special needs of troubled girls.

Developmental Assets

Growing out of its research with schools and communities across the nation conducted in the 1980s and early 1990s, the Search Institute offered a list of forty "developmental assets." The Institute's research showed that the more of these assets a youth has, the more that child is likely to demonstrate positive behavior. It measured this both by the child's being less likely to be involved with drugs and alcohol and less likely to be sexually irresponsible, on the one hand, and by her or his being more likely to do well in school, control impulses and delay gratification, have healthy habits, and value diversity, on the other hand.

The forty assets are grouped into eight categories. They include things about the family (e.g., "Family has clear rules and consequences, and monitors the young persons' whereabouts"). They assess aspects of the school (e.g., "School provides clear rules and consequences"). They tap into the neighborhood (e.g., "Neighbors take responsibility for monitoring young people's behavior"). They explore positive peer influence (e.g., "Young person's best friends model responsible behavior") and high expectations (e.g., "Both parent(s) and teachers encourage the young person to do well"). And they include what's inside the kid's head (e.g., "Young person reports that 'My life has a purpose'").

In its research, the Search Institute found that among kids with zero to ten assets, the rate of drug abuse is 42 percent, and of problem alcohol use is 53 percent. In contrast, among kids with thirty-one to forty assets, the rate of drug abuse is 1 percent, and of problem alcohol use is 3 percent. When we turn to positive outcomes we find that for kids with thirty-one to forty assets, the rate of school success is 53 percent, maintaining good health is 88 percent, and delaying gratification is 71 percent, while for kids with zero to ten assets the corresponding figures are 53, 88, and 72 percent. The picture is clear: The more assets youths have, the more likely it is that they are living up to the kinds of ideals we as parents and citizens hope for in our children and youths, girls and boys alike.

What about aggression? The more assets children and teenagers have, the less likely they are to be plagued with problems of violence, defined in this research as "Has engaged in three or more acts of fighting, hitting, injuring a person, carrying a weapon, or threatening physical harm in the past 12 months."

With zero to ten assets, 61 percent of the kids were in the violent category; with eleven to twenty assets 35 percent; with twenty-one to thirty assets 16 percent, and with thirty-one to forty assets only 6 percent. Overall only 8 percent of kids report thirty-one to forty assets, and 20 percent report zero to ten. How does gender fit into these patterns? For a start we should note that the average number of assets reported by girls (from sixth to twelfth grade) is 19.5 whereas for boys it is 16.5. This alone speaks to why traditionally we might observe more aggressive behavior among boys than among girls. If more assets predict less aggression, then even if everything else were the same, we should expect to find more aggression among boys because of their having fewer assets than girls, on average.

Even at the same level of assets, we see the traditional gender patterns at work: Boys are more physically aggressive than girls. Among sixth- to eighth-grade boys with thirty-one to forty assets the rate of violent behavior is 14 percent, but for girls in the same situation it is 5 percent. For ninth- to twelfth-grade boys with thirty-one to forty assets, the figure is 8 percent, but for girls it is 2 percent. These differences continue as the number of assets declines, but the magnitude of the difference declines among the more "high-risk" youths. Thus, for sixth- to eighth-grade boys with zero to ten assets the percentage involved in violence is 74 percent whereas for girls it is 60 percent. For ninth- through twelfth-grade boys, it is 64 percent while for ninth- through twelfth-grade girls with zero to ten assets it is 47 percent. This is quite consistent with what we saw in Chapter 6; among kids at risk because of social conditions in their lives, girls' protection against antisocial physical aggression is reduced.

But what about physical aggression against the self? The Search Institute research includes a measure of "depression and suicide risk." Here we find that 58 percent of girls with zero to ten assets report high levels of depression and risk for suicide compared with 29 percent of boys. The difference is still apparent but much smaller for kids with thirty-one to forty assets (5 percent for girls and 3 percent for boys).

The good news in these data are the findings that girls on average have more developmental assets than boys of the same age and that these assets are more powerful in preventing violence for girls than boys (except in the cases of self-directed aggression and depression).

But we cannot assume that the level of developmental assets for girls is fixed. Like almost everything else in the human ecology of children and youths, the number of assets is a variable. While we don't have the data to make firm historical comparisons, I believe that other evidence points to declining assets for kids in recent decades, a trend that is part of rising social toxicity. For example, numerous studies have documented declining rates of supervision during nonschool hours, reductions in adult-child interaction, lessened responsiveness to adult norms, and rising cynicism and declining social trust. Each of these bears on Search Institute developmental assets. Each predicts declining asset totals for kids.

We know that the average number of assets for kids declines as they move through adolescence, from 21.5 in sixth grade to 17.2 in twelfth grade. Adolescence is a time when most kids experience a decline in assets, and in our current environment this is particularly the case. Social toxicity erodes precisely the developmental assets girls will need to protect themselves from falling prey to the aggressive influences they confront more and more openly as they are unleashed from the "protection" of traditional femininity.

One way that social toxicity translates into the day-to-day lives of kids is in diminishing developmental assets—in the family, in the school, in the neighborhood, in the community, and inside kids' heads. All told, these data on developmental assets highlight the importance of protecting and encouraging the positive forces in girls' lives in the face of rising social toxicity. This may involve specific programs that seek to cultivate assets (e.g., the kinds of sports and arts programs implicit in some of the assets) as well as more general community mobilization, parent education, and character education initiatives designed indirectly to promote clusters of developmental assets (like increasing parental supervision and kids' relationships with nonparental adults).

Empowerment Programs

The modern feminist movement began with the publication of Betty Friedan's book *The Feminine Mystique* nearly half a century ago. Except for some subcultures that are fighting feminism (mostly fundamentalist religious groups), there is no going back to the old patriarchal cultural models. Nonetheless, much remains to be done to bring about a true and pervasive egalitarianism between women and men. Girls still need empowerment, despite the fact that the progress made over the last fifty years is not going to be reversed.

For example, many girls are still oppressed. They earn less money than boys do when they work in comparable jobs (about seventy cents on the dollar). They are sexually victimized in numbers that far exceed the levels of victimization experienced by boys. And there are still far too many girls who believe that the only way for them to experience the satisfactions of physical power is through sex, through the use of their bodies as sexual tools.

Here's one girl's honest account of her use of sex to exercise power. Her name is Carol, and she is a nineteen-year-old sophomore studying chemistry. She grew up in Baton Rouge, Louisiana, with her parents and two brothers.

Growing up, I had always been taught to be ladylike—you know, to sit with my legs crossed and be polite to others. When I wanted to deal with my frustrations, it was not acceptable for me to use physical force, so instead I would usually go for a run or exercise physically to get out my frustrations. Screaming also seemed to work. I would regularly see many males engaging in rough play, physical fighting, and more, yet this was not "acceptable" for a young lady. This of course led me to even more frustration, and I eventually had to seek out other ways to deal with my feelings. When I got slightly older, I found sex to be a particular effective way in which I could express my frustrations in a more physical way. I was able to act more aggressive in the bedroom because there was no one there telling me to be ladylike. It was a way that I could express my feelings and use my body in a physical way that wasn't regarded as boylike or socially inappropriate.

Carol's experience with sex as the culturally available option for physical response to frustration is not unique to her. Research by psychologist Anne Campbell and her colleagues reveals that much of women's aggression is traditionally "expressive, emerging as a release only after they could no longer control their pent-up frustration and anger. Sex is a form of expression in many women and may take place when they are frustrated." As the larger picture of girls getting physical changes, it will permit and encourage changes in the sexuality of women (as it does and has for boys and men).

Both sex and aggression are powerful drives in the human psyche, drives that people are prone to intertwine in confused, self-defeating, and often socially dangerous ways. The complex dynamics of rape testify to this in the case of men and boys. For the New American Girl and the woman she will become, it will be vital to make positive sense of sex and aggression as separable issues, each with its own ethic and emotional rules and values. Without such a sorting out, girls will continue to experience a dangerous confusion, as in the case of Tanya, an eighteen-year-old engineering student who grew up in New York City, with her single mother and brother. She reports: "I view sex as a way for me to be dominant over other individuals. I enjoy the feeling of control and being able to influence the males in my life. Society allows males to lead in so many ways that are collectively acceptable, thus forcing women to take a secondary role. The feeling of power that is given to me through sex is something I cannot gain any other way."

We shall be better off if this girl and the many like her see ways to be powerful without using sex to gain that power. The issue is not the suppression of sensuality or sexuality or in other ways the disempowering of girls like her, but rather the shift of the focus of their legitimate yearning for power. It will no longer do simply to say, "Assertiveness is not ladylike." Using that framework, we end up stuck in the view that all physical aggression in girls is bad, but that "[aggressive] boys will be boys." This puts girls in an untenable position with respect to aggression, boxed in by outmoded gender stereotypes, stuck between the rock of male physical intimidation and the hard place of the social realities of modern life. It's no wonder that some girls see using their bodies sexually as the one path to power open to them.

And it may be that presexual girls are vulnerable to an analogous danger when it comes to misplaced assertiveness. The issue is not merely a matter of replacing passivity with assertiveness. Assertiveness is a force. It has no inherent direction. In our socially toxic society undirected assertiveness can lead to arrogance and power assertion because adult society is often lax in teaching the elements of character that provide positive direction for girl power and counter the corrupting effects of our society's love affair with violence. I find evidence of this misdirected assertiveness in what nineteen-year-old Rebecca, a college student majoring in parks and recreation management, told me of her experiences as a counselor in a summer camp for girls:

> I was placed in charge of a group of eight-year-old girls, and it was rare for a day to go by without some physical aggression breaking out among these girls. I thought that one of the reasons physical aggression did occur among these girls was simply that they felt very comfortable in their own skins, so to speak. They had a strong sense of identity. They constantly wanted to give voice to their opinions in self-expressive activities and rarely felt shy around anyone, the counselors or their peers. As a result, if something didn't go their way, the girls who had the strongest convictions were also the first to hit other girls. All they wanted was to get their own way and these girls felt very comfortable with who they were. When they did not know how to voice their concerns properly or did not think to compromise or were too impatient for it, they started hitting each other. I noticed one of the girls whom the counselors had the most trouble with as far as the hitting was concerned. If she had to use the rest room— which was quite often—she refused to wait for someone to take her without making a fuss. If she was hungry, she would demand a snack. She opened up in discussions all the time with counselors and with peers. She just felt extremely comfortable with how she was and confident in whatever she did. And that included hitting other children when they got in her way. Confident. Assertive. Aggressive.

This echoes what I have seen and heard working with some aggressive boys. Sometimes the problem is not low self-esteem and passivity, but rather an exaggerated self-concept that slips into narcissism and egocentrism. It's always hard to find a good balance. That balance is the combining of traditionally feminine and masculine traits (androgyny) rather than the substituting of masculine for feminine traits. It is a complicated challenge for both genders. Boys who are asked to add feminine traits to complete their androgyny may fear they risk being labeled "gay" and subject to homophobic bias if they become too "soft." Girls who are asked to add masculine traits may fear they will be labeled "unladylike."

There are consequences and risks for both genders, but with boys the movement to androgyny seems to pose little risk to society; more emotionally sensitive and nurturing males seem to be an unambiguous good. However, there may be social costs for girls if one of the masculine traits added is the male propensity to physical violence. This is *not* to say we should try to stop the movement to androgyny. No, it is essential as a strategy for increasing resilience in the face of social toxicity and as a matter of social justice. But we must promote it with our eyes open to one of the fundamental laws of human ecology—namely, that you can never do just one thing. There are always side effects and unanticipated consequences to human intervention.

There are programs that explicitly seek to encourage the positive empowerment of girls. One is Girls Incorporated. This organization is "dedicated to inspiring all girls to be strong, smart and bold." In fact its main focus is poor and minority girls, girls who most need empowerment and are probably at greatest risk for becoming troubled, violent girls. Its program statement includes this: "Today, innovative programs help girls confront subtle societal messages about their value and potential, and prepare them to lead successful, independent and fulfilling lives." It offers a variety of efforts aimed at empowering girls: Friendly PEERsuasion (drugs), Preventing Adolescent Pregnancy, Operation SMART (science and technology skills), and FUTURE (substance abuse, sexual and physical abuse, and gang involvement).

Besides providing local service and educational programs (particularly to low-income girls), Girls Incorporated operates a National Resource Center. Among its offerings is a 2001 fact sheet titled "Girls and Violence." However, of the two dozen sets of facts reported, virtually all concern physical violence directed *at* girls rather than violence committed *by* girls. The three exceptions are data on girls carrying guns to school (6 versus 29 percent for boys during a thirty-day period), increasing rates of arrests for aggravated assault (up 57 percent during the 1990s), and the relatively greater likelihood of black girls compared with white girls reporting that they had been in a physical fight. In the future, empowerment programs will have to do a better job of recognizing the possibility of physical aggression as an unanticipated side effect of empowerment in girls and program accordingly.

Another front in the efforts to empower girls positively is of course their involvement in sports. As I noted before, whereas once it was rare for girls to play interscholastic sports (one for every thirty-two boys), now it is common (approaching one to one). It is clear that legislation has played a role in stimulating this change. Congress outlawed discrimination in sports (and other public settings) on the basis of gender through passage of Title IX of the Civil Rights Act in 1975. This led to cascading changes in schools across the country with respect to the participation of girls in athletics. That work is mostly done. Indeed, recent reports indicate a leveling off of the upward trend in girls' participation in high school sports as it nears parity.

Beyond the national legal prompt created by Title IX (violators are threatened with the loss of federal funding), much of the change that has come in athletic empowerment has come as a matter of local schools and communities' opening up sports for girls. Has there been a concomitant focus on issues of character and physical aggression in girls' sports? My experience as a consultant and lecturer in schools around the country tells me that the answer is generally no. In fact, despite the many decades of experience with boys participating in organized sports, awareness of the need to program for issues of character and physical aggression is spotty and uneven where males are concerned.

It is not surprising, then, that issues of character and aggression stand mostly unconsidered with respect to girls and sports. A casual conversation with two teachers in Texas reveals that a local middle school girls' field hockey tournament degenerated into a brawl, but no one seemed to know much about it. Chatting with teachers in Ohio, I learn of a girls' soccer game that had to be ended prematurely because of a fight on the field. After a lecture in Florida, a parent came to tell me how her daughter had had to quit the basketball team because she was frightened of being physically intimidated by other players. A girl in California told me of a locker room brawl that took place between her softball team and its crosstown rival. A powder-puff football game in Illinois degenerated into a brutal hazing incident that sent several girls to the hospital. So long as events such as these are treated as mystifying aberrations rather than as indicators of social changes affecting girls' aggression, we shall be stuck with an awareness gap.

Here are two perspectives on the way girls and boys are dealing with aggression in the context of sports. Tom, a twenty-year-
old martial arts instructor from St. Louis, reports:

I received my black-belt first degree in Sho-Tae-Ryu martial
arts when I was ten years old. When I was sixteen, I began teaching martial arts classes, and because I was the youngest black
belt, I taught more of the beginner-youth classes. Regardless of
the class age, we had more females than males in what is usually
thought of as a male-dominated sport. We try to make the point
throughout the beginner levels that students must control their
anger and never lose control of their emotions. Sometimes, however, when sparring or competing for rank, students have been
known to get a little too aggressive and lose their control. This
was a rare occurrence, but more common among boys. They
would usually push each other around or pull at their uniforms,
making quick jabs or kicks, but it never amounted to much. They
made it fairly noticeable, and the fights were not very long.
When girls got into these aggressive fights, it was very different.
One day, while we were letting some students spar and others cri-
tique their form, two girls suddenly got into a serious fight (not
related to the sparring). The girls were around ten to twelve
years old, and both were yellow belts (a low rank). This fight was
very different from the boys' spontaneous fights of aggression.
Without any of the protective gear on, these girls went right for
each other, screaming, clawing, and swinging away. It was very
surprising to me and the other instructors because unlike the
boys, who would make little jabs and comments before they
started fighting, the girls went straight into fighting. As another
instructor and I began to separate the girls, we realized this was

very different from the boys. The girls did not seem to notice we were there and kept on fighting. They were bleeding on their arms from nail scratches. Their hair and uniforms were pulled during the fight. Once we finally did separate the girls we found that the dispute was over ranking, but also because one of the girls had made a rude (or wrongly interpreted as rude) remark, and it built up quickly from there. These girls held a grudge for a long time, unlike the boys, who usually forgot about the hostility in few weeks.

Joan, now a college student majoring in child development, tells this story of her experience in Dallas, Texas:

> As an athlete in high school I encountered dozens of situations in which aggression among females was a common accompaniment to the sport that was being played. Often girls would start fights with each other on the soccer field as the result of one tripping the other "on purpose." Whether each kick or push was intentional or not, girls often interpreted this as a personal attack on themselves and responded to this assault in a similar manner to which it had been received. I admit that on occasion I wanted to physically hurt another player for the wrong she had done me, but my parents had previously warned me that if I ever started a fight, I would never be able to play sports again.

The shifting culture of aggression for girls in sports raises many important questions for programming. Some will merely require the same strategies that have developed for boys (even if these strategies are too often neglected for boys). Some will require gender-specific programmatic efforts, like Shelley Frost and Ann Troussieux's *Throw Like a Girl: Discovering the Body, Mind and Spirit of the Athlete in You*, and John DeWitt's *Coaching Girls' Soccer.*

These efforts will have to recognize the legacy of relational aggression in girls and the greater focus of girls on the emotional quality of relationships generally. This is one reason why I think it is important that institutions have arisen to analyze the psychological impact of athletics and document their effects. For example, the University of Minnesota hosts the Tucker Center for Research on Girls and Women in Sports. In addition, the Ms. Foundation and the Feminist Majority Foundation have sponsored research on girls and the effects of participation in sports. More information about these programs is available in the Resource Guide at the end of this book.

Beyond these gender-specific efforts there are institutions concerned more generally with the impact of modern athletics on the social, psychological, and moral development of kids. For example, Notre Dame University inaugurated a center to study the role of sports in character education in response to concerns that athletic participation has a downside for boys and men. Then there is the National Alliance for Youth Sports, which seeks to reduce the emotionally and socially destructive effects of excessive and premature competition in organized sports for all children. It too will have to adapt to the new realities of girls getting physical.

Efforts to Deal with Relational Aggression

Relational aggression is currently the big thing in programming for girls. Add recent books like Rosalind Wiseman's *Queen Bees and Wannabes*, Rachel Simmons's *Odd Girl Out*, and Marion Underwood's *Social Aggression Among Girls* to the previous generation of books on the special developmental issues faced by modern girls, like Mary Pipher's *Reviving Ophelia* and Carol Gilligan's *In a Different Voice*, and there are enough books dealing with this topic to fill a nice-size shelf. There are also efforts to translate the insights and analyses of these books into programs. For example, a group called the Girls' Initiative Network has developed a program called Allies in Action to deal with relational aggression. Here's its description of the goals: "Relational aggression is behavior that goes largely ignored because it is normalized in our culture by girls and adults alike. It is also ignored because it can be so frustrating to curb. With increased public awareness about female aggression and its impact on self-esteem and learning, parents and schools are asking critical questions about why girls harm one another and what can be done to prevent or change these behaviors. Through didactic and experiential techniques, the Allies in Action workshop explores the nature of relational aggression between girls and offers culturally relevant and age-appropriate prevention and intervention strategies."

Some "Ophelia Groups" have taken on the task of dealing with relational aggression. Named after Mary Pipher's book *Reviving Ophelia*, these groups are offering girls workshops on how to recognize, to deal with, and ultimately to prevent relational aggression. For example, Monroe County in upstate New York is part of the National Ophelia Sister Project and has taken on the issue of relational aggression among middle school girls. Teaming with a variety of community agencies, including the Community Conflict Resolution Program, the Ophelia project is working with girls "to understand how to change negative and destructive behaviors without sacrificing their assertiveness or strong sense of self."

Rachel Simmons's book *Odd Girl Out* has also spawned programs to help girls deal with relational bullying. One issue these programs address is helping girls accept the idea that aggression between girls need not be the end of their relationship. That's a good start. It should also provide the organizational foundation for dealing with issues of physical aggression as they arise if adults are willing to do so.

But have these books spawned efforts to deal with physical aggression as part of their general efforts to support girls in positive ways of dealing with the sexual and other pressures placed upon girls in our socially toxic culture? As far as I can tell, the answer is mostly no.

There are some scholarly compendiums of research on female aggression than include some discussion of delinquent violence (e.g., K. Bjorkvist and P. Niemla's *Of Mice and Women*, Marlene Moretti, Candice Odgers, and Margaret Jackson's *Girls and Aggression*, and Martha Putallaz and Karen Bierman's *Aggression, Antisocial Behavior, and Violence Among Girls.*) But while these books do deal with physical aggression in girls as a concern for research and theory, the role of "normal" physical aggression in the lives of girls seems largely absent as a concern in programming beyond the confines of university laboratories.

In the world of programming, most people still see incidents of physical aggression by girls mostly as aberrations and exceptions rather than as evidence of an emerging new rule. That new rule is that girls—not all girls, but girls in increasing numbers—can and will be physically aggressive in ways that are much more like what has traditionally been seen in boys. The lethality of their aggression remains lower, the protective effect of developmental assets remains greater, and the biological protections of having two X chromosomes remains unchanged. But the fact is, troubled girls are leading the way in narrowing the aggression gap, and other girls are following suit.

I think in the coming years existing programs for girls will have to address physical aggression more systematically. It will not be sufficient to focus exclusively on relational and verbal aggression. I believe school- and community-based character education programs must focus on the issue of physicality with a new urgency and comprehensiveness. I think the confusion and ambivalence that many girls feel about physical aggression will continue. In fact they will probably escalate as conditions change in the day-to-day lives of girls and in the world of the mass media, where the life of the New American Girl is writ large in characters and plots.

Treatment and Intervention Programs for Aggressive Troubled Girls

If there was one truism about troubled kids when I was being professionally educated, it was that boys act out and girls act in. Traditionally, troubled boys exhibited externalizing problems—hitting people, hurting animals, and setting fires, for example—and troubled girls exhibited internalizing problems: low self-esteem, depression, headaches, for example. They allowed others to hurt them; many of those were precisely the troubled boys who manifested externalizing problems. This was accepted knowledge among clinicians.

Among sociological theorists of delinquency, troubled girls were largely a nonentity. In her book *Sex, Power, & the Violent School Girl*, youth care specialist Sibylle Artz offers a tour of these theorists and the virtual absence of girls in their models.

She writes: "Few mainstream sociological theories appear to have dealt with female crime and delinquency. Content with the assumption that crime and delinquency were masculine forms of behavior, and bolstered in that assumption by statistical evidence of the overwhelming participation of males in such behavior, the majority of theorists (who were themselves male) focused on males. Those who did address female participation in crime and delinquency still grounded most of their thinking in male experience."

Of course social workers and psychologists actually working in residential facilities, community programs, and schools did see girls and dealt with them regardless of how they appeared in academic theories. Nonetheless, the lack of intellectual foundations for programs based upon the distinct needs and characteristics of girls has been a problem, one that continues to this day.

There have been preliminary efforts to address the state of intervention and treatment for troubled and delinquent girls. For example, an Ohio-based Gender Specific Working Group in 1997 released a report entitled *Moving Toward Juvenile Justice and Youth-Serving Systems That Address the Distinct Experience of the Adolescent Female*. But the vague prescriptions offered were not really much more than an exhortation to pay attention to girls in the juvenile justice system, and they were stated in very general terms: "meet the unique needs of females"; "acknowledge the female perspective"; "support the female experience through positive female role models," "recognize the contributions of girls and women"; "respect female development"; "empower girls and young women to reach their full potential"; "work to change established attitudes that prevent or discourage young women from recognizing their potential." Those are good messages, but they are hardly the prescriptions necessary for programming. In many ways and in many places troubled girls are left in a kind of program limbo.

What has emerged is not a good situation for girls. In theory and traditionally they were confined to the role of victim or, in some cases, perpetrators of "sexual crimes" or just delinquency groupies who engaged in antisocial behavior simply as a means to establish sexual relationships with bad boys. The fact that girls bore most of the costs themselves (internalizing problems) while boys were costly to the community (externalizing problems) reduced society's motivation to deal with troubled girls. In a sense, their suffering was devalued. When girls did act out, they were seen as betraying both their society and their gender, presumably on the ground that it was normal for boys to act out—"boys will be boys"—but was not so for girls, who were seen as pathological for acting in a manner that was both antisocial and nonfeminine.

All this is changing. Troubled girls are unleashed. More and more they are manifesting their troubles as externalizing problems that get people's attention rather than suffering in silence as they might have in the past. Victims are demanding justice, in the legal system, in their families, in their intimate relationships, and in the court of public opinion. That's good. Communities are also taking notice of troubled girls and their needs for psychological services. That's good. When all is said and done, it seems simply fair that troubled girls will express their hurt and rage assertively rather than swallow it and make themselves sick, as they have for so long. That's better than it was, even if it is not as good as preventing their traumas in the first place. But converting trauma-related rage in troubled girls from acting in to acting out can involve them in the very same antisocial and ultimately self-destructive physical aggression that plagues hurt and sad boys.

In her Associated Press story on female violence in 2004, Wiley Hall quoted numerous professionals who were concerned that girls are implementing the shift from acting in to acting out in ways that are dangerous to themselves and the community. "We're seeing girls doing things now that we used to put off on boys," the former Baltimore school police chief Jansen Robinson said. "This is vicious, 'I-want-to-hurt-you' fighting. It's a nationwide phenomenon and it's catching us all off guard."

I thought of this when I sat with the director of a secure facility for delinquent girls in New York as she explained her view of physical aggression in the troubled girls with whom she works: "I think the girls who are most aggressive are generally more healthy psychologically than those who hurt themselves or passively allow other people to hurt them. I wish both groups were not hurt in the first place, but honestly, I think girls have taken too much over the years, and it is better for their own mental health to act it out rather than just suffer in silence." This view is not unusual and has its merits. If push comes to shove, I would rather have girls push back than get passively pushed over. That's a better alternative than the self-victimizing internalizing response of the past. I'll have something to say about the best alternative later.

The national data point to increasing rates of violent delinquency among girls. But at the same time, the very high levels of victimization among girls continue, in the form of abuse, neglect, assault, and emotional deprivation. These same data show that the girls most likely to be victimized in these ways are always least empowered in other ways—coming disproportionately from poor families, for example. Also, despite the increased empowerment of women generally, there are still a lot of men and boys in our society hurting women and girls. For example, about one in ten girls experiences sexual abuse in some form. This means that there is a deep reservoir of hurt in girls. If all that hurt is converted into physically aggressive acting out because of the breaking down of barriers to girls' physical assertion and the influence of social toxicity, there is going to be a lot more physical violence among girls in the years to come.

So what can communities and institutions do about girls who have a problem with violence, not just with "normal" aggression? To answer this question, we turn to the many programs and research studies that deal with interventions to reduce problematic aggression in children and adolescents, particularly those that have addressed the special needs of girls.

The American Bar Association in 2002 published a report entitled "Justice by Gender: The Lack of Appropriate Prevention, Diversion and Treatment Alternative for Girls in the Justice System." It offers specific recommendations to address long-standing inequities in the treatment of girls and boys in the system (for example, the fact that the money spent per institutionalized girl is much less than that spent for boys).

Meda Chesney-Lind and Larry Selden's 1997 book *Girls, Delinquency, and Juvenile Justice* provides a valuable perspective. The authors offer conclusions about three elements common to successful programs: comprehensive counseling to address multiple problems, including sexual abuse and exposure to violence; support for educational and vocational development; and special support for girls separated from their families and in need of surrogate parental figures. All three factors recognize some of the forces at work in the development of violence in girls, although on its face none particularly differentiates delinquent girls from delinquent boys.

The area that most differentiates the troubles of girls from the troubles of boys that are likely to lead to aggressive delinquency is early out-of-wedlock pregnancy because it conveys social injuries that put girls on a fast track to negative life pathways, including delinquency and violence. But as always there is not a simple and universal effect of early out-of-wedlock pregnancy. What matters is how girls make sense of the experience, a fact that returns us to the risky thinking (social cognition problems) and problems with basic relationships (insecure attachment and rejection sensitivity) that I highlighted in Chapter 6 as the key to understanding how and why abused kids develop conduct disorder.

What is the nature of current efforts to deal with violent behavior in girls? There is a significant and growing base of clinical interventions addressing the issue of whether or not the variety of programs developed to deal with aggression generally have different effects for girls and boys.

Research shows that the most successful violence reduction programs aimed at teenagers combine efforts to change the way kids think about violence (cognitive restructuring) and to provide practice in nonviolent alternatives (behavioral rehearsal). It is not enough to do one or the other to achieve successful violence reduction. Programs must engage kids in efforts to understand violence and their own aggressive behavior in new, alternative ways. After all, it is risky thinking about social situations that provides the link between being abused and developing a chronic pattern of aggression, bad behavior, acting out, and violating the rights of others. But the gap between knowing and doing is always a problem for human beings. Thus, the second key element is to offer kids experiences in what their new way of thinking implies for behavior so they can see how it feels to respond nonviolently through role playing and other exercises.

Two programs that accomplish these goals for children are the Good Behavior Game, developed by Sheppard Kellam and his colleagues at Johns Hopkins University, and Let's Talk About Living in a World with Violence, developed by me and my colleagues at the Erikson Institute (information about both is presented in the Resource Guide). The Good Behavior Game is a strategy for first-grade teachers to take charge of the social process of the classroom and use it to direct aggressive children toward nonaggressive behavior. It prevents antisocial peer groups from forming in the classroom. Instead it offers the children a set of positive, nonaggressive norms and then puts the power of the peer group behind those new norms in a series of exercises. Research reveals that it is effective in blunting the trend toward escalating aggression by high-risk kids, a process that extends its influence through sixth grade. Thus it can prevent high-risk kids from developing by age ten the pattern of aggression, bad behavior, acting out, and violating the rights of others (early-onset conduct disorder) that puts kids on the fast track for violent delinquency.

Let's Talk About Living in a World with Violence is aimed at fourth to sixth graders and involves them in a process of learning and reflection about the existence and meaning of physical aggression and violence in their lives. Through a workbook format, the program considers violence in all aspects of life (including the mass media) and points the way to alternative, nonviolent strategies for dealing with conflict and negative arousal. Research on the program indicates it does reduce aggressive attitudes and behavior.

Programs that emphasize uncontrolled peer group experience (rather than adult direction and control of the content of peer interaction) tend to produce more rather than less aggressive and antisocial behavior in kids. A generation of research on programs to reduce antisocial behavior demonstrates that peer group programs can easily be taken over by aggressive youths with an antisocial orientation, the result being that the "good" kids move in the negative direction modeled by the "bad" kids. This is the conclusion drawn by a review of three decades of research published in the American Psychological Association's journal in 1999 by psychologist Thomas Dishion and his colleagues entitled "When Interventions Harm: Peer Groups and Problem Behavior."

I think that ultimately the most successful programs have a spiritual orientation. By this I mean that they deal with questions of ultimate meaning and thus buffer children against the negative social and cultural forces around them. If I had to identify one element in the boys who kill I have known, it would be a spiritual emptiness. Rather than know and feel that they are part of something larger than day-to-day material life, these troubled kids believe they are alone in the universe. This spiritual isolation makes them a high-risk group in a socially toxic environment because it gives them nothing to resist the allure of the dark side of human experience, because it does not invoke a sense that human material actions are limited by virtue of larger spiritual realities, and because it does not give them a positive place to stand in the world when they are besieged with sadness.

A spiritually grounded youth, in contrast, can be sustained and guided by saying, "I do not have a hole in my heart. I know there is more to any interaction than my physical power. I know too that despite how bad things look, I need not slip into emotional free fall because there is a positive spiritual meaning to my life no matter what happens." I believe this belief system sustains kids, and research documents that youths involved in this sort of spiritual life are indeed buffered from many of the social pathologies that concern us, like violent delinquency (and drug abuse). Two of the Search Institute's developmental assets speak directly to these matters: "spends one or more hours per week in activities in a religious institution" and "reports that 'my life has a higher purpose.'"

With these findings in mind, we can look for these elements in whatever programs are offered to help troubled and aggressive girls. Too many of the programs for kids are not based upon sound theory and research. Often they are based upon a naively appealing idea or on "common sense" or are the pet projects of powerful, influential, or rich individuals or groups, without being grounded in the developmental realities of violence and delinquency. When this happens, these programs either have no effect at all or make things worse. This has been true of a variety of popular interventions, including the original version of the DARE program (which was shown to have little effect overall on substance abuse and to be associated with increased drug use in suburban kids). They include Scared Straight, a program to reduce delinquency in which prisons delivered scary messages to kids that turned out to make the high-risk kids behave in a more delinquent fashion, and boot camps, in which the use of tough power assertion produced no generally significant results. As a droll bumper sticker once said, "You can change the world . . . but unless you know what you are doing, please don't."

Some programs have moved beyond these pitfalls. They have been grounded in coherent theory and a familiarity with well-designed and well-executed research on the origins of antisocial violence in girls' lives. They are implementing psychologist Kurt Lewin's maxim "There is nothing so practical as a good theory." When good theory and good research form the bedrock of an intervention program, there are still no guarantees that it will be powerful enough to change deeply rooted problematic behavior, but at least the effort is not capricious.

A positive case in point is the Earlscourt Girls Connection, in Toronto. The experience of this program is distinctive in that it arose out of consciousness of the fact that program models for boys do not necessarily work for girls. Earlscourt Child and Family Centre is a family-focused treatment center for aggressive children between five and eleven. The standard program involved anger management and skill-building interventions and did not differentiate between boys and girls. As one study of the project put it, "Preliminary assessments of the program indicated that the girls' inclusion in 'gender-neutral' interventions were . . . found to be associated with negative outcomes. Some of the girls showed increases in aggression and others withdrew from participation in the group program."

So what did the people at Earlscourt do? They devised special elements of intervention on the basis of understanding of girls' development. These elements included concurrent parent and child groups and a mother-daughter group. Within the structure provided by these three groups, the programs include three separate efforts. For parents, there is the SNAP parent program, a twelve-session parent-training effort that teaches more effective techniques for child management and anger control. It includes a special focus on how to handle various forms of aggression in girls' lives and utilizes role playing to communicate new ways of viewing and responding to girls' behavior. For girls, there is the Girls Club, a twelve-session course that focuses on teaching effective self-regulation and problem-solving strategies. Activities focus on the various triggers for aggression in girls' lives, triggers that are often related to exaggerated or inaccurate thinking about peers and adults. Issues of appearance and social status dominate the sessions, and triggers for physical aggression are an important area of emphasis. For the mother-daughter pairs, there is a program called Girls Growing Up Healthy, which concentrates on improving skills in enhancing the relationship between a girl and her mother. Activities include cooperative projects emphasizing health and safety issues as well as competent communicating.

Evaluation of the Earlscourt Girls Connection program is encouraging. During the first year of involvement, girls in the program showed more effective regulation of their anger (fewer blowups), decreases in defiant attitudes and behavior (less "attitude"), more prosocial relationships (cooperative friendships), and less aggression (both relational and physical). However, these changes had not translated into reduced delinquency and vandalism by the end of the first year. We can only hope that with the changes in the attitudes and behaviors that underlie delinquency there will be an eventual positive change in this area as well. In any case, the well-designed research accompanying the intervention program reassures us that those responsible for the program will at least know why they are doing what they are doing and will know if it is working (and, one hopes, why it isn't, so they can redress the program's inadequacies). Realistically, you can't ask for more in any intervention program, except perhaps that it deal directly with the spiritual needs of troubled, violent girls.

At the core of the youth violence is a spiritual crisis. Human beings are not simply animals with complicated brains. We are spiritual beings having a physical experience. Research conducted by psychiatrist Kathleen Kovner Kline and her colleagues dealing with the beneficial effects of a spiritual orientation for troubled youths found that "strong nurturing can reduce or eliminate the harmful effects that are associated with aggression, anxiety, depression or substance abuse." They further found that "primary nurturing relationships influence early spiritual development" and that "spirituality is associated with lower levels of stress hormones, with more optimism, and with commitment to helping others." Their conclusion? "The human brain appears to be organized to ask ultimate questions and seek ultimate answers."

This recognition directs our attention to the multiple spiritual crises in the lives of the most violent girls. They often have a sense of meaninglessness, in which they are cut off from a sense that life has a higher purpose. By the same token, they often have difficulty envisioning themselves in the future. This terminal thinking undermines their motivation to contribute to their community and to invest their time and energy in schooling and healthy lifestyles. Finally, they often have lost confidence in the ability and motivation of the adults in their world to protect and care for them. This leads them to adopt the orientation of juvenile vigilantism. A boy once said to me, "If I join a gang, I am fifty percent safe; if I don't join a gang, I am zero percent safe." His girlfriend looked on and nodded. The point is that adults don't enter the equation.

Nonpunitive, love-oriented religion institutionalizes spirituality and functions as a buffer against social pathology, according to research reviewed by psychologist and pastoral counselor Andrew Weaver and his colleagues. On the other hand, the toxic materialist culture in which we live undermines spirituality and exacerbates these problems. One way to deal with these issues is to have treatment programs committed to cultivating deep meaning for the troubled girls they serve. This can take the form of character education, as developed, for example, by psychologist Thomas Lickona.

Character education is an effort to infuse every element of kids' lives with a values perspective. It asks kids and adults to monitor their behavior constantly and ask, "Is this consistent with our core values?" It goes beyond slogans to embed these core values in everyday life in schools and communities. In this way, it provides a framework in which to pursue an agenda that nourishes spirituality (without bumping into constitutionally insoluble issues of church and state). Violent, troubled girls are wandering in a spiritual wilderness. Our task is to do more than teach them social skills and provide therapeutic insights. Our goal should be find them and to lead them back down the path of goodness, in spiritual terms that most religiously motivated individuals will find compatible, be they Christian, Jewish, Muslim, Buddhist, or Hindu. Even nonreligious humanists can find a home in this broad commitment to spirituality as a source of meaningfulness.

My colleagues and I have explored strategies for accomplishing this through a pilot program we called From Boot Camp to Monastery. Although the institution in which we explored this approach served only boys, I believe it has direct application to the lives of troubled and aggressive girls as well, for the spiritual crisis that spawns destructive violence crosses gender lines. Others have experimented with using deep meditation programs. These efforts have produced success with incarcerated women and demonstrated positive results that extend to many of our core concerns with meaningfulness and prosocial behavior. There is every reason to expect the same with girls, that a From Boot Camp to Nunnery approach will prove beneficial for girls. Several spiritual traditions, including both the Christian and Buddhist heritages, teach us to expect this. Zen Buddhism particularly, with its emphasis on being more an applied psychology than a religion, offers a great deal.

The writings and practical experience of Thich Nhat Hanh are exemplary in this regard. Adding a detailed reading and reflection program based upon his book *Creating True Peace* would go a long way toward meeting the programmatic goal of a spiritual dimension. Imagine the benefits to troubled, aggressive girls to live with the "mindfulness" precepts embodied in Nhat Hanh's words:

> The Mindfulness Trainings help us learn to exercise self-protection. They present clear, practical ways to implement the spirit of peace in our daily lives. They are our tools for peace. We tend to think that the violence we suffer comes only from outside ourselves, but this is not correct. We inflict violence upon our own body and consciousness by our way of eating, drinking or working. . . . Our consciousness as well as our body can be victim to mindless consumption. When we consume something that is not healthy for our body we are not loving ourselves. . . . We often live our daily life in forgetfulness. . . . With the Mindfulness Training we can learn to detect these elements when they manifest and protect ourselves from them. . . . All of these trainings help keep us conscious of our thought and actions. They help us cultivate nonviolent thoughts and non-violent actions . . . we cannot only talk about doing what is beneficial, we have to put it into practice. By practicing these trainings, we gain more awareness of the suffering caused by the violent in our thoughts, words, and actions. On the basis of this awareness, we are then motivated to relieve suffering and to foster peace in ourselves and others.

I believe that the best programming for troubled, aggressive girls will unite the kind of psychological interventions pioneered by the Earlscourt Girls Connection with spiritual training for mindfulness of the sort espoused and perfected by Thich Nhat Hanh. Such an effort will meet the scientific criteria emergent in a generation of psychological research with the well-tested applied wisdom of spirituality.

This review of the three categories of programs (empowerment, aggression prevention, treatment for violent troubled girls) sets the stage for a final effort to take stock of where things are headed for girls getting physical. What will things look like in the world of girls in the coming years and decades of the twenty-first century? This is our final question.

9

Female Aggression in the Twenty-first Century: What Lies Ahead for the New American Girl?

You could say that Sally, a twenty-year-old English major from a small town in rural Pennsylvania, speaks with the voice of the Old American Girl:

I endured female aggression during my high school years. A lot of these hostile attacks did not happen face-to-face, but rather behind another girl's back in the form of verbal aggression. I have found that girls use rumors and gossip as a way to express their aggression without actually confronting those their attacks are aimed at. For example, I have been in several situations where girls have used such forums as parties, lunch tables, and classrooms in order to announce reasons to dislike another girl. The most common reasons for these feelings of anger and aggression involve boys in some way. Whether a girl likes to use her body as a way to attract boys or likes to flirt with a boy who already has a girlfriend or dresses in a way that shows more skin than is covered up, these are reasons for aggression. In many cases it is a group of girls that utilize this verbal aggression to gang up on a single girl to isolate her. At times the target girl is even one whom they considered a friend, but of course they do not share their true feelings to the person's face. Personally, I feel that girls are much more cutthroat toward other girls, always sizing them up, than boys are toward other boys. There is a popular feeling that girls are much more dramatic than boys, making a big deal out of little problems and small disagreements. I believe that this drama is caused by the spreading of malevolent rumors and the ganging up of girls on other girls in the form of verbal aggression.

Now listen to Jodie, a nineteen-year-old psychology major from Boston, as she speaks for the New American Girl:

> I learned aggression right away. I knew that if I pushed my brothers, they would push back. It was very interesting having brothers. They made me much tougher than all my girlfriends. I was a little rougher around the edges but could handle more and fit in well with the boys. Having brothers allowed me to be very physical. Where I couldn't hit other people (my friends, my parents), my brothers were the people that I could hit. When I was angry, it felt good to let out aggression on them. I also played ice hockey since I was six years old. This was another outlet for aggression. I played with my brothers and two of my male cousins. This brought us very close, because we were almost always on the same team. On the ice I was just another player. I could hit the boys and what other few girls there may have been, and it didn't matter. When I got into high school, I played on the boys'

team. There was one other girl on the team, and we were close friends. Here I continued to be aggressive, and the guys on the team became close friends. They became like my brothers too because they were able to be physical with me on the ice and know that it wouldn't affect our friendship off the ice.

What lies ahead for our girls in the coming decades of the twenty-first century? Will the trend toward greater physical aggression among girls continue? Will it eventually match the levels of aggression found in boys? Will troubled girls become increasingly violent?

Prognosticating when it comes to social issues affecting children and youth is a risky proposition. For example, it was only a decade ago that some observers raised the alarm that a whole generation of male "superpredators" that would overwhelm society with remorseless young killers was coming along. A few years later the youth homicide rate had dropped dramatically across America, and talk of the epidemic of superpredators faded away.

A great deal happened to short-circuit the superpredator prediction. Some of the prediction problems stemmed from inadequate analysis of the data in the first place. For example, some analysts assumed that most of the youths involved in murder were actually of the psychopathic disposition that did (and does) characterize a small minority of kids who kill. As a result, they projected inaccurately what the future would bring. Some of the prediction problems arose from the politicized use of the data available. This was part of what some have seen as a larger scare tactic to demonize youth for political purposes—for example, promoting the concept of the superpredator to justify passage of legislation designed to reduce investment in rehabilitation in favor of harsher punishment for all juvenile offenders.

Other prediction problems stemmed from society's deliberate interventions in response to the rising youth homicide rate in the early 1990s. These interventions may well have prevented some kids from becoming killers, thus invalidating the predictions by reaching at-risk boys early and then redirecting or healing them. Additional sources of error in this case have been attributed to the more liberal abortion policies in the 1970s that resulted in fewer unwanted and high-risk births, which in turn led to fewer violently aggressive youths in the later 1990s.

Still other of the prediction problems were attributable to the vagaries of the ripple effect in human affairs, an example of the butterfly effect I brought up in Chapter 1. Forces are always at work one way or another in youth development with the power to magnify some events (like the first school shooting by a middle-class white kid to receive national publicity) into an outbreak of similar events (like the wave of school shootings that followed the first ones from 1997 on, culminating in the Columbine school massacre in 1999). Whatever the constellation of reasons, the superpredator scare was a case of bad prognostication. That doesn't mean that prognostication is always in error, but rather that we should learn some lessons about the process of prediction.

What does the example of the superpredator tell us about our efforts to predict the future with respect to physical aggression among girls? It tells us to be cautious but not immobilized. If we work hard without bias to see clearly what has been happening, figure out why it happened, and anticipate how these historical trends will play themselves out in the future, we may be able see the possible paths ahead of us.

In trying to predict the future of girls' physical aggression, we must always remember that scientific complexities abound. Indeed, from our ecological perspective we must always answer, "It depends," when asked, "Will X lead to Y?" The interaction of systems and the fact that human beings respond when they are alerted make this inevitable. Just your act of reading this book and approaching girls differently can be a factor in whether current trends become future patterns.

Think of the impact of Rachel Carson's book *Silent Spring* published in 1962. Carson alerted America to the dangers of DDT and forecast dire consequences if the trends she observed were allowed to continue. In response to her book, DDT was banned, and the future was changed. Carson was right in her analysis and persuasive in her arguments *and thus was wrong in her predictions*. It is the best a scientific prophet can ask for.

Sometimes the good news about "failed" predictions is the fact that human beings are not passive in the face of experience and information. We act in response to what we see and hear, and this complicates efforts to extrapolate the future from past trends. I learned this in the early 1980s, when I chaired the Research Committee of Prevent Child Abuse America (then known as the National Committee to Prevent Child Abuse). At a board of directors' meeting, the group's founder, Donna Stone, challenged the organization to a bold commitment, "Reduce Child Abuse by 20 percent in Five Years." The board eventually voted unanimously to support this goal and turned to the Research Committee to document the success or failure of the effort.

We struggled with that responsibility. There were many problems facing our group, including where and how to get reliable measures to assess change in the coming years. One of our challenges was to deal with the fact that the efforts of the National Committee and many others around the country were already being directed at child abuse prevention. We realized that if the organization's new mobilization were successful, such efforts would increase. That was the whole point of the campaign, of course. But was our task simply to measure a 20 percent decrease in the rate compared with when we began the new initiative—e.g., from 100 to 80 on some measurement yardstick? Was it to measure the decrease compared with the rate we would have predicted in light of evidence of deteriorating social conditions for families—e.g., finding that without our intervention it would have risen from 100 to 120, but that with our intervention it stayed at 100? In fact, we concluded that we could be successful in meeting our goal if the rate of child abuse five years later was 20 percent lower than it would have been predicted to have been (what it "should" have been) without our new initiative. With all this in mind, I proceeded to write a professional article on the subject, entitled "Can We Measure Success in Preventing Child Abuse?," which was published in the professional journal *Child Abuse and Neglect* in 1986. By the way, we didn't meet the 20 percent goal but agreed that just setting the goal motivated and focused the organization's efforts.

So what do I now predict about girls' aggression? I predict that the forces that have generated increased physical aggression in girls will continue. I predict that the various human systems of families, schools, and communities will respond to these trends in ways designed to ameliorate them, but that this will not stop them in their tracks immediately. I also predict that biology and residues of culture will put the brakes on these trends, with the result that girls in general will never be on average as physically aggressive as boys, nor will troubled girls be as physically violent as troubled boys. Those are my predictions. Here are my reasons for making them:

The Trend Toward Increased Physical Aggression in Girls Will Continue

As I observed in Chapter 3, the empowerment of girls is still a work in progress. There remains much to be done to empower girls to feel good about their bodies, to believe that there is more to being a powerful physical presence than sex. The stories girls have told me convince me that many girls are still stuck on the sex = power equation. They need the positive messages of physicality.

On the negative side we must recognize that despite decades of improving conditions and empowerment, most women still live with the fear that they will be sexually assaulted (as they do with the fear that they will develop breast cancer after a similar period of national attention to prevention and treatment). This fear of sexual assault may be a vague and mostly remote fear for most girls, but it is there, even if below the surface much of the time. One evidence of this is that each year women (and sympathetic men) engage in Take Back the Night marches and demonstrations. They do this because the factual data and the emotional lives of girls and women dictate it. Women's fear is fed by mass media images. For example, studies show that paranoia increases in direct proportion to the amount of television people watch. Its influence competes with efforts to empower girls and women as they are unleashed from traditional femininity. All told, efforts to empower girls physically are still incomplete and, in many places and for many girls, are still fragmentary.

There is every reason to believe that efforts to shift the physicality of girls away from the "sex = power" equation toward a "my body is powerful through nonsexual action" mindset will continue. More girls will play sports (although the most recent data indicate a leveling off of participation rates after decades of dramatic increase). More girls will study martial arts (but this number too is likely to reach a ceiling before it equals or exceeds the rate for boys). More girls will revel in their physical power (even though biology dictates that most girls will not exceed most boys in physical stature and strength). And almost inevitably, as a result, levels of physical aggression among girls will continue to rise but will not exceed those of boys.

In an article entitled "Bad Heroines," journalist Mary Spicuzza writes elegantly of her own experience with the new female physical aggression:

When I began studying martial arts nearly four years ago, a former boyfriend was appalled by the thrill I received from practicing roundhouse kicks, elbow jabs and punches to the solar plexus. "Why do you want to do that?" he finally asked, with a mixture of confusion and disgust. "It's so violent!" Several weeks later, after wrestling with the image of myself as a violent bully, I ended up locked out of a friend's apartment in San Francisco's Mission District, pre-gentrification. While walking past a group of 20 men hanging out on a quiet, dark corner, drinking 40-ouncers from paper bags, my first thought wasn't "What could they do to me?" but "What could I do to them?" It was then that I realized what training in Tae Kwon Do, a Korean martial art, had given me. I never have had the privilege of living without the fear of being a victim, but martial arts has taught me that I am much more than a walking target. And that, if need be, even the littlest women can kick some serious ass.

Recently I asked a Natasha, a twenty-year-old petite woman in my Body Combat aerobics class, how she felt about all the aggressive images contained in the movements and the instructor's aggressive commentary. She smiled, her eyes lit up, and here's what she said: "It feels great. I love the punching and the kicking, and I love the power."

You know, so do I. And that touches on the issue of basic justice wrapped up in all this: Why should I as a male get a chance to feel the power and she as a female not? The writing is on the wall here: Girls can and do kick ass, and they mostly like it. But my experience as a child psychologist and my knowledge of a generation of research on aggression in boys tell me there is more to this story. Sometimes, for some kids, there is a spillover from liking the sense of empowerment that comes with practicing acts of physical aggression in the gym to actually committing acts of aggression outside the gym. At least some girls who *can* hit *will* hit.

The involvement of girls in sports that generate physical contact will also continue. This too will stimulate more situations in which physical aggression is a likely by-product of physical prowess, as we saw in Chapter 3. Girls are not immune to the combination of hormonal and behavioral effects of participation in sports. As their participation increases, so, I believe, will more girls fall prey to the risk that hitting people on the sports field will spill over to hitting people off the field.

Listen to nineteen-year-old Erin's illuminating discussion of why she finds the "boys' world" of sports so empowering in this regard. Erin grew up in a suburb of Syracuse, New York, with her two parents and four siblings. She looks back and reports:

> I have played football for the past five years. Although I usually get along with males better than with females and generally

have almost all male friends, some still find my participation in a "male" sport threatening. One day during a game a boy on the other team started making nasty remarks, calling me some unsavory names and belittling me. Some of my teammates intervened on my behalf, but I decided to prove that I belonged and deserved to be on the team. When the boy who called me names received a pass, I barreled toward him as if my life depended on it. I was always taught to perform a tackle around the chest or below. But my anger got the better of me, and I wrapped my arms around his neck and swung with all my might, slamming him into the ground—hard. I felt great. My adrenaline was flowing, and I could feel my pulse in my stomach. My knee was hurting, but I didn't care. I was king (queen). I had won. It's the kind of feeling you get only from athletics or from completing some physical feat that you never thought you could. The guys all slapped me on the back in the comradely fashion accepted only in sports, and the boy who had offended me jumped up red-faced and breathless. The rest of the game he tried to break me. I think he would have succeeded if I hadn't outrun him each time he came after me. It felt fabulous slamming into that fool and flinging him to the ground.

What else lies beyond the playing fields on which girls are exploring the forbidden pleasures of being physically aggressive? There is the increasingly active involvement of girls in gangs. This too predicts more physically aggressive behavior by girls. Some girls join gangs for precisely the reasons their male counterparts do—namely, for access to power in a threatening world. Here's what one girl said: "There are students in school afraid of our gang, the Black Widows, and because I am in the gang, people show me respect and won't mess with me. I like that feeling of power."

In the past girls were largely confined to relatively passive roles in the aggressive behavior of gangs as well as to being the target of violence within the gang structure. This appears to be changing. Girls in gangs are more actively aggressive than before. In some gangs girls participate in the ritual of "jumping in" new members (in which they are beaten by other gang members as an initiation). A thirteen-year-old girl reports: "When I walked the line, there were about fourteen or sixteen of my homeys gang members there. Some just used their fists or were kicking me, but I remember that one homeboy had on brass knuckles that broke my nose, and this one girl hit me with a stick."

And there's this report from eighteen-year-old Latoya, who grew up in San Diego:

> My high school is a very large public high school filled with students from many different backgrounds. The worst violence I witnessed arose from the girl gangs. One day, as everyone was leaving school to get on the buses or into cars, I noticed a huge group of people standing in one spot. As I approached, I saw one girl running to her car while another was chasing after her. The first girl went to the trunk of her car and pulled out a baseball bat. The second girl came up behind her, grabbed the bat from her hand, and started beating her with it. As soon as this happened, three or four more girls came over and started kicking and beating the girl who originally had the bat but was now on the ground screaming. Nobody in the crowd knew what to do. Finally a few security guards came and broke up the fight. The one girl was badly hurt, and all of them were suspended for a period of time.

In addition to these social influences in the day-to-day lives of girls, there are the ongoing trends in the depiction of female characters in the mass media. There is every indication that television, movies, music videos, and video games will continue to expand the range of physically aggressive roles played by girls and women that are exposed to the next generation of girls. For example, in the 2004 science-fiction action film *Alien vs. Predator,* twenty men and one woman set out to explore an underground pyramid that turns out to be the site of a battle between two species of vicious extraterrestrial killers. One species is that of the serpentlike creatures initially battled by Sigourney Weaver and her colleagues in *Alien.* The other is that of the relentless intergalactic hunter-warriors battled by Arnold Schwarzenegger and his ill-fated squad of men in *Predator.*

By the end of *Alien vs. Predator* all the men are dead, and it is the woman (Lex) who is left standing to join forces with the remaining Predator warrior to save Earth from the ravages of the vicious serpent creatures. Lex even earns a ritualistic facial scar to celebrate her success in killing the serpents, a scar that marks her acceptance into the fellowship of the Predator warriors.

Girls are responding to these images. Nineteen-year-old Sarah, a computer science major from Cleveland, reports: "I saw *The Matrix* when it first came out in theaters and *Underworld* several years later on video. Both these movies star strong, aggressive, and capable women who wear tight black clothes, big black boots, and long black trench coats. Both women are such expert fighters that nothing can even come close to threatening them, and they illustrate this in multiple fight scenes throughout the films. I have posters of both women on my walls, and I proudly wear a long black trench coat that most people immediately recognize as coming from one of the two movies."

Nineteen-year-old Shauna, who grew up with her single mother in San Francisco, echoes the sentiment: "The first time I saw *The Fifth Element*, I was awe-struck. Leeloo was the most incredible character: She was sexy, had superpowers, and was strong and assertive enough to do whatever she wanted. My favorite scene in the entire movie is when she kicks the crap out of the evil aliens. Watching that movie made me want to be just like her." I expect this trend of validating physical aggression in girls and women will continue, and with it the cultural impetus for real-life physical aggression in girls that I outlined in Chapter 4.

A recent report from Great Britain leads with this: "The number of women who are seeking treatment at hospital casualty units [emergency rooms] after being injured in drunken cat fights is rising sharply. . . . Late-night brawls between women who have been binge-drinking are resulting in horrific injuries such as facial wounds caused by 'glassing' (using broken bottles to cause injuries), broken jaws and bleeding scalps where girls have had their hair pulled out." It sounds too much like reports in the American press—for example, the accounts of a hazing incident at Glenbrook High School outside Chicago. In this incident an off-campus football game between junior and senior girls turned violent as the junior girls were beaten and brutalized. The "fun" initiation turned gross as urine, feces, and animal intestines were thrown at the girls. Four girls were hospitalized with injuries that included a gash in the head from being hit with a paint can, a broken ankle, and a fractured tailbone resulting from being kicked and punched. Is this what the future holds for more and more girls? All the signs point in that direction.

Families, Schools, and Communities
Will Respond

Our culture has a lot of experience trying to contain, channel, focus, ritualize, suppress, and tame physical aggression in boys, just as it has a lot of experience stimulating and mobilizing that aggression for socially approved purposes (notably to meet military and athletic goals). Remember, despite the widespread social and cultural support for physical aggression among boys, "only" about 5 percent of men have a significant problem with chronic antisocial violence in adulthood. And only a small minority of males engage in any serious physical assault during adulthood (even including spousal assault, which is characteristic of about 12 percent of men, and severe assault, which characterizes about 5 percent of men). Most men, even most "violent" men, are not physically aggressive most of the time, indeed the vast majority of the time.

So, as psychologist Richard Tremblay has persuasively argued, society actually does a very good job of dealing with the nearly universal "problem" of physical aggression in male infants and toddlers. Families have developed a range of interventions to accomplish this job with little boys. Like young mammals across the board, human boy pups learn how to use their bodies in an elaborate dance of wrestling and play fighting. Fathers wrestle and play fight with their sons, and one important consequence is that boys learn when and how to be physically aggressive.

This of course is one reason for the troubles evidenced by boys who don't grow up with their fathers (or some other males who play this role for and with them). These fatherless boys are put at risk if they don't have this hands-on instruction in how to be physically aggressive but not violent. What are they left with if they don't have real-life flesh-and-blood fathers to wrestle with? In many cases, the role models available to them are the distant, unrealistic, and hyperaggressive males they witness in pop music, on television, and in the movies.

While fathered boys may be tempted by these fantastic figures, they tend to be held closer to social realities by their experiences with the real men who are their fathers. Fatherless boys are more likely to be taken in by these fantastically violent males. As a result, the crucial process of neutralizing boys' natural aggression is stunted or warped, and their natural physical aggression misdirected or magnified to grotesque proportions. I know some of these boys. They filled the pages of my book *Lost Boys* and my memories of my interviews as an expert witness in death penalty cases, just as they fill prisons and detention centers around the country.

Even the "new man" as father must find a way to deal with the issue of dealing with aggression. In his book *Finding Our Fathers*, psychologist Samuel Osherson offers this perspective on how even "new" fathers take on this task with their sons. He writes:

> *As I sit at a playground with my young son on a pleasant spring Sunday, we are surrounded by other parents and children. It being a weekend, there are many fathers with their kids. Suddenly across the playground I see a familiar scene. An older boy, about seven, goes up to a younger one and punches him on the shoulder. The blow is not particularly savage, and the littler kid seems more shocked than hurt. The older boy seems quite angry and upset; he's clearly working something out. One could easily imagine that boy getting a good spanking from his father. I wonder what I'd do if he comes near my boy.*

As I watch, though, the boy's father comes over and gently picks him up. The boy writhes and protests, crying in his father's arms, while the man carries him over to a nearby bench. Despite his son's fighting the father does this forcefully, yet also gently. He sits and rocks the boy in his lap, and then I hear him whispering, almost singing, in his son's ear: "I'm not going to let you go until you say, 'I am a gentle boy and I do not hit other children.'" As they sit there, the boy sheltered in his arms, the father repeats the refrain: "I am a gentle boy and I do not hit other children." Finally the boy seems soothed, sings along with his father, and runs off to play by himself.

How does all this apply to girls? Historically, girls have not needed their parents to do much about physical aggression because the culture has presented a unified front that made physical aggression by girls mostly a cultural and thus psychological impossibility. Everywhere a girl turned in the culture she found a consistent message: "Girls don't hit because hitting is not ladylike." Girls have mostly realized that they *could* express their aggressive impulses through relational and verbal aggression without being thought "unladylike."

I think that as the cultural affirmation of physical aggression for girls in the mass media increases, we shall no longer be able to assume that culture will take care of the task of taming the natural physical aggression of girls. Girls will need wrestling parents to do the same job that effective fathers have done with their sons. For many fathers this will be a bit of a stretch.

Must it be fathers? Can it be mothers? Is it better if it is one, the other, or both? I think there is a good case to be made that it should be fathers—at least in the short run, until most mothers are up to speed on the matter of wrestling and play fighting. I did this with my own daughter, just as I did with my son and my father had done for me (but not with my sister). I suspect many mothers are still too uncomfortable with physical aggression to play this role for their daughters.

But are fathers ready to play ball with their daughters the way they have with their sons? As David Salter puts it in his book *Crashing the Old Boys' Network*, "It probably hasn't been a very masculine thing . . . for a father to come home from work and ask his daughter is she wants to throw the ball around. But while evidence supports the contention that attitudes have changed in this regard, behavior has not followed the same course. . . . It is time for fathers to step up to the plate."

Of course, when fathers are ready to do this, will their wives let them? Are the mothers who were once the Old American Girl ready to do what is needed by the New American Girl who is their daughter? Here's eighteen-year-old Jessica's account, and her family experience speaks to this:

> As a kid I was fairly aggressive, fighting with all three of my brothers (and constantly getting trounced by the older two). I remember my mother would always shout, "Stop it, George, you're encouraging her violent tendencies!" to my dad as we wrestled on the living room couch. By the time I was eleven, however, everything calmed down quite a bit, and instead my brothers and I became competitive in sports and academically. I never fought with my peers or my sister, just with the guys in my family. I still wrestle around with my brother and my boyfriend, but it is almost always in fun with no intent to hurt anyone. I consider myself much more sensitive and "girlie" now than I was as a little girl.

For this girl the process worked, as it does for most boys. She learned how to manage her physical aggressiveness through play fighting with her dad. Rather than make her more aggressive, as her mother feared ("encouraging her violent tendencies"), it helped her become a well-socialized but *physical* teenager—like her brothers.

My sister, like many girls with brothers before her, wrestled with me and my brother. That was probably useful, but I doubt my brother and I were as good at this with her as our father was with us boys. We boys were indeed much older than our sister (eleven years in my case, seven years in the case of my brother), but we weren't men yet. We were more inclined to make "mistakes" in our roughhousing with our sister. Our rough-and-tumble play with her often took the form of a kind of football game played on the living room rug in which my brother and I stayed on our knees while our sister stayed on her feet and carried "the ball" (actually a cushion from the couch). The riskiness of this enterprise was captured by our mother's lament each time we started to play this game: "Someone's going to end up crying!" She was right, of course, and it was mostly our sister. But this never happened when Dad wrestled with me and my brother; he was much better at it than we were. I think the message is clear: "Fathers, wrestle with your daughters!" And "Mothers, let them do it!" And "Maybe give it a try yourself."

Beyond family responses there are and will be schools responding to increased physical aggression in girls in ways that may put the brakes on these trends. As we saw in Chapter 8, some schools are already gearing up for this, for example, with Ophelia Groups, which focus on aggression, and employing the Good Behavior Game to tame highly aggressive young children before they band together in aggressive peer groups and amplify each other's behavior. What is more, the national movement toward putting character education at the center of the educational process is gaining momentum and is a natural intervention to reduce girl aggression as it becomes apparent. Issues of character education naturally arise in the athletic arena, and we can expect that there will be more attention paid to the moral education of girls in sports in the future.

The increasing rates of girls' participation in martial arts can be a positive step in this direction. At its best martial arts instruction seeks to ritualize aggression and infuse the student with a more spiritual and disciplined approach to life, including conflict and aggressive impulses. This has worked wonders for some boys who struggle with aggression issues, and it could accomplish the same worthwhile goals with girls.

More generally, the Search Institute's approach to identifying and encouraging developmental assets is important as well, as we saw in Chapter 8. For both boys and girls more assets are correlated with lower violence toward self and others. Therefore, community-based initiatives to increase girls' access to developmental assets should support nonviolence generally both because of the cultural changes that have unleashed girls and because of the social toxicity that undermines positive development across the board.

Communities are already starting to respond to the increase in girls' physical aggression. Professionals are rethinking how violence reduction programs aimed at incarcerated and detained boys apply to girls, as we also saw in Chapter 8. Several books for professionals have been published in recent years. This feeds both professional interest and competence. The more community agencies see violence by girls as part of a social trend rather than as an individual aberration, the more they will be inclined to program for it.

The core principles of violence reduction are the same for boys and girls: changing thinking about violence (cognitive restructuring); practicing alternative ways of acting (behavioral rehearsal); and developing a sense of meaningfulness through spiritual development. The differences lie in the specifics of implementation. That in turn depends upon recognizing the issue in the first place. With community agencies moving to a state of heightened consciousness about the expanding role of physical aggression in troubled girls and girls in general, I believe this will happen.

Biology and Culture Will Set Limits to Girls' Physical Aggression

It seems clear that there are biological factors that put a brake on physical aggression in girls, particularly at the antisocial end of the violence continuum. The story of the MAOA gene I recounted in Chapter 6 is a prime example. Just by virtue of having two X chromosomes, girls are mostly protected from the severe information processing deficiencies associated with low levels of MAOA. This means a dramatically reduced likelihood that girls will walk down the path from being abused to being involved in antisocial violence. Remember that 85 percent of the kids who were abused and had the MAOA deficient gene on all their X chromosomes (that is, on the only one for boys) ended up with conduct disorder in childhood, whereas only 40 percent of the abused kids who had a normal MAOA gene were so afflicted.

Beyond the MAOA gene there are the other disabilities that increase a child's vulnerability to frustration, social rejection, and coping difficulties generally. Most of these are more common in boys for reasons that are mostly genetic in nature (the old empty Y chromosome at work). Thus boys are more likely than girls to face the world with strikes against them even before we factor social deprivation into the equation.

One of the processes at work in child development is what Dan Freedman and other investigators have called the magnification of initially small differences. Freedman's initial work was with puppies. He found that often one of the pups was slightly smaller and slower than the others at birth and that this initially small difference magnified over the days and weeks that followed because the littlest one was slow to get to the mother's teats and thus got less milk and became increasingly slower and smaller in comparison with the other pups in the litter. Before long, the slower, smaller one was identifiably "the runt of the litter," despite the initially small difference.

The same may be true for the emergence of aggression in boys and girls; it reflects the magnification of an initially small difference. Biological evidence points to an initially small difference between girls and boys in rough-and-tumble play because of prenatal exposure to the male sex hormones (androgens). Rough-and-tumble play is one of the behavioral building blocks for physical aggression. Boys on average start out more inclined to rough-and-tumble play for this biological reason. They thus have a head start on embedding the physical aggression that comes naturally in early childhood while because of their generally lower level of androgens, girls have a head start on shedding it. Traditionally, biology and culture have worked in concert to reduce aggression by girls more effectively than in boys. Even as this changes, and the gap between boys and girls narrows still further, I believe that the rates of physical aggression will not equalize.

When it comes to the link between being troubled and being

violent, most of the same arguments apply in making the case against equalization. This is a trend that has been evolving for decades. For example, as criminologist Ralph Weisheit reports, whereas in 1940 robbery-murders accounted for 18 percent of female homicides, by 1983 that type of crime was accounting for 42 percent of female homicides. The fact that troubled girls tend to have a load of rage associated with sexual violation is the starting point. Add to this the fact that these victimized girls must cope with being in subordinate social positions in negative environments. This combination predicts that troubled girls are particularly receptive to antisocial violence as a response to that anger.

Boys may well have already reached an upper ceiling; troubled boys are already about as violent as they can get. We didn't see the epidemic of superpredators that some observers predicted in the 1990s in part because for boys, things in the 1990s were about as bad as they can get. To use a crude economic analogy, with girls, there is greater opportunity to increase violent behavior because the "market" of troubled girls with the kinds of psychological issues that generate antisocial violence in boys is still "underdeveloped." The market for cultural images that validate physical aggression is still largely untapped for girls, just as it is mostly saturated for boys. There is thus "growth potential" for girls' physical aggression and not much for boys.

What will the future bring? As always, it depends. It depends upon how soon we as a society wake up to the new fact that girls are not immune to acting in a physically aggressive way. It depends upon how well the institutions of family, school, and community respond to the changing facts of cultural and psychological life for the New American Girl. We can no longer take it for granted that the culture will suppress and redirect impulses to physically aggressive behavior in girls. The mass media are moving in exactly the opposite direction. The general liberation and empowerment of girls are moving in exactly the opposite direction, and doing so in the socially toxic environment of twenty-first century America. It's also possible, of course, that as they reach adulthood, some of America's new girls will rebel against the mass media's agenda for them and will seek to reclaim elements of traditional femininity on their own new terms.

The future course of female development in America depends upon how soon we see the trends that are emerging: "Normal" girls are engaging in more physical aggression, and troubled girls are engaging in more antisocial violent behavior. The future course of female development in America depends upon how soon and how well we respond to these changes. As always, it depends.

Acknowledgments

This book owes its inspiration to Victoria Sanders, my literary
agent. Victoria and I first worked together in developing my
1999 book *Lost Boys: Why Our Sons Turn Violent and How We
Can Save Them*. In the years since then we have worked together
on two other projects, and I have come to appreciate her as a
smart and savvy advocate. So I was responsive when she sent me
a newspaper article on rising assault rates for females and suggested that I explore the changing role of physical aggression in
the lives of girls. This book is the result.

I've been writing books for thirty years. It's always a struggle.
Scott Moyers at Penguin took an interest in the project and didn't
let go. I have worked with many editors but no one as smart and
tenacious as Scott. Much of whatever is good about this book is
due to his intelligent prodding.

I should also like to thank the individuals who commented

upon early drafts and suggested improvements, most notably Claire Bedard. A group of Cornell University students helped me track down content material during the 2004 fall semester: Katrina Davy, Renee Gewercman, Jenna Goldstein, and Erica Kerman. My daughter, Joanna Garbarino, a Cornell alum herself, provided invaluable editorial assistance in the final stages of the project. My colleague Ellen de Lara also provided useful feedback. Thanks too to my assistant at Cornell, Jolan Balog, who kept track of the various versions of the manuscript along the way.

I should also like to thank the two hundred or so Cornell students who contributed memoirs of their experiences with physical aggression. They shared their feelings about their experiences of female aggression in ways that were illuminating. I have protected their privacy by changing some details of their accounts and by camouflaging their identities. In addition, my thanks go to the incarcerated girls and young women (and boys and young men) from whom I have learned a great deal. I also thank the numerous professionals around the country who shared their observations of female aggression.

I must also thank the instructors and participants in the Body Combat classes at Courtside Fitness Center in Ithaca, New York, for their contributions to my understanding of how physicality and aggression are embedded in female empowerment (and for all the fun we have had together).

Finally, I offer my thanks to Cornell University's College of Human Ecology and Dean Lisa Staiano-Coico for providing my academic home since 1994. As a faculty member in the Human Development Department I have found the intellectual and material support needed to take on the challenge of this book and develop it to fruition, even as I left Cornell to join the faculty of Loyola University, Chicago in 2005.

References

Chapter 1: The New American Girl Gets Physical

3 **Twenty-five years ago:** For a review, see D. Prothrow-Stith and H. Spivak's 2005 book, *Sugar and Spice and No Longer Nice: How We Can Stop Girls' Violence* (San Francisco: Jossey-Bass). The data change from year to year and decade to decade, but the shift identified is reflected in a variety of sources. It includes reports from the Office of Juvenile Justice and Delinquency Prevention and other agencies of the Justice Department—for example, E. Poe-Yamagat, J. Butts, and S. Bilchik (1996), *Female Offenders in the Juvenile Justice System* (Pittsburgh: National Center for Juvenile Justice). It is also reflected in independent analyses—e.g., P. C. Giordano (1978), "Girls, Guys and Gangs: The Changing Social Context of Female Delinquency," *Journal of Criminal Law and Criminology*, 69, pp. 126–32. However, these official data are not the whole story. Criminologist Meda Chesney-Lind and her colleagues have challenged the significance of the report data: M. Chesney-Lind and J. Belknap (2004), in M. Putallaz and K. L. Bierman (eds.), *Aggression, Anti-social Behavior, and Violence Among Girls: A Developmental Perspective* (New York: Guildford Press), pp. 203–20. Like all such government statistics (for example, the number of reported child abuse cases), arrest rates for assault depend to some de-

gree upon policies and practices of law enforcement, and it does appear that these policies and practices have been shifting (for both boys and girls).

5 **"A pervasive myth has taken hold":** M. Winn (1983), *Children Without Childhood* (New York: Penguin Books), p. 14.

5 **The overwhelming majority of children:** For a review of this research, see J. Garbarino, C. Schellenbach, and J. Sebes (1986), *Troubled Youth, Troubled Families* (New York: Aldine).

5 **most high school dropouts:** H. E. Garnier, J. A. Stein, and J. K. Jacobs (1997), "The Process of Dropping Out of High School: A 19 Year Prospective," *American Educational Research Journal*, 34, pp. 395–419.

5 **Most teenagers who have trouble:** J. Elicker, M. Englund, and L. A. Sroufe (1992), "Predicting Peer Competence and Peer Relationships in Childhood from Early Parent-Child Relationships," in R. D. Parke and G. Ladd, eds., *Family-Peer Relationships: Modes of Linkage* (Hillsdale, N.J.: Laurence Erlbaum), pp. 77–106; R. L. Paikoff and J. Brooks-Gunn (1991), "Do Parent-Child Relationships Change During Puberty?," *Psychological Bulletin*, 110, pp. 47–66.

5 **Most violent youth:** L. D. Eron, J. H. Gentry, and P. Schlegel, eds., *Reason to Hope: A Psychosocial Perspective on Violence and Youth* (Washington, D.C.: American Psychological Association).

5 **Research reveals that many personality traits:** For a review of this point, see L. Berk (2005), *Infants, Children and Adolescents* (Boston: Allyn and Bacon).

5 **while many young teenagers:** For a fascinating and accessible investigation of this research, www.pbs.org/wgbh/pages/frontline/shows/teenbrain.

6 **Similarly, most adolescents:** D. Elkind (1994), *A Sympathetic Understanding of the Child: Birth to Sixteen*, 3rd ed. (Boston: Allyn and Bacon).

6 **The impulse to peer conformity:** B. Brown, M. Lohr, and E. McClenahan (1986), "Early Adolescents' Perceptions of Peer Pressure," *Journal of Adolescence*, 6, pp. 139–54.

6 **adolescence does bring on shifts:** D. Buhrmester (1996), "Need Fulfillment, Interpersonal Competence, and the Developmental Contexts of Early Adolescent Friendship," in W. M. Bukowski, A. F. Newcomb, and W. W. Hartup, (eds), *The Company They Keep: Friendships During Childhood and Adolescence* (New York: Cambridge University Press).

6 **Research reveals that antisocial:** R. Dishion, J. McCord, and F. Poulin (1999), "When Interventions Harm: Peer Groups and Problem Behavior," *American Psychologist*, 54, pp. 755–64.

7 **The fact is, children:** R. E. Tremblay (2002), "Prevention of Injury by Early Socialization of Aggressive Behavior," *Injury Prevention*, 8, pp. 17–21.

7 **But traditionally most little girls:** N. R. Crick and J. K. Grotpeter (1995), "Relational Aggression, Gender, and Asocial–psychological Functioning," *Child Development*, 66, pp. 710–22.

7 **First, little girls developed:** B. I. Fagot and M. D. Leinbach (1989), "Gender La-

beling, Gender Stereotyping, and Parenting Behaviors," *Developmental Psychology*, 28, pp. 225–30.

7 **What is more:** Ibid.

7 **They will also become more likely:** B. Yeoman (November/December 1999), "Bad Girls," *Psychology Today*, available at cms.psychologytoday.com/articles/pto-19991101-000037.html.

8 **For more than thirty years:** For example, J. Garbarino, K. Kostelny, and N. Dubrow (1991), *No Place to Be a Child: Growing Up in a War Zone* (New York: Lexington Books); J. Garbarino, N. Dubrow, K. Kostelny, and C. Pardo (1992), *Children in Danger: Coping with the Consequences of Community Violence* (San Francisco: Jossey-Bass); J. Garbarino (1993), *Let's Talk About Living in a World with Violence* (Chicago: Erikson Institute); J. Garbarino, J. Eckenrode, and Family Life Development Center (1997), *Understanding Abusive Families* (San Francisco: Jossey-Bass).

8 **In my 1999 book:** J. Garbarino (1999), *Lost Boys: Why Our Sons Turn Violent and How We Can Save Them* (New York: Free Press).

8 **I believe this shift transcends:** M. Chesney-Lind and J. Belknap (2004), in M. Putallaz and K. L. Bierman, eds., *Aggression, Antisocial Behavior, and Violence Among Girls: A Developmental Perspective* (New York: Guildford Press), pp. 203–20.

9 **Criminal violence perpetrated by adolescent females:** M. Morretti, C. Odgers, and M. Jackson, eds. (2004), *Girls and Aggression: Contributing Factors and Intervention Principles* (New York: Kluwer Academic/Plenum Publishers).

9 **Criminal violence among girls:** Ibid.

9 **Troubled girls have long engaged in self-destructive behavior:** G. Downey, L. Irwin, M. Ramsay, and O. Auduk (2004), "Rejection Sensitivity and Girls' Aggression," in M. Morretti, C. Odgers, and M. Jackson, eds., *Girls and Aggression: Contributing Factors and Intervention Principles* (New York: Kluwer Academic/Plenum Publishers).

10 **The elements of this social toxicity:** J. Garbarino (1995), *Raising Children in a Socially Toxic Environment* (San Francisco: Jossey-Bass).

12 **I think most effective parents:** R. Tremblay (2000), "The Development of Aggressive Behaviour During Childhood: What Have We Learned in the Past Century?," *International Journal of Behavioral Development*, 24, pp. 129–41.

13 **The German poet Goethe once wrote:** S. W. Goethe, Xenien *as dem Nachlass*, 45.

13 **A study of physical aggression:** R. Tremblay (2000). "The Development of Aggressive Behavior During Childhood."

13 **Thirty years ago:** L. R. Huesmann, J. Moise-Titus, C. Podolski, and L. D. Eron (2003), "Longitudinal Relations Between Children's Exposure to TV Violence and Their Aggressive and Violent Behavior in Young Adulthood: 1977–1992," *Developmental Psychology*, 39 (2), pp. 201–21.

13 A study of aggression in eleven thousand children: L. J. Aber, J. L. Brown, and S. M. Jones (2003), "Developmental Trajectories Toward Violence in Middle Childhood: Course, Demographic Differences, and Response to School-based Intervention," *Developmental Psychology*, 39 (2), pp. 324–48.

13 U.S. Department of Health and Human Services data: National Center for Education Statistics: http://nces.ed.gov/pubs2003/schoolcrime.

13 According to the most widely cited study of spousal violence: R. Gelles and C. P. Cornell (1990), *Intimate Violence in Families*, 2nd ed. (Thousand Oaks, Calif.; Sage).

14 According to the American Humane Association: American Humane Association (2002), *Highlights of Official Child Neglect and Abuse Reporting* (Denver: American Humane Association).

14 a dramatic change occurs: M. Gladwell (2000), *The Tipping Point: How Little Things Can Make a Big Difference* (Boston: Little, Brown).

15 Another cause of our blindness: J. Glieck (1988), *Chaos: Making a New Science* (New York: Penguin).

22 "The women were especially brutal": M. Sholokov (1943/1975), *The Don Flows Home to the Sea* (New York: Vintage/Ebury), p. 250.

22 "Their bosoms were much enlarged": J. Hargreaves (1997), *Body and Society*, 3 (4), pp. 33–49.

22 psychologist Larry Aber and his colleagues: "Developmental Trajectories Toward Violence."

27 When I told Sheila of research: R. E. Tremblay (2002), "Prevention of Injury by Early Socialization of Aggressive Behavior."

28 That is an *enormous* shift!: "Title IX Facts Everyone Should Know," at www.womenssportsfoundation.org.

28 A report from Oregon: A. Jude (May 7, 2001), "Girls Can Hit Too," *Oregon Daily Emerald*.

28 two classes developed and marketed: The Les Mills Web site is www.lesmills.com.

29 "though we can't guarantee": The Web site is www.iCircle.com.

30 "Go down fighting": A. Leary, March 17, 2004, "Girl Recalls Dad's Lesson: Fight," *St. Petersburg Times* online.

30 The first law of human ecology: G. Hardin (1993), *Living Within Limits: Ecology, Economics, and Population Taboos* (New York: Oxford University Press).

30–31 the rate at which American kids: T. Achenbach and C. Howell (1993), "Are American Children's Problems Getting Worse?: A Thirteen-Year Comparison," *Journal of the American Academy of Child and Adolescent Psychiatry*, 32 (6), pp. 1145–54.

Chapter 2: To Hit or Not to Hit:
Are Girls and Boys Wired Differently
for Aggression?

33 **From this perspective:** For an excellent review of several theoretical perspectives on the origins of violence and the relevance of these theories to sex difference in various types of aggression, see J. Archer (2004), *Review of General Psychology*, 8 (4), pp. 291–322.

33 **This nature-nurture debate:** R. Tremblay (2000), "The Development of Aggressive Behaviour During Childhood: What Have We Learned in the Past Century?," *International Journal of Behavioural Development*, 24, pp. 129–41.

34 **"Yet when we know how to cultivate the seeds of love":** Thich Nhat Hanh (2003), *Creating True Peace: Ending Violence in Yourself, Your Family, Your Community and the World* (New York: Free Press).

35 **Tremblay's research:** R. Tremblay (2000). "The Development of Aggressive Behaviour During Childhood."

35 **"If you put your four-month-old to bed":** Cited in E. Anderssen and A. McIlroy (April 3, 2004), "The Most Violent People on Earth," *University of Victoria Faculty Newsletter.*

36 **Up to that point:** R. E. Tremblay (2002), "Prevention of Injury by Early Socialization of Aggressive Behavior," *Injury Prevention*, 8, pp. 17–21.

36 **Think of Lennie:** J. Steinbeck (1937/1978), *Of Mice and Men* (New York: Penguin).

36 **In my work as an expert witness:** J. Garbarino (1999), *Lost Boys: Why Our Sons Turn Violent and How We Can Save Them* (New York: Free Press).

38 **The process of retrospection:** R. Tremblay (2000), "The Development of Aggressive Behaviour During Childhood."

38 **Most children quickly learn:** R. E. Tremblay (2002), "Prevention of Injury by Early Socialization of Aggressive Behavior."

39 **if a child lives in an environment:** Ibid.

40 **Girls were taught by word and deed:** B. I. Fagot, M. D. Leinbach, and C. O'Boyle (1992), "Gender Labeling, Gender Stereotyping, and Parent Behaviors," *Developmental Psychology*, 28, pp. 225–30.

40 **With that recognition:** B. I. Fagot (1984), "The Child's Expectations of Differences in Adult Male and Female Interactions," *Sex Roles*, 11, pp. 593–600.

40 **Prenatal exposure to the male sex hormone:** M. L. Collaer and M. Hines (1995), "Human Behavioral Sex Differences: A Role for Gonadal Hormones During Early Development?," *Psychological Bulletin*, 118, 55, pp. 1–7.

40 **Boys' rough and tumble:** L. Berk (2005), *Infants, Children and Adolescents* (Boston: Allyn and Bacon).

41 **In 1982 Carol Gilligan:** C. Gilligan (1982), *In a Different Voice* (Cambridge: Harvard University Press).

42 **Some have come on scientific grounds:** For example, L. J. Walker (1991), "Sex Differences in Moral Reasoning," in W. M. Kurtines and J. L. Gewirtz, eds., *Handbook of Moral Behavior and Development* (Hillsdale, N.J.: Lawrence Erlbaum), vol. 2, pp. 333–64.

42 **the differences are primarily a matter of power:** S. Harter, P. L. Walters, N. R. Whitesell, and D. Kastelic (1998), "Level of Voice Among Female and Male High School Students: Relational Context, Support, and Gender Orientation," *Developmental Psychology*, 34 (5), pp. 892–901; C. Woods (1996), "Gender Differences in Moral Development and Acquisition: A Review of Kohlberg's and Gilligan's Models of Justice and Care," *Social Behavior and Personality*, 24 (4), pp. 375–84; K. M. Galotti (1989), "Gender Differences in Self-reported Moral Reasoning: A Review and New Evidence," *Journal of Youth and Adolescence*, 18 (5), pp. 475–88.

43 **Women in power:** J. Manza and C. Brooks (1998), "The Gender Gap in U. S. Presidential Elections: When? Why? Implications?" *American Journal of Sociology*, 103 (5), pp. 1235–66.

44 **commonly reported differences:** X. Ge, R. D. Conger, and G. H. Elder (2001), "The Relation Between Puberty and Psychological Distress in Adolescent Boys," *Journal of Research on Adolescence*, 11, pp. 49–70; J. Brooks-Gunn (1998), "Antecedents and Consequences of Variations in Girls' Maturational Timing," *Journal of Adolescent Health Care*, 9, pp. 365–73.

44 **Late-maturing boys:** M. C. Jones (1965), "Psychological Correlates of Somatic Development," *Child Development*, 36, pp. 899–911.

44 **the advantage has gone to girls:** J. Brooks-Gunn, loc. cit.

45 **They did accrue advantage:** N. Livson and H. Peskin (1980), "Perspectives on Adolescence from Longitudinal Research," in Adelson, eds., *Handbook of Adolescent Psychology* (New York: Wiley), pp. 49–98.

45 **may not be good for their mental health:** S. Stryzewski (1976), "Biological Maturation Rate, Acceptance, and Rejection in Informally Structured School Classes," *Psychologica Wychowawcza*, 19 (1), pp. 73–79.

46 **That is a topic well developed:** X. Ge, R. Conger, and G. H. Elder (2001), "Pubertal Transitions, Stressful Life Events, and the Emergence of Gender Differences in Adolescent Depressive Symptoms," *Developmental Psychology*, 37 (3), pp. 404–17; J. Graber, P. M. Lewinsohn, J. T. Seeley, and J. Brooks-Gunn (1997), "Is Psychopathology Associated with the Timing of Pubertal Development?," *Journal of the American Academy of Child and Adolescent Psychiatry*, 36 (12), pp. 1768–76.

47 **Girls resort to relational aggression:** D. Kindlon and M. Thomson (1999), *Raising Cain: Protecting the Emotional Life of Boys* (New York: Ballantine); W. Pollack (1999), *Real Boys: Rescuing Our Sons from the Myths of Boyhood* (New

York: Owl Pubishing); J. Pleck (1983), *The Myth of Masculinity* (Cambridge: MIT Press); M. Gurien (1997), *The Wonder of Boys* (New York: Putnam).

47 **"Boys generally harm others":** Berk, op. cit., p. 377.

47 **"This behavior is consistent":** N. R. Crick and J. K. Grotpeter (1995), "Relational Aggression, Gender, and Social–Psychological Functioning," *Child Development*, 66, p. 711.

47 **"Their relationships are more intimate":** E. Maccoby (1995), "The Two Sexes and Their Social Systems," in P. Moen, G. Elder, and K. Luscher, eds., *Examining Lives in Context* (Washington, D.C.: APA), p. 351.

48 **"girls are trying to attract boys":** C. Hanna (2000), "Bad Girls and Good Sports: Some Reflections on Violent Female Juvenile Delinquents, Title IX, and the Promise of Girl Power," *Hastings Constitutional Law Quarterly*, 27, pp. 667–716.

51 **In our increasingly toxic social environment:** J. Garbarino (1995), *Raising Children in a Socially Toxic Environment* (San Francisco: Jossey-Bass).

51 **adolescent culture is more and more infusing:** D. Elkind (2001), *The Hurried Child: Growing Up Too Fast Too Soon.* (New York: Perseus).

57 **At every point after age four:** R. Tremblay (2000). "The Development of Aggressive Behaviour During Childhood."

58 **To use the current psychological terminology:** N. R. Crick, et al. "Relational Aggression, Gender, and Social–psychological Functioning."

58 **The more relationally aggressive a girl is:** A. J. Rose, L. P. Swenson, and E. M. Waller (2004), "Overt and Relational Aggression and Perceived Popularity: Developmental Differences in Concurrent and Prospective Relations," *Developmental Psychology*, 40 (3), pp. 378–87.

60 **This is not a fact in contemporary China:** S. X. He and D. Lester (1997), "The Gender Difference in Chinese Suicide Rates," *Archives of Suicide Research*, 3 (2), pp. 81–89.

60 **When we look at the development:** U. Bronfenbrenner (1979), *The Ecology of Human Development: Experiments by Nature and Design* (Cambridge: Harvard University Press); J. Garbarino and Associates (1992), *Children and Families in the Social Environment, 2nd ed.* (New York: Aldine).

60 **Sarnoff Mednick and Elizabeth Kandel:** S. A. Mednick and E. Kandel (1998), "Genetic and Perinatal Factors in Violence," in S. A. Mednick and T. Moffitt, eds., *Biological Contributions to Crime Causation* (Dordrecht: Martinus Nijhoff), pp. 121–134.

60 **Rolf Loeber and David Farrington:** R. Loeber and D. Farrington (1998), *Serious and Violent Juvenile Offenders: Risk Factors and Successful Interventions* (Thousand Oaks, Calif.: Sage).

61 **when Diana Baumrind repeated:** For a discussion of these studies, see J. Garbarino and C. Bedard (2001), *Parents Under Siege: Why You Are the Solution, Not the Problem, in Your Child's Life* (New York: Free Press).

61 **consistent with the findings:** A. Baldwin, C. Baldwin, and R. Cole (1990), "Stress-resistant Families and Stress-resistant Children," in J. Rolf et al., eds., *Risk and Protective Factors in the Development of Psychopathology* (New York: Cambridge University Press).

62 **Urie's books:** U. Bronfenbrenner (1970), *Two Worlds of Childhood: U.S. and U.S.S.R.* (New York: Russell Sage Foundation); Bronfenbrenner (1979), op. cit.

62 **it is the accumulation of risk factors:** M. Rutter (1989), "Pathways from Childhood to Adult Life, *Journal of Child Psychology and Psychiatry,* 30 (1), pp. 23–51.

62 **research on the effects of televised violence:** L. R. Huesmann, J. Moise-Titus, C. Podolski, and L. D. Eron (2003), "Longitudinal Relations Between Children's Exposure to TV Violence and Their Aggressive and Violent Behavior in Young Adulthood: 1977–1992," *Developmental Psychology,* 39 (2), pp. 201–21.

Chapter 3: Girls Unleashed

65 **But if the child were a girl:** M. Mead (1989), *Blackberry Winter: My Earlier Years* (New York: Peter Smith Publisher).

67 **women still earn on average:** F. D. Blau and L. M. Kahn (2000), "Gender Differences in Pay," *Journal of Economic Perspectives,* 14, (4), pp. 75–99.

67 **the "adult male" list:** I. Broverman, D. Broverman, F. Clarkson, P. Rosencrantz, and S. Vogel (1970), "Sex-role Stereotypes and Clinical Judgments of Mental Health," *Journal of Consulting and Clinical Psychology,* 34 (1), pp. 1–7. Also, I. Broverman, S. Vogel, D. Broverman, F. Clarkson, and P. Rosencrantz (1972), "Sex-role Stereotypes: A Reappraisal," *Journal of Social Issues,* 28, pp. 59–78.

68 **psychologist Emmy Werner and others:** E. Werner (2000), "Protective Factors and Individual Resilience," in J. Shonkoff and S. Meisels, eds., *The Handbook of Early Interventions,* pp. 115–34.

69 **there is tremendous competition:** J. McNeal (1999), *The Kids Market: Myths and Realities* (New York: Paramount Market Publishing).

69 **Writing in *Mothering* magazine:** G. Ruskin (1997), "Why They Whine," *Mothering,* available at www.mothering.com/articles/growing_child/consumerism/whine.html.

69 **This is business as usual:** R. Clay (2000), "Advertising to Children: Is It Ethical?," *Monitor on Psychology,* 31(8), pp. 52–53.

69 **In *Reviving Ophelia*:** M. Pipher (1995), *Reviving Ophelia: Saving the Selves of Adolescent Girls* (New York: Ballantine Books).

70 **One emerging danger:** *Hello! Magazine* (February 15, 2005). Available at: www.hellomagazine.com/profiles/annakournikova/.

71 Social historian Joan Brumberg: J. J. Brumberg (1998), *The Body Project: An Intimate History of American Girls* (New York: Vintage).

71 And how especially painful this is: The Center for Health and Health Care in Schools, available at www.healthinschools.org/sh/obesityfacts.asp.

72 In his book *Listening to Prozac:* P. D. Kramer (1997), *Listening to Prozac* (New York: Penguin Books).

73 In a June 2004 issue of *Newsweek:* A. Quindlen (June 28, 2004), "To Hell with Well Behaved," *Newsweek*, p. 66.

73 These communities still abhor: B. Reed and K. Pollit, eds. (2002), *Nothing Sacred: Women Respond to Religious Fundamentalism and Terror* (New York: Nation Books).

73 research by psychologist Madeline Heilman: M. E. Heilman, A. S. Wallen, D. Fuch, and M. M. Tamkins (2004), "Penalties for Success: Reactions to Women Who Succeed at Male Gender-typed Tasks," *Journal of Applied Psychology*, 89 (3), pp. 416–27.

74 For the past twenty years: K. Berkeley (1999), *The Women's Liberation Movement in America* (New York: Greenwood Press).

74 Today's empowered queen bees: R. Wiseman (2003), *Queen Bees and Wannabes: Helping Your Daughter Survive Cliques, Gossip, Boyfriends, and Other Realities of Adolescence* (New York: Three Rivers Press).

78 A study of adolescents in Finland: K. Bjorkvist and P. Niemla, eds. (1991), *Of Mice and Women: Aspects of Female Aggression* (New York: Academic Press).

78 the lack of socialization experiences: R. E. Tremblay (2002), "Prevention of Injury by Early Socialization of Aggressive Behavior," *Injury Prevention*, 8, pp. 17–21.

79 nearly three million girls: National Federation of State High School Associations (2003) Survey Resources, "Participation Sets Record for Fifth Straight Year," September 2, 2003, available at www.nfhs.org.

79 studies do at least document: See "Athletic Participation as an Education and Psychological Asset" at womenssportsfoundation.org.

80–81 sexual fascination with feminine aggression: J. Hargreaves (1997), "Women's Boxing and Related Activities: Introducing Images and Meanings," *Body and Society*, 3 (4), pp. 33–49.

82 When Jeffrey Goldstein wrote: J. Goldstein (1986), *Aggression and Crimes of Violence* (New York: Oxford University Press).

83 a news story from Chicago: K. Christiansen (2001), "Hormones and Sport: Behavior Effects of Androgen in Men and Women," *Journal of Endocrinology*, 170, pp. 39–48.

86 what Thich Nhat Hanh means: Thich Nhat Hanh (2003), *Creating True Peace: Ending Violence in Yourself, Your Family, Your Community and the World* (New York: Free Press).

86 June 7, 2004, issue of *U.S. News & World Report:* P. Cary (June 7, 2004), "Rescuing Children's Games from Crazed Coaches and Parents," *U. S. News & World Report*, p. 46ff.

87 **The intensity of all this competitiveness:** F. Engh (2002), *Why Johnny Hates Sports* (New York: Square One Publishers).

87 **Women's Sports Foundation:** See womenssportsfoundation.org.

Chapter 4: From Powder Puff to Powerpuff Girls: How Pop Culture Celebrates Aggressive Girls

91 **Researchers in the 1950s:** R. Hamilton and R. Lawless (1956), "Television Within the Social Matrix," *Public Opinion Quarterly*, 20 (20), pp. 393–444.

91 **By 1969 more than 25 percent:** C. Anderson, L. Berkowitz, Donnerstein, E. L. R. Huesmann, J. Johnson, W. D. Linz, N. Malamuth, and E. Wartella (in press), "Influences of Media Violence on Youth," *Psychological Science in the Public Interest*.

91 **Like most children of her age:** B. Bushman and C. Anderson (2001), "Media Violence and the American Public: Scientific Facts Versus Media Misinformation," *American Psychologist*, 56, pp. 477–89.

91 **Children spend more time with media:** G. Comstock and H. Paik (1991), *Television and the American Child* (New York: Academic Press).

91 **One study reported:** J. Lyle and H. R. Hoffman (1972), "Children's Use of Television and Other Media," in E. A. Rubinstein, G. A. Comstock, and J. Murrey, eds., *Television and Social Behavior*, vol. 4, *Television in Day-to-Day Life: Patterns of Use* (Washington, D.C.: U.S. Government Printing Office), pp. 129–256.

91 **at ten on any Saturday morning:** G. Comstock and H. Paik, *Television and the American Child*.

92 **The premier long-term study:** L. D. Eron, L. R. Huesmann, M. M. Lefkowitz, and L. O. Walder (1972), "Does Television Violence Cause Aggression?," *American Psychologist*, pp. 253–63.

92 **Eron and Huesmann's research shows:** L. R. Huesmann, J. Moise-Titus, C. Podolski, and L. D. Eron (2003), "Longitudinal Relations Between Children's Exposure to TV Violence and Their Aggressive and Violent Behavior in Young Adulthood: 1977–1992," *Developmental Psychology*, 39, (2), pp. 201–21.

92 **The authors speculate:** L. R. Huesmann and L. D. Eron (1986), "The Development of Aggression in American Children as a Consequence of Television Violence Viewing," in L. R. Huesmann and L. D. Eron, eds., *Television and the Aggressive Child: A Cross-national Comparison* (Hillsdale, N.J.: Lawrence Erlbaum), pp. 45–80.

92 **For the first few decades of television viewing:** Ibid.

92 **"Females who were high-volume viewers":** L. R. Huesmann et al. "Longitudinal Relations Between Children's Exposure to TV Violence."

References

93 **a 50 percent increase in aggressive behavior:** T. M. Williams, ed., *The Impact of Television: A Natural Experiment in Three Communities* (San Diego: Academic Press).

93 **Robert Centerwall's study:** B. S. Centerwall (1989a), "Exposure to Television as a Cause of Violence," in G. Comstock, ed., *Public Communication and Behavior* (New York: Academic Press), vol. 2, pp. 1–58.

93 **"shift in aggressive female role models":** L. R. Huesmann, et al. "Longitudinal Relations Between Children's Exposure to TV Violence."

94 **the episode titled "Bubble Trouble":** L. Dower (2000), *Bubble Trouble* (New York: Scholastic).

94 **Saturday morning programming:** C. Anderson, et al. "Influences of Media Violence on Youth."

94 **over the course of her childhood:** Children Now (1997) Survey, "Reflections of Girls in the Media" (Menlo Park, Calif.: Kaiser Family Foundation).

95 **no apparent consequence associated with a violent act:** National Television Violence Study (1997), "Content Analysis of Violence in Television Programming," issue briefs (Studio City, Calif.: Mediascope Press).

95 **particularly likely to contain violence:** Ibid.

95 **"greater identification with same-sex aggressive characters":** L. R. Huesmann, et al. "Longitudinal Relations Between Children's Exposure to TV Violence."

96 **61 percent said they watch what they want:** Anderson et al. "Influences of Media Violence on Youth."

98 **girls actually had higher levels of aggressive fantasies:** L. J. Aber, J. L. Brown, and S. M. Jones (2003), "Developmental Trajectories Toward Violence in Middle Childhood: Course, Demographic Differences, and Response to School-Based Intervention," *Developmental Psychology*, 39 (2), pp. 324–48.

98 **Hermione's aggressive response:** Children Now "Reflections of Girls in the Media."

98 *aggression works*: "National Television Violence Study."

99 **Although most antisocial behaviors do not pay off:** Children Now "Reflections of Girls in the Media."

99 **less effective than boys:** Ibid.

100 **The male heroes of the 1950s:** See J. Katz and J. Earp (1999), *Tough Guise: Violence, Media, and the Crisis in Masculinity*, video available from Media Education Foundation (www.mediaed.org).

101 **Concern about the impact of television:** T. H. Pear (1936), "What Television Might Do," *Listener*, p. 18.

101 **the results of a new report:** U.S. Surgeon General's Scientific Advisory Committee on Television and Social Behavior (1972), *Television and Growing Up: The Impact of Televised Violence.* DHEW Publication No. HSM 729086. Washington, D.C.

102 **The American Psychological Association's 2001 report:** C. Anderson et al. "Influences of Media Violence on Youth."

104 **girls have been less likely than boys:** B. Bushman and C. Anderson, "Media Violence and the American Public."

105 **those who played violent games were more aggressive:** C. Anderson, et al. "Influences of Media Violence on Youth."

105 **Psychiatrist Lenore Terr:** L. Terr (1995), *Unchained Memories: True Stories of Memories Lost and Found* (New York: Basic Books).

106 **Joanne Cantor and her colleagues:** J. Cantor (1998), *Mommy, I'm Scared: How TV and Movies Frighten Children* (New York: Harcourt Brace).

106 **The findings of the traumatic impact of mass media images:** Ibid.

106 **echoes the findings from Kuwait:** M. Macksoud, L. J. Aber, and I. Cohen (1996), "Assessing the Impact of War on Children," in R. Apfel and B. Simon, eds., *Minefields in Their Hearts: The Mental Health of Children in War and Communal Violence* (New Haven: Yale University Press), pp. 218–30.

107 **This may be one area of particular concern:** C. Anderson et al. "Influences of Media Violence on Youth."

107 **Studies have demonstrated:** N. L. Carnagey, B. J. Bushman, and C. A. Anderson (2003), "Violent Video Game Exposure and Aggression: A Literature Review." Under review.

108 **A study conducted by Michael Rich:** M. Rich (1998), "Aggressors or Victims: Gender and Race in Music Video Violence," *Pediatrics*, 101 (4), pp. 669–74.

108 **positive correlation between amount of MTV watching and physical fights:** D. A. Gentile, ed. (2003), *Media Violence and Children* (Westport, Conn.: Ablex Publishing).

109 **They may put on a socially conscious face:** E. Miller (2000), *What It's Like for the Material Girl*, available at www.popmatters.com/music/videos/m/madonna-what.shtml.

109 **Children Now's ongoing content analysis:** Children Now "Reflections of Girls in the Media."

110 **Asked to choose three roles:** Ibid.

112 **In 1974, Maccoby and Jacklin:** K. Bjorkvist and P. Niemla, eds. (1991), *Of Mice and Women: Aspects of Female Aggression* (New York: Academic Press), p. 7.

Chapter 5: The Evolution of Mean: The New Language of Girl Violence

115 **when girls want to hurt people:** N. R. Crick and J. K. Grotpeter (1995), "Relational Aggression, Gender, and Social-Psychological Adjustment," *Child Development*, 66, pp. 710–22.

115 **the reality of day-to-day life among kids:** J. Archer (2004), "Sex Differences in Aggression in Real-World Settings: A Meta-analytic Review," *Review of General Psychology*, 8 (4), pp. 291–322.

115 **These findings are repeated in study after study:** Ibid.

115 **Researcher Eleanor Maccoby:** E. E. Maccoby, E. M. Dowley, J. W. Hagen, and R. Degerman (1965), "Activity Level and Intellectual Functioning in Normal Preschool Children," *Child Development*, 36 (3), pp. 761–70.

117 *desensitization:* D. Grossman (1996), *On Killing* (New York: Little, Brown).

117 **the very process of desensitization:** Ibid.

120 **They absorb this imagery:** For a nice review prepared by the Internet consulting company Caslon Analytics, see www.caslon.com.au/emailprofile4.htm.

120 **a set of five studies:** C. A. Anderson, N. L. Carnagey, and J. Eubanks (2003), "Exposure to Violent Media: The Effects of Songs with Violent Lyrics on Aggressive Thoughts and Feelings," *Journal of Personality and Social Psychology*, 84 (5), pp. 960–71.

120 **As a footnote to this:** For resources on this issue, visit the National Center's Web site at www.missingkids.com.

120–121 **Several incidents have occurred:** For resources on this issue, visit www.wildxangel.com/netcrime1.html.

121 **Spend some time in the hallways:** J. Garbarino and E. de Lara (2002), *And Words Can Hurt Forever: How to Protect Adolescents from Bullying, Harassment, and Emotional Violence* (New York: Free Press).

121 **I laid these out first:** J. Garbarino, J. Seeley, and E. Guttmann (1986), *The Psychologically Battered Child* (San Francisco: Jossey-Bass).

121 **rejection is universally a psychological malignancy:** R. Rohner (1975), *They Love Me, They Love Me Not* (New Haven: Human Relations Area Files Press).

121 **steeped in rejection:** R. Simmons (2003), *Odd Girl Out: The Hidden Culture of Aggression in Girls* (New York: Harvest Books).

125 **characters in Chaim Potok's *The Chosen*:** C. Potok (1987), *The Chosen* (New York: Fawcett).

126 **the work of Eudora Welty:** E. Welty (1995), *One Writer's Beginnings* (Cambridge: Harvard University Press).

126 **Once isolated:** E. Aronson (2001), *Nobody Left to Hate* (New York: Owl Books).

126 **And consider this example:** J. Garbarino and E. de Lara (2002). *And Words Can Hurt Forever.*

127 **These children rarely report:** J. Garbarino and C. Bedard (2001), *Parents Under Siege: Why You Are the Solution, Not the Problem, in Your Child's Life* (New York: Free Press).

127 **In our study:** Ibid.

128 **Research shows that this negative language:** T. J. Dishion, J. McCord, and F.

Poulin (1999), "When Interventions Harm: Peer Groups and Problem Behavior," *American Psychologist*, 54 (9), pp. 755–64.

130 **There *is* a correlation:** D. Grossman (1996), *On Killing* (New York: Little, Brown).

131 **Boys often report:** R. Simmons (2003), *Odd Girl Out*.

134 **psychologist Mary Pipher:** M. Pipher (1995), *Reviving Ophelia: Saving the Selves of Adolescent Girls* (New York: Ballantine Books).

134 **historian Joan Brumberg:** J. J. Brumberg (1998), *The Body Project: An Intimate History of American Girls* (New York: Vintage).

135 **Psychologists studying aggression between girls:** J. Archer, "Sex Differences in Aggression in Real-world Settings."

136 **Female gang wannabes:** C. E. Molidor (1996), "Female Gang Members: A Profile of Aggression and Victimization," *Social Work*, 41 (3), pp. 251–58.

Chapter 6: Cinderella Strikes Back: Girls Who Are Sad, Mad, and Hurt

144 **Many studies have linked early experiences:** J. Garbarino, J. Eckenrode, and Family Life Development Center (1996), *Understanding Abusive Families* (San Francisco: Jossey-Bass).

144 **abused children (girls and boys):** K. A. Dodge, G. S. Pettit, and J. E. Bates (1997), "How the Experience of Early Physical Abuse Leads Children to Become Chronically Aggressive," in D. Cicchetti and S. Toth, eds., *Rochester Symposium on Developmental Psychology* (Rochester: University of Rochester Press).

144 **conduct disorder:** American Psychiatric Association (1994), *Diagnostic and Statistical Manual, 4th ed.* (Washington, D.C.: American Psychiatric Association).

144 **girls are less likely to be accurately identified:** Ibid.

144 **a majority end up troubled:** Ibid.

145 **what makes a child turn to conduct disorder:** J. Garbarino (1999), *Lost Boys: Why Our Sons Turn Violent and How We Can Save Them* (New York: Free Press).

145 **The social map:** J. Garbarino and Associates (1992), *Children and Families in the Social Environment* (New York: Aldine).

145 **a girl's social map must contain:** J. Garbarino, E. Guttmann, and J. W. Seeley (1986), *The Psychologically Battered Child* (San Francisco: Jossey-Bass).

145 **Psychologist Daniel Goleman:** D. Goleman (1997), *Emotional Intelligence: Why It Can Matter More Than IQ* (New York: Bantam).

146 **attachment:** Ibid.

146 secure attachments are mostly consistent and uniform: M. D. Ainsworth, M. C. Blehar, E. Wates, and S. Wall (1978), *Patterns of Attachment* (Hillsdale, N.J.: Lawrence Erlbaum).

146 this effect is particularly important: A. Sroufe (1985), "Attachment Classification from the Perspective of Infant-Caregiver Relationships and Infant Temperament," *Child Development*, 56, pp. 1–14.

147 troubled children and youths: M. M. Moretti, D. Kimberly, and R. Holland (2004), "Aggression from an Attachment Perspective," in M. M. Moretti, C. L. Odgers, and M. A. Jackson, eds., *Girls and Aggression: Contributing Factors and Intervention Principles* (New York: Kluwer Academic/Plenum Publishers), pp. 41–56.

147 girls and boys tend to differ: Ibid.

147 the child is "unable to anticipate": Ibid.

147 Marlene Moretti: Ibid.

147 "seem uninterested in attachment relationships": Ibid., p. 47.

148 only 6 percent of the troubled girls: Ibid., pp. 41–56.

148 third type of insecure attachment: Ibid.

148 it is the differences in the type of attachment difficulty: Ibid.

149 The insecure-preoccupied group: Ibid.

149 The insecure-dismissive group: Ibid.

149 The insecure-fearful group: Ibid.

151 children have a universal craving for acceptance: Ibid.

151 rejection sensitivity: G. Downey, L. Irwin, M. Ramsay, and A. Ozlem (2004), "Rejection Sensitivity and Girls' Aggression," in M. M. Moretti, C. L. Odgers, and M. A. Jackson, eds., *Girls and Aggression: Contributing Factors and Intervention Principles* (New York: Kluwer Academic/Plenum Publishers), p. 9.

151 rejection sensitivity readily stimulates a vicious cycle: Ibid.

153 Many of the traditional sources of success: L. J. Alpert-Gillis and J. P. Connell (1989), "Gender and Sex-Role Influences On Children's Self-Esteem," *Journal of Personality*, 57, pp. 97–114.

155 a girl's aggression is therefore more likely to arise: G. Downey et al. "Rejection Sensitivity and Girls' Aggression."

155 It is not surprising: P. Chamberlain and K. J. Moore (2002), "Chaos and Trauma in the Lives of Adolescent Females with Antisocial Behavior and Delinquency," in R. Greenwald, ed., *Trauma and Juvenile Delinquency: Theory, Research, and Interventions* (New York: Haworth Press), pp. 79–108.

156 "Boys are more concerned with competition": E. Maccoby (1995), "The Two Sexes and Their Social Systems," in P. Moen, G. Elder, and K. Luscher, eds., *Examining Lives in Context* (Washington, D.C.: APA).

158 one form of physical aggression: L. S. Abrams and A. L. Gordon (2003), "Self-harm Narratives of Urban and Suburban Young Women," *Affilia*, 18 (4), pp. 429–44.

158 females' assaults on themselves: L. Macaian (2001), "Cutting Voices: Self-injury in Three Adolescent Girls," *Psychosocial Nursing and Mental Health Services*, 39 (11), pp. 22–29.

158 assault against oneself: R. A. Sansone and J. L. Levitt (2002), "Self-harm Behaviors Among Those with Eating Disorders: An Overview," *Eating Disorders*, 10, pp. 205–13.

160 Self-assault of this type: L. Macaian, "Cutting Voices."

160 A girl filters all these "data": G. Downey et al. "Rejection Sensitivity and Girls' Aggression."

160 the results of these differences: K. A. Dodge, et al. "How the Experience of Early Physical Abuse Leads Children to Become Chronically Aggressive."

161 the odds that an abused girl (or boy): Ibid.

163 eight times more likely: Ibid.

163 which abused children develop risky thinking: A. Caspi, J. McClay, T. E. Moffitt, J. Mill, J. Martin, I. W. Craig, A. Taylor, and R. Poulton (2002), "Role of Genotype in the Cycle of Violence in Maltreated Children," *Science*, 297, 851–54.

164 Although this is only one study: Ibid.

165 the pathway from there into an antisocial life: D. P. Farrington and R. Loeber (1999), *Serious and Violent Juvenile Offenders: Risk Factors and Successful Interventions* (London: Sage).

165 the odds that a child with conduct disorder: Ibid.

166 "MAOA is an X-linked gene": A. Caspi et al. "Role of Genotype in the Cycle of Violence in Maltreated Children."

167 Nonmaltreated girls can become troubled girls: R. Dishion, J. McCord, and F. Poulin (1999), "When Interventions Harm: Peer Groups and Problem Behavior," *American Psychologist*, 54, pp. 755–64.

167 disrupt the process of unlearning aggression: M. Rutter (1989), "Pathways from Childhood to Adult Life," *Journal of Child Psychology and Psychiatry*, 30 (1), pp. 23–51.

167 Some cases of conduct disorder: J. D. Coie and K. A. Dodge (1998), "Aggression and Antisocial Behavior," in N. Eisenberg, ed., *Handbook of Child Psychology*, vol. 3, *Social, Emotional and Personality Development*, 5th ed. (New York: Wiley), pp. 779–862.

168 A classic study found: A. Thomas and S. Chess (1977), *Temperament and Development* (New York: Brunner/Mazel).

168 Few girls are totally immune: R. Dishion et al. "When Interventions Harm."

168 meticulous observations of parents: G. R. Patterson (1982), *Coercive Family Processes* (Eugene, Ore.: Castilia Press).

169 "Don't give in to terrorists": J. Garbarino and C. Bedard (2001), *Parents Under Siege: Why You Are the Solution, Not the Problem, in Your Child's Life* (New York: Free Press).

169 A long-term study: A. Caspi, G. H. Elder, and D. J. Bem (1987), "Moving

Against the World: Life-course Patterns of Explosive Children," *Developmental Psychology*, 23 (2), pp. 308–13.

169 **Ross Greene has studied children:** R. W. Greene (2001), *The Explosive Child: A New Approach for Understanding and Parenting Easily Frustrated, Chronically Inflexible Children* (New York: HarperCollins).

170 **if a boy predisposed to aggression:** S. G. Kellam, G. W. Rebok, N. Ialongo and L. S. Mayer (1994), "The Course and Malleability of Aggressive Behavior from Early First Grade into Middle School: Results of a Developmental Epidemiology-based Preventive Trial," *Journal of Child Psychology and Psychiatry and Allied Disciplines*, 53 (2), pp. 259–81.

171 **published estimates of conduct disorder:** A. Caspi et al. "The Role of Genotype in the Cycle of Violence in Maltreated Children."

171 **These problems in diagnosis:** M. S. Atkins, M. McKernan, J. McKay, E. Talbott, and P. Arvanitis (1996), "DSM-IV Diagnosis of Conduct Disorder and Oppositional Defiant Disorder: Implications and Guidelines for School Mental Health Teams," *School Psychology Review*, 25 (3), pp. 274–83.

171 **research by psychologist Tom Achenbach:** T. Achenbach and C. Howell (1993), "Are American Children's Problems Getting Worse?: A Thirteen-Year Comparison," *Journal of the American Academy of Child and Adolescent Psychiatry*, 32 (6), pp. 1145–54.

172 **narrow still further:** D. P. Farrington and R. Loeber, *Serious and Violent Juvenile Offenders.*

172 **stop short of lethal violence:** Office of Juvenile Justice and Delinquency Prevention (2003), *Person Offenses in Juvenile Court, 1990–1999*, FS 200303 (Washington, D.C.: Office of Juvenile Justice and Delinquency Prevention).

172 **Services for troubled girls:** M. Chesney-Lind (2001), "Out of Sight, Out of Mind: Girls in the Juvenile Justice System," in C. Renzetti and L. Goodstein, eds., *Women, Crime and Criminal Justice: Original Feminist Readings* (Los Angeles: Roxbury Publishing), pp. 27–43; American Bar Association (2002), "Justice by Gender: The Lack of Appropriate Prevention, Diversion and Treatment Alternatives for Girls in the Justice System," *William and Mary Journal of Women and the Law*, 9 (1), pp. 73–97.

172 **64 percent of the girls:** P. Chamberlain and K. J. Moore (2002), "Chaos and Trauma in the Lives of Adolescent Females with Antisocial Behavior and Delinquency," in R. Greenwald, ed., *Trauma and Juvenile Delinquency: Theory, Research, and Interventions* (New York: Haworth Press), pp. 79–108.

Chapter 7: Girls Who Kill . . . Themselves or Others

174 **Female juveniles commit:** Office of Juvenile Justice and Delinquency Prevention (2003), *Person Offences in Juvenile Court, 1990–1999*, FS 200303 (Washington, D.C.: Office of Juvenile Justice and Delinquency Prevention).

174 **the rate at which American girls commit murder:** L. A. Fingerhut and J. C. Kleinman (1990), "International and Interstate Comparisons of Homicide Among Young Males," *Journal of the American Medical Association*, 263, pp. 3292–95.

175 **Females are more likely to kill:** L. A. Greenfeld and T. L. Snell (December 1999), *Women Offenders.* Bureau of Justice Statistics Special Report. NCJ 175688. Washington, D.C.: U.S. Department of Justice. Available at www.ojp.usdoj.gov/bjs/pub.

175 **more likely to suffer from overt depression:** C. R. Mann (1996), *When Women Kill* (Albany: State University of New York Press).

176 **Most of the murders that girls commit:** G. Downey, L. Irwin, M. Ramsay, and A. Ozlem (2004), "Rejection Sensitivity and Girls' Aggression," in M. M. Moretti, C. L. Odgers, and M. A. Jackson, eds., *Girls and Aggression: Contributing Factors and Intervention Principles* (New York: Kluwer Academic/Plenum Publishers), pp. 7–26.

178 **There is a long history linking honor and violence:** Ibid.

178 **As chronicled by Fox Butterfield:** F. Butterfield (1996), *All God's Children: The Bosket Family and the American Tradition of Violence* (New York: Perennial).

178 **the belief that one's reputation in the community:** B. Wyatt-Brown (1982), *Southern Honor: Ethics and Behavior in the Old South* (New York: Oxford University Press).

179 **Honor above all else:** F. Butterfield, *All God's Children.*

179 **this has exacerbated the victimization of women:** H. Mayell (February 12, 2002), "Thousands of Women Killed for Family 'Honor,'" *National Geographic News*, available at http:news.nationalgeographic.com/news/2002/02/0212_020212_honorkilling.html.

180 **Fewer than three thousand:** R. N. Anderson and B. L. Smith (2003), "Deaths: Leading Causes for 2001," *National Vital Statistics Report*, 52 (9), pp. 1–86.

180 **the suicide rate for girls increased:** H. N. Snyder and M. H. Swahn (March 2004), "Juvenile Suicides: 1981–1998," *Youth Violence Research Bulletin*.

180 **girls have been subject to higher levels of depression:** D. M. Fergusson, L. J. Woodward, and L. J. Horwood (2000), "Risk Factors and Life Processes Associated with the Onset of Suicidal Behaviour During Adolescence and Early Adulthood," *Psychological Medicine*, 30, pp. 23–39.

180 Terrence Real's book: T. Real (1997), *I Don't Want to Talk About It: Overcoming the Secret Legacy of Male Depression* (New York: Scribner).

181 gender differences in methods of assault: H. N. Snyder and M. H. Swahn, "Juvenile Suicides: 1981–1998."

181 By the end of the 1990s: Ibid.

181 In the case of suicides: Ibid.

182 a majority of teenagers: J. Garbarino (1995), *Raising Children in a Socially Toxic Environment* (San Francisco: Jossey-Bass). For further information, see www.kidsandguns.org. Also: K. M. Jones, J. Tabor, J. T. Beuhring, T. Sieving, R. E. Shew, M. Ireland, M. Bearinger, and L. H. Udry (1997), "Protecting Adolescents from Harm: Findings from the National Longitudinal Study on Adolescent Health," *Journal of the American Medical Association*, 278 (10), pp. 823–32.

182 Kids routinely overestimate: J. W. Graham, G. Marks, and W. B. Hansen (1991), "Social Influence Processes Affecting Adolescent Substance Use," *Journal of Applied Psychology*, 76, pp. 291–98.

182 Each killing says something: J. Garbarino (1999), *Lost Boys: Why Our Sons Turn Violent and How We Can Save Them* (New York: Free Press).

182 In the worst war zones: J. Garbarino, K. Kostleny, and N. Dubrow (1991), *No Place to Be a Child: Growing Up in a War Zone* (New York: Lexington Books).

183 inadvertently mislabeled: D. Lester (1992), *The Cruelest Death: The Enigma of Adolescent Suicide* (New York: Charles Press Publishers).

183 "the number of boy burglars": R. Shepherd (1997), *Juvenile Justice Update*.

183 A child psychiatrist working in Manhattan's juvenile court: (March 27, 1954), "Manhattan's Child Criminals Are My Job," *Saturday Evening Post*.

184 numerous cases of juveniles: J. Brumberg (2003), *Kansas Charley: The Story of a 19th-Century Boy Murderer* (New York: Viking).

184 a sevenfold increase in per capita aggravated assault cases: D. Grossman (1999), "Increase in Violent Crime," available at: www.killology.com.

184 rate of criminal activity for female adolescents: Bureau of Justice Statistics (1999), *Special Report: Women Offenders* NCJ 175688 (Washington, D.C.: Greenfeld and Snell).

184 the proportion of girls arrested: H. Snyder and M. Sickmund (1999), *Juvenile Offenders and Victims: 1999 National Report* (Washington, D.C.: Office of Juvenile Justice and Delinquency Prevention).

184 tried and incarcerated as adults: J. Brumberg, *Kansas Charley*.

184 It was not until 2005: Information available at www.deathpenaltyinfo.org/.

185 One study concluded: A. R. Harris, S. H. Thomas, G. A. Fisher, and D. J. Hirsch (2002), "Murder and Medicine: The Lethality of Criminal Assault 1960–1999," *Homicide Studies*, 6, pp. 128–66.

186 in contemporary China: E. Rosenthal (January 24, 1999), "Suicides Reveal Bitter Roots of China's Rural Life, *New York Times*.

186 In the United States: National Center for Health Statistics (2000), "Deaths

from 282 Selected Causes by Year Age Groups, Race, and Sex: Each State and the District of Columbia, 1995–1998."

186 **78 percent of suicide attempts:** *Oregon Vital Statistics Report* 1996, Department of Health.

186 **about 3 percent of high school girls:** U.S. Department of Health and Human Services (December 17, 2003), *Bulletin on Mental Health and Mental Disorders.*

186 **some experts estimate:** National Mental Health Association, "Suicide: No Suicide Attempt Should Be Dismissed or Treated Lightly," available at www.nmha.org/infoctr/factsheets/81.cfm.

186 **Our own study:** J. Garbarino and C. Bedard (2001), *Parents Under Siege: Why You are the Solution, Not the Problem, in Your Child's Life* (New York: Free Press).

191 **that is not to say:** Ibid.

191 **perpetrators who were scarred:** J. Garbarino, J. Eckenrode, and Family Life Development Center (1996), *Understanding Abusive Families* (San Francisco: Jossey-Bass).

191 **lost boys:** J. Garbarino, *Lost Boys.*

192 **violent girl gangs:** M. Chesney-Lind and J. M. Hagedorn, eds. (1999), *Female Gangs in America* (New York: Lake View Press).

192 **gang-related violence:** C. E. Molidor (1996), "Female Gang Members: A Profile of Aggression and Victimization," *Social Work,* 41 (3), pp. 251–58.

Chapter 8: Lifelines and Safety Nets: Helping Girls Get Physical Without Getting Hurt or Hurting Other People

198 **the Search Institute offered:** Search Institute (1997), "The Assets Approach: Giving Kids What They Need to Succeed," available at: www.search-institute.org.

198 **The forty assets:** N. Leffert, P. K. Benson, P. C. Scales, A. R. Sharma, D. R. Drake, and D. Blyth (1998), "Developmental Assets: Measurement and Prediction of Risk Behaviors Among Adolescents," *Applied Developmental Science,* 2 (4), pp. 209–30.

199 **The more assets youths have:** Ibid.

200 **among kids at risk:** Ibid.

200 **The difference is still apparent:** Ibid.

201 **declining rates of supervision:** J. Garbarino (1995), *Raising Children in a Socially Toxic Environment* (San Francisco: Jossey-Bass).

201 **the average number of assets:** Search Institute (1997) "The Assets Approach."

202 **The modern feminist movement:** B. Friedan (2001/1963), *The Feminine Mystique* (New York: W. W. Norton).

203 **Psychologist Anne Campbell:** A. Campbell, S. Muncer, and D. Bibel (2001), "Women and Crime: An Evolutionary Feminist Approach," *Aggression and Violent Behavior,* 6, pp. 481–97.

206 **Sometimes the problem:** J. Garbarino (1999), *Lost Boys: Why Our Sons Turn Violent and How We Can Save Them* (New York: Free Press).

206 **you can never do just one thing:** Ibid.

206 **Girls Incorporated:** Information available at www.girls-inc.org.

206 **Its program statement:** Ibid.

207 **Among its offerings:** National Resource Center (2001), "Girls and Violence," available at www.girls-inc.org.

210 ***Throw Like a Girl:*** S. Frost and A. Trossieux (2000), *Throw Like a Girl: Discovering the Mind, Body, and Spirit of the Athlete in You* (Hillsboro, Oregon: Beyond Words Publishing).

211 ***Coaching Girls' Soccer:*** J. DeWitt (2001), *Coaching Girls' Soccer* (New York: Three Rivers Press).

211 **Tucker Center for Research on Girls and Women in Sports:** Information available at www.education.umn.edu/tuckercenter.

211 **the Ms. Foundation:** Information available at www.ms.foundation.org and www.feminist.org.

211 **athletic participation has a downside:** Information on the Mendelson Center for Sports, Character, and Community available at www.nd.edu.

211 **National Alliance for Youth Sports:** Information available at www.nays.org.

211 **Relational aggression:** A Google search of the term *relational aggression in girls* turned up twenty thousand entries.

211 ***Queen Bees and Wannabes:*** R. Wiseman (2003), *Queen Bees and Wannabes: Helping Your Daughter Survive Cliques, Gossip, Boyfriends and Other Realities of Adolescence* (New York: Three Rivers Press).

211 ***Odd Girl Out:*** R. Simmons (2003), *Odd Girl Out: The Hidden Culture of Aggression in Girls* (New York: Harvest Books).

212 ***Social Aggression Among Girls:*** M. Underwood (2003), *Social Aggression Among Girls* (New York: Guildford Press).

212 ***Reviving Ophelia:*** M. Pipher (1995), *Reviving Ophelia: Saving the Selves of Adolescent Girls* (New York: Ballantine Books).

212 ***In a Different Voice:*** C. Gilligan (1993), *In a Different Voice: Psychological Theory and Women's Development* (Cambridge: Harvard University Press).

212 **description of the goals:** Information available at www.girlsinitiativenetwork.org/allies.html.

212 **National Ophelia Sister Project:** Information available at www.opheliaproject.org.

213 **Of Mice and Women:** K. Bjorkvist and P. Niemla, eds. (1991), *Of Mice and Women: Aspects of Female Aggression* (New York: Academic Press).

213 **Girls and Aggression:** M. M. Moretti, C. L. Odgers, and M. A. Jackson, eds., *Girls and Aggression: Contributing Factors and Intervention Principles* (New York: Kluwer Academic/Plenum Publishers).

213 **Aggression, Antisocial Behavior, and Violence Among Girls:** M. Putallaz and K. Bierman, eds., *Aggression, Antisocial Behavior, and Violence Among Girls: A Developmental Perspective* (New York: Guildford Press).

214 **school- and community-based character education programs:** For an excellent discussion of character education, see T. Lickona (2004), *Character Matters: How to Help Our Children Develop Good Judgment, Integrity and Other Essential Virtues* (New York: Touchstone).

214 **Sex, Power & the Violent School Girl:** S. Artz (1998), *Sex, Power, & the Violent School Girl* (Toronto: Trifolium Books).

215 **"Few mainstream sociological theories":** Ibid.

215 **an Ohio-based Gender Specific Working Group:** J. Belknap, M. Dunn, and K. Holsinger (1997), *Moving Toward Juvenile Justice and Youth-Serving Systems That Address the Distinct Experiences of the Adolescent Female* (Columbus, Ohio: Office of Criminal Justice Services), available at www.ocjs.oh.us.

216 **confined to the role of victim:** A. Cohen (1995), *Delinquent Boys: The Culture of the Gang* (New York: Free Press).

217 **Wiley Hall:** W. Hall (April 29, 2004), "Girls Getting Increasingly Violent," Associated Press.

217 **very high levels of victimization:** For the most recent national data compiled by the government, www.acf.hhs.gov/programs/cb/publications/cmreports.htm.

218 **"Justice by Gender":** American Bar Association (2002), "Justice by Gender: The Lack of Appropriate Prevention, Diversion and Treatment Alternatives for Girls in the Justice System," *William and Mary Journal of Women and the Law*, 9 (1), pp. 73–97.

218 **Girls, Delinquency, and Juvenile Justice:** M. Chesney-Lind and R. G. Selden (1997), *Girls, Delinquency, and Juvenile Justice*, 2nd ed. (Pacific Grove, Calif.: Brooks/Cole).

219 **The area that most differentiates:** P. Chamberlain and K. Moore (2002), "Chaos and Trauma in the Lives of Adolescent Females with Antisocial Behavior and Delinquency," in R. Greenwald, ed., *Trauma and Juvenile Delinquency: Theory, Research, and Interventions* (New York: Haworth Press), pp. 79–108.

219 **cognitive restructuring:** P. Tolan and N. Guerra (1993), *What Works in Reducing Adolescent Violence* (Chicago: University of Chicago Press).

220 **the Good Behavior Game:** S. G. Kellam, G. W. Rebok, N. Ialongo, and L. S. Mayer (1994), "The Course and Malleability of Aggressive Behavior from Early First Grade into Middle School: Results of a Developmental Epidemiology-Based Preventive Trial," *Journal of Child Psychology and Psychiatry and Allied Dis-*

ciplines, 53 (2), pp. 259–81. Information available at www.emstac.org/registered/topics/posbehavior/schoolwide/good.htm.

220 **Let's Talk About Living in a World with Violence:** Information available from www.teacher.scholastic.com/professional/teachstrat/worldwithviolence.htm.

221 **"When Interventions Harm":** T. Dishion, J. McCord, and F. Poulin (1999), "When Interventions Harm: Peer Groups and Problem Behavior," *American Psychologist*, 54, pp. 755–64.

221 **spiritual emptiness:** J. Garbarino (1999), *Lost Boys: Why Our Sons Turn Violent and How We Can Save Them* (New York: Free Press).

221 **this belief system:** A. J. Weaver, L. T. Flannelly, K. J. Flannelly, H. G. Koenig, and D. B. Larson (1998), "An Analysis of Research on Religious and Spiritual Variables in Three Major Mental Health Nursing Journals, 1991–1995," *Issues in Mental Health Nursing*, 19 (3), pp. 263–76.

222 **Two of the Search Institute's:** Search Institute (1997), "The Assets Approach."

222 **"There is nothing so practical as a good theory":** K. Lewin (1951), *Field Theory in Social Science: Selected Theoretical Papers*, ed., D. Cartwright (New York: Harper & Row), p. 169.

223 **Earlscourt Girls Connection:** D. Pepler, M. M. Walsh, and K. S. Levene (2004), "Interventions for Aggressive Girls: Tailoring and Measuring the Fit," in Moretti, Odgers, and Jackson, op. cit., pp. 131–46; K. S. Levene, M. M. Walsh, L. K. Augimeri, and D. J. Pepler (2004), "Linking Identification and Treatment of Early Risk Factors for Female Delinquency," in Moretti, Odgers, and Jackson, op. cit., pp. 147–64.

223 **"Preliminary assessments of the program":** Pepler, Walsh, and Levene, op. cit.

224 **Evaluation of the Earlscourt Girls Connection:** Ibid.

224 **psychiatrist Kathleen Kovner-Klein:** K. Kovner-Kline et al. (2003), *Hardwired to Connect: The New Scientific Case for Authoritative Communities* (Washington, D.C.: Commission on Children at Risk).

225 **This terminal thinking:** J. Garbarino, *Lost Boys*.

225 **Andrew Weaver:** A. J. Weaver et al. "An Analysis of Research on Religious and Spiritual Variables."

225 **character education:** R. Lickona, *Character Matters*.

226 **From Boot Camp to Monastery:** J. Garbarino, *Lost Boys*.

227 ***Creating True Peace*:** Thich Nhat Hanh (2003), *Creating True Peace: Ending Violence in Yourself* (New York: Free Press), pp. 72–73.

Chapter 9: Female Aggression in the Twenty-first Century: What Lies Ahead for the New American Girl?

231 male "superpredators": J. J. Dilulio, W. J. Bennett, and J. P. Walters (1996), *Body Count* (New York: Simon and Schuster).

231 Some of the prediction problems: P. Elikann (2002), *Superpredators: The Demonization of Our Children by the Law* (New York: Perseus).

231 a larger scare tactic: Ibid.

232 society's deliberate interventions: Center for the Study and Prevention of Violence. Information available at www.colorado.edu/cspv/blueprints.

232 Additional sources of error: J. Donohue and S. Levitt (2000), *Legalized Abortion and Crime*. Working Paper Series number 8004. (Washington, D.C.: National Bureau of Economic Research).

232 vagaries of the ripple effect: J. Glieck (1988), *Chaos: Making a New Science* (New York: Penguin).

233 *Silent Spring:* R. Carson (1962), *Silent Spring* (New York: Houghton Mifflin).

233 Research Committee of Prevent Child Abuse America: Information available at www.preventchildabuse.org.

234 "Can We Measure Success in Preventing Child Abuse?": J. Garbarino (1986), "Can We Measure Success in Preventing Child Abuse?: Issues in Policy, Programming, and Research," *Child Abuse and Neglect: The International Journal*, 10, pp. 143–56.

235 Take Back the Night: Information available at www.campusaction.net/activis.

236 "Bad Heroines": M. Spicuzza (March 15, 2001), "Bad Heroines," *Metroactive*, available at www.metroactive.com/papers/metro/03.15.01/cover/womanfilm 0111.html.

238 Some girls join gangs: C. E. Molidor (1996), "Female Gang Members: A Profile of Aggression and Victimization," *Social Work*, 41 (3), pp. 251–58.

239 "When I walked the line": Ibid.

240 in the 2004 science-fiction action film: Information available at www.imdb.com/title/tt0370263.

241 "The number of women": J. Henry and N. Day (September 19, 2004), "Ladettes Log Casualty Units After Catfights," *London Telegraph*, available at www.telegraph.co.uk/news.

241 Glenbrook High School: C. Flynn and L. Black (May 12, 2003), "Glenbook North Moves to Expel Students in Hazing," *Chicago Tribune*, available at: www.chicagotribune.com/news/local/chi-030512hazing.story.

242 widespread social and cultural support: R. Tremblay (2000), "The Development of Aggressive Behaviour During Childhood: What Have We Learned in

References

the Past Century?," *International Journal of Behavioural Development*, 24, pp. 129–41.

242 **only a small minority of males:** R. Gelles and C. P. Cornell (1990), *Intimate Violence in Families*, 2nd ed. (Thousand Oaks, Calif.: Sage).

242 **society actually does a very good job:** R. Tremblay, "The Development of Aggressive Behaviour During Childhood."

242 **one reason for the troubles:** M. Lamb (1981), *The Role of the Father in Child Development* (New York: John Wiley).

243 **They filled the pages:** J. Garbarino (1999), *Lost Boys: Why Our Sons Turn Violent and How We Can Save Them* (New York: Free Press).

243 **As I sit at a playground:** S. Osherson (2001), *Finding Our Fathers: How a Man's Life Is Shaped by His Relationship with His Father* (New York: McGraw-Hill), pp. 227–28.

245 **"It is time for fathers":** D. F. Salter (1996), *Crashing the Old Boys' Network* (New York: Praeger Publishers), p. 22.

248 **core principles of violence reduction:** P. Tolan and N. Guerra (1993), *What Works in Reducing Adolescent Violence* (Chicago: University of Chicago Press).

248 **having two X chromosomes:** A. Caspi, J. McClay, T. E. Moffitt, J. Mill, J. Martin, I. W. Craig, A. Taylor, and R. Poulton (2002), "Role of Genotype in the Cycle of Violence in Maltreated Children," *Science*, 297, pp. 851–54.

249 **One of the processes at work:** D. Freedman (1974), *Human Infancy: An Evolutionary Perspective* (Hillsdale, N.J.: Lawrence Erlbaum).

250 **criminologist Ralph Weisheit:** R. Weisheit (1984), "Female Homicide Offenders: Trends Over Time in an Institutionalized Population," *Justice Quarterly*, 1 (4), pp. 471–89.

Resources

General Web Sources

http://www.safeyouth.org/scripts/teens/bullying.asp
   site about bullying in general, not gender specific
   offers suggestions on what to do if you or someone you know is being bullied
   explains why individuals are bullies
http://www.safeyouth.org/scripts/teens/fighting.asp#references
   facts about physical aggression in teens
   more boys (44 percent) in fights than girls (27 percent) Centers for Disease
      Control and Prevention (June 9, 2000). Youth risk behavior surveillance—
      United States, 1999. *Morbidity and Mortality Weekly Report*, 49(SS-5), 7.
http://www.cdc.gov/ncipc/dvp/bestpractices.htm
   guidelines for effective youth violence interventions
http://www.sfu.ca/gap/
   a project on gender and aggression to find the differences and examine female
      aggression
   current publications available on the Web site
http://www.knowgangs.com/school_resources/menu_026.htm
   review of violent girls and reference list

http://www.wi-doc.com/SOGS.htm

   Web site for Southern Oaks School for Girl Delinquents

http://www.ilppp.virginia.edu/Juvenile_Forensic_Fact_Sheets/FemJuv.html

   Web site with facts and ideas on relational aggression

http://www.fitness.gov/girlssports.html

   President's Council on Physical Fitness (report on girls and sports)

http://www.caaws.ca/Girls/girls_self-est.htm

   self-esteem in girls and its relationship to sports

http://faculty.ncwc.edu/toconnor/428/428lectl1.htm

   interesting facts on female serial killers

   clever names for different types of female killers

Books

Adler, Freda. *Sisters in Crime: The Rise of the New Female Criminal*. New York: Mc-Graw-Hill, 1975.

Artz, Sybille. *Sex, Power, and the Violent School Girl*. Toronto, Ontario: Trifolium, 1998.

Chesney-Lind, Meda, and Randall G. Shelden. *Girls, Delinquency, and Juvenile Justice*. London: Wadsworth, 2003.

Corrado, R., R. Roesch, S. Hart, and J. Gierowski, eds. *Multi-problem Violent Youth: A Foundation for Comparative Research*. Amsterdam: IOS Press, 2002.

Deak, JoAnn. *Girls will be Girls: Raising Confident and Courageous Daughters*. New York: Hyperion, 2002.

Dekeseredy, Walter. *Women, Crime and the Canadian Criminal Justice System*. Cincinnati: Anderson, 2000.

Eagly, A. H. *Sex Differences in Social Behavior: A Social Role Interpretation*. Mahwah, NJ: Erlbaum, 1987.

Flannery, D.J. *School Violence: Risk, Preventive Intervention, and Policy*. Urban Diversity Series No. 109. New York: Teachers College, ERIC Clearinghouse on Urban Education (ERIC Abstract), 1997.

Flannery, Daniel, and C. Ronald Huff, eds. *Youth Violence: Prevention, Intervention, and Social Policy*. Washington, D.C.: American Psychiatric Press, 1999.

Gilligan, Carol. *In a Different Voice: Psychological Theory and Women's Development*. Cambridge, MA: Harvard University Press, 1982.

Girls Incorporated. *Prevention and Parity: Girls in Juvenile Justice*. Indianapolis: Girls Incorporated National Resource Center, 1996.

Hagen, John, and Ruth D. Peterson, eds. *Crime and Inequality*. Stanford: Stanford University Press, 1995.

Huff, C. Ronald, ed. *Gangs in America*. Thousand Oaks, CA: Sage, 1996.

Jenson, Jeffrey M., and Matthew O. Howard. *Youth Violence: Current Research and Recent Practice Innovations*. Washington, D.C.: NASW Press, 2003.

Moretti, Marlene M.; Candice Odgers; Margaret Jackson, eds. *Girls and Aggression: Contributing Factors and Intervention Principles*. New York: Plenum, 2004.

Mosatche, Harriet, and Elizabeth Lawner. *Girls: What's So Bad About Being Good?: How to Have Fun, Survive the Preteen Years, and Remain True to Yourself*. New York: Prima Lifestyles, 2001.

Pearson, Patricia. *When She was Bad: Violent Women and the Myth of Innocence*. London: Virago Press, 1998.

Peplar, Debra. *The Development and Treatment of Girlhood Aggression*. Mahwah, NJ: Erlbaum, 2005.

Prothrow-Stith, D., and H. Spivak. *Sugar and Spice and No Longer Nice: How We Can Stop Girls' Violence*. San Francisco: Jossey-Bass, 2005.

Rosaldo, Michelle Z., and Louise Lamphere, eds. *Woman, Culture and Society*. Stanford, CA: Stanford University Press, 1974.

Sadker, Myra, and David Sadker. *Failing at Fairness: How Our Schools Cheat Girls*. New York: Touchstone, 1994.

Sikes, Gini. *8 Ball Chicks: A Year in the World of Violent Girl Gangsters*. New York: Anchor, 1998.

Articles

Artz, S. "Considering Adolescent Girls' Use of Violence: A Researcher's Reflections on Her Inquiry." *The B.C. Counselor* 22, 1 (2000): 44–54.

———. "A Community-based Approach for Dealing with Chronically Violent Under Twelve-year-old Children." Report for the Department of Justice Crime Prevention Initiative. 2002.

Campbell, A. "The Girls in the Gang." Cambridge, MA: Blackwell, ERIC Abstract, 1991.

Campbell, A., and S. Muncer. "Female-female Criminal Assault: An Evolutionary Perspective." *Journal of Research in Crime and Delinquency* 35 (1998): 413–28.

Campbell, A., S. Muncer, and D. Bibel. "Women and Crime: An Evolutionary Feminist Approach." *Aggression and Violent Behavior* 6 (2001): 481–97.

Eagly, A. H. and V. J. Steffen. "Gender and Aggressive Behavior: A Meta-analytic Review of the Social Psychological Literature." *Psychological Bulletin* 100 (1986): 303–30.

Hyde, J. S. "How large are gender differences in aggression? A developmental meta-analysis." *Developmental Psychology* 20 (1984): 722–36.

Joe, K., and M. Chesney-Lind. "Just Every Mother's Angel: An Analysis of Gender and Ethnic Variations in Youth Gang Membership," *Gender & Society* 9 (1995): 408–31.

Koroki, J., and Chesney-Lind, M. " 'Everything Just Going Down the Drain': Interviews with Female Delinquents." Honolulu: Youth Development and Research Center Report No. 319. ERIC Abstract, 1985.

Krakowski, M., and P. Czobor. "Gender Differences in Violent Behaviors: Relationship to Clinical Symptoms and Psychosocial Factors." *The American Journal of Psychiatry* 161:3, 459–65.

Leschied, A., A. Cummings, M. Van Brunschot, A. Cunningham, and A. Saunders, "Female Adolescent Aggression: A Review of the Literature and the Correlates of Aggression." Ottawa, Ontario: Solicitor General Canada, 2000, User Report No. 2000-04.

Moretti, M., R. Holland, and S. McKay. "Self-other Representations and Relational and Overt Aggression in Adolescent Girls and Boys." *Behavioral Science and the Law* 19, 1 (2000): 109–26.

Muncer, S., A. Campbell, V. Jervis, and R. Lewis. " 'Ladettes': Social Representations and Aggression." *Sex Roles* 44 (2001): 33–44.

Odgers, Candice L., and Marlene Moretti. "Aggressive and Antisocial Girls: Research Update and Challenges." *International Journal of Forensic Mental Health* 1 (2) (2002): 103–19.

Owens, L. "Sticks and Stones and Sugar and Spice: Girls' and Boys' Aggression in Schools," *Australian Journal of Guidance and Counseling* 6 (1996): 45–55.

Pepler, D. "Aggressive Girls in Canada," Ottawa, Ontario: Human Resources Development Canada, 1998.

Rankin, J. H. "School Factors and Delinquency: Interaction by Age and Sex." *Sociology and Social Research* 64 (1980): 420–34.

Webster, D. W., P. S. Gainer, and H. R. Champion. "Weapon Carrying Among Inner-city Junior High School Students: Defensive Behavior Versus Aggressive Delinquency." *American Journal of Public Health* 83 (1993): 1604–08.

Zoccolillo, M., and K. Rogers. "Characteristics and Outcome of Hospitalized Adolescent Girls with Conduct Disorder." *Journal of the American Academy of Child and Adolescent Psychiatry* 30 (1991): 973–81.

Interventions
Designed Specifically
for Girls

Girls Incorporated
30 East 33rd Street
New York, NY 10016
(212) 689-3700
www.girlsinc.org

For ages six through eighteen. Provides packaged programs for healthy peer relationships, pregnancy prevention, and academic encouragement.

Female Intervention Team
321 Fallsway
Baltimore, MD 21202
(410) 333-4564

For adjudicated girl delinquents ages eleven through eighteen. Case managers direct girls toward gender specific activities such as mentoring by older women and Girl Scouts, as well as community service and recreational activities.

Harriet Tubman Residential Center
6752 Pine Ridge Road
Auburn, NY 13021
(315) 255-3481

For adjudicated delinquent girls ages thirteen through seventeen. Residential center that provides full range of interventions, including reproductive health, mediation training, parenting, and strategies for dealing with victimization.

PACE Center for Girls Inc.
100 Laura Street
10th Floor
Jacksonville, FL 32202
(904) 358-0555

For ages twelve through eighteen. Community based program offering educational and therapeutic services to girls. Students participate in educational programs, life management classes, counseling, and community service.

Sistas'
7828 Allendate Drive
Landover, MD 20785
(202) 675-9175

For ages twelve through seventeen in low income settings. Emphasis on cognitive strategies to overcome destructive belief systems, alternatives to destructive behavior, and decision making.

OTHER PROGRAMS

The Empowerment Program runs a School Violence Prevention Institute that tries to prevent bullying, gossiping, dating violence, homophobia, cliques, and sexual harassment. They work equally with young men and women through school and youth service based programs. According to pre/post testing, the program increased the knowledge and awareness of violence in 66 percent of participants. Eighty-three percent experienced a decrease of both verbal and physical aggression.

http://www.empowered.org/svpi.htm

The Empowerment Program
4420 Connecticut Ave. NW
Suite 250
Washington, D.C. 20008
(Phone) 202-686-1908 (Fax) 202-686-1951

GOVERNMENT RESOURCES IN CANADA

Earlscourt Child and Family Centre

46 St. Clair Gardens, Toronto, Ontario M6E 3V4. Telephone: (416) 654-8981. Fax: (416) 654-8996. E-mail: mailus@earlscourt.on.ca. Web site: www.earlscourt.on.ca.

Girls Connection Program and the "Early Assessment Risk List for Girls," Consultation Edition, 2001.

Department of Justice Canada

284 Wellington Street Ottawa, Ontario K1A 0H8 (canada.justice.gc.ca/en/ps/yj)

Index

Index

social toxicity (*cont.*)
   resilience as counterweight to, 70–71, 75–77
   sports as counterweight to, 80
Spears, Britney, 70
Spicuzza, Mary, 236
spirituality, 18
   crisis in youth today, 224–25
   in intervention programs, 221–22
sports
   benefits of, 79–80
   character development vs. aggression through, 17
   coaches' and parents' defining meaning of, 83–84
   female aggression, empowerment and, 207–11
   girls' increased participation in, 4, 26, 79
   new interaction of sexes through, 80–82
   as social toxicity counterweight, 80
   violent behavior in, 86–87
Steinbeck, John, 36
Stewart, Martha, 43, 74
Stone, Donna, 233
suicide
   attempted, statistics on, 186–87
   depression and, 180
   gender differences in methods of, 180–81
   history of juvenile, 183
   statistical differences between sexes, 59–60
   statistics on juvenile, 180
Symonds, Percival, 61

Take Back the Night, 235
television
   aggression, effect on, 101–4
   consumerism, sexuality and popularity links on, 69–71
   hours spent watching, 94
   socially acceptable violence on, 95–96
   studies on aggression and, 92–93
   violence and its effects, 62
   violent incidents on, 94–95

   watching habits, 91
   youth violence reports on, 3–8
Television and Growing Up: The Impact of Televised Violence, 101
temper tantrums, 169
Terr, Lenore, 105
terrorizing as nonphysical aggression, 123–25
testosterone and aggression, 84–85
Thatcher, Margaret, 43
They Love Me, They Love Me Not (Rohner), 121
Thompson, Michael, 46
Throw Like a Girl (Frost and Troussieux), 210–11
Title IX, 88, 207–8
"traveling teams," 87
Tremblay, Richard, 27, 35–36, 38, 39, 41, 59, 74, 78, 113, 242
Troussieux, Ann, 210–11
Tucker Center for Research on Girls and Women in Sports, 211
Two Worlds of Childhood (Bronfenbrenner), 62

Unchained Memories (Terr), 105
Underworld, 240
University of Minnesota, 211

verbal skills of the sexes, 116
video games' effect on aggression, 104–5

Weisheit, Ralph, 250
Welty, Eudora, 126
Werner, Emmy, 68
White House Summit on Youth Violence, 14
Why Johnny Hates Sports (Engh), 87
Winn, Marie, 5
Wiseman, Rosalind, 74, 96, 211
women's liberation, 66–67
   impact on today's girls, 71–72
Women's National Basketball Association, 27, 88
Women's Sports Foundation, 87
Wonder of Boys, The (Gurian), 46
workplace bias against assertive women, 73–74

294

FOR THE BEST IN PAPERBACKS, LOOK FOR THE

In every corner of the world, on every subject under the sun, Penguin represents quality and variety—the very best in publishing today.

For complete information about books available from Penguin—including Penguin Classics and Puffins—and how to order them, write to us at the appropriate address below. Please note that for copyright reasons the selection of books varies from country to country.

In the United States: Please write to *Penguin Group (USA), P.O. Box 12289 Dept. B, Newark, New Jersey 07101-5289* or call 1-800-788-6262.

In the United Kingdom: Please write to *Dept. EP, Penguin Books Ltd, Bath Road, Harmondsworth, West Drayton, Middlesex UB7 0DA.*

In Canada: Please write to *Penguin Books Canada Ltd, 90 Eglinton Avenue East, Suite 700, Toronto, Ontario M4P 2Y3.*

In Australia: Please write to *Penguin Books Australia Ltd, P.O. Box 257, Ringwood, Victoria 3134.*

In New Zealand: Please write to *Penguin Books (NZ) Ltd, Private Bag 102902, North Shore Mail Centre, Auckland 10.*

In India: Please write to *Penguin Books India Pvt Ltd, 11 Panchsheel Shopping Centre, Panchsheel Park, New Delhi 110 017.*

In the Netherlands: Please write to *Penguin Books Netherlands bv, Postbus 3507, NL-1001 AH Amsterdam.*

In Germany: Please write to *Penguin Books Deutschland GmbH, Metzlerstrasse 26, 60594 Frankfurt am Main.*

In Spain: Please write to *Penguin Books S. A., Bravo Murillo 19, 1° B, 28015 Madrid.*

In Italy: Please write to *Penguin Italia s.r.l., Via Benedetto Croce 2, 20094 Corsico, Milano.*

In France: Please write to *Penguin France, Le Carré Wilson, 62 rue Benjamin Baillaud, 31500 Toulouse.*

In Japan: Please write to *Penguin Books Japan Ltd, Kaneko Building, 2-3-25 Koraku, Bunkyo-Ku, Tokyo 112.*

In South Africa: Please write to *Penguin Books South Africa (Pty) Ltd, Private Bag X14, Parkview, 2122 Johannesburg.*